THE ENVIRONMENT AND THE PRESS

Medill School of Journalism
VISIONS *of the* AMERICAN PRESS

GENERAL EDITOR
David Abrahamson

Other titles in this series

HERBERT J. GANS
*Deciding What's News: A Study of CBS Evening News, NBC Nightly News,
Newsweek, and Time*

MAURINE H. BEASLEY
First Ladies and the Press: The Unfinished Partnership of the Media Age

PATRICIA BRADLEY
Women and the Press: The Struggle for Equality

DAVID A. COPELAND
The Idea of a Free Press: The Enlightenment and Its Unruly Legacy

MICHAEL SWEENEY
The Military and the Press: An Uneasy Truce

PATRICK S. WASHBURN
The African American Newspaper: Voice of Freedom

DAVID R. SPENCER
The Yellow Journalism: The Press and America's Emergence as World Power

KARLA GOWER
Public Relations and the Press: The Troubled Embrace

TOM GOLDSTEIN
Journalism and Truth: Strange Bedfellows

JAMES BRIAN MCPHERSON
*The Conservative Resurgence and the Press: The Media's Role
in the Rise of the Right*

THE ENVIRONMENT
AND THE PRESS
FROM ADVENTURE WRITING
TO ADVOCACY

Mark Neuzil

Foreword by Russell E. Train

MEDILL SCHOOL OF JOURNALISM

Northwestern University Press
Evanston, Illinois

Northwestern University Press
www.nupress.northwestern.edu

Printed in the United States of America

10 9 8 7 6 5 4 3 2 1

Library of Congress Cataloging-in-Publication Data

Neuzil, Mark.
    The environment and the press : from adventure writing to advocacy /
Mark Neuzil ; foreword by Russell E. Train.
        p. cm. — (Medill School of Journalism Visions of the American Press)
    Includes bibliographical references and index.
    ISBN-13: 978-0-8101-2403-5 (pbk. : alk. paper)
    ISBN-10: 0-8101-2403-3 (pbk. : alk. paper)
    1. Mass media and the environment. 2. Communication in science. I. Title.
P96.E57N48 2008
070.4'493337—dc22
                                                          2008008602

For Amy, Elena, Maria, Gabriel

CONTENTS

FOREWORD

Russell E. Train

This excellent book by Mark Neuzil goes well beyond the apparent framework of its title, *The Environment and the Press: From Adventure Writing to Advocacy.* I think of the "press" as being pretty synonymous with journalism, whatever the media. Professor Neuzil covers this narrower scope in detail, but he goes well beyond it—and rightly so—to give us a detailed picture of environmental writing over the years, principally in the United States. Indeed, in his preface he defines "environmental journalism . . . as the gathering, writing, editing, and distribution of information about the interaction of people and the natural world, and issues related to that interaction." You can't get much broader than that!

Of the environmental writers discussed in this book who actually influenced my own thinking, I would single out Aldo Leopold. His concept of land as a "community" rather than just as a "commodity" had (and has) strong appeal for me, intellectually as well as emotionally. I like to think that the concept was one of the building blocks of the National Land Use Policy Act drafted by the Council on Environmental Quality (CEQ) under my chairmanship in 1970 and submitted by President Richard Nixon to two successive Congresses.[1]

I was privileged to hold three highly visible government jobs during the eight years of the Nixon and Ford administrations: undersecretary of the Department of the Interior, chairman of the CEQ, and administrator of the Environmental Protection Agency (EPA), in that order. The Department of the Interior had very significant environmental jurisdictions, including national parks, fish and wildlife, outdoor recreation, public lands, and the Federal Water Pollution Control Administration (prior to its transfer to the EPA when the latter was created toward the end of 1970).

That was a time, particularly from 1969 to 1972, when the environment was high on the public agenda and was being given an equally high priority by both the Nixon White House and the Congress. Reflecting this state of affairs, many major newspapers had reporters assigned to the environmental beat, as well as reporters who did occasional environmental articles.

I particularly recall Ned Kenworthy, Gladwin Hill, Bob Semple, Bill Shannon, and Phil Shabecoff at the *New York Times,* Al Otten and Burt Schorr at the *Wall Street Journal,* George Wilson, Elsie Carper, Carroll Kilpatrick, Don Oberdorfer, Bob O'Toole, and Margot Hornblower at the *Washington Post,* Stan Benjamin at the Associated Press (AP), Roberta Hornig at the *Washington Star,* and Jim Bishop at *Newsweek.* There were also Bob Cahn and Godfrey Sperling Jr. of the *Christian Science Monitor.* On a more regional level, I recall Casey Bukro of the *Chicago Tribune,* Howard Scarlett of the *Houston Post,* and Bill Wyant of the *St. Louis Post-Dispatch.* There were, of course, many others.

I believed then, as I do now, that a close and positive relationship with the press was a vital part of the environmental responsibilities I filled in government. And even though they had to maintain something of an "arm's-length" relationship to protect the objectivity of their reporting, I also assumed that a good working rapport was important for members of the press assigned to cover environmental developments. Furthermore, from my standpoint, my relationship with the press was important not only for building and sustaining public support for the environment generally, but also for specific environmental issues in which I became engaged.

Thus, in 1976 I gave a speech at the National Press Club in Washington on the Toxic Substances Control Act (TOSCA), which had been developed at the CEQ and submitted by President Nixon to Congress in 1971. Five years later, the act's fate in Congress was increasingly uncertain. Unlike my usual style, I used alarmist language to describe the potential threats to the public from the continued introduction into the environment of untested chemicals, and a recent toxic scare involving a chemical called Kepone lent some urgency to the issue. The speech and the Q&A that followed were carried live by 183 public broadcasting radio stations. It was on the evening news and was covered by both the AP and United Press International (UPI). I was interviewed by National Public Radio on *All Things Considered* and by NBC-TV. The *New York Times* carried an extensive article by Ned Kenworthy, and the *Washington Post* did an editorial on the speech. In any event, TOSCA subsequently was passed by Congress and has been the law now for thirty years. I have no doubt that the unusual press coverage helped light a fire under Congress—and helped persuade President Ford to sign the bill.

In a less dramatic instance, in 1971 President Nixon proposed to Congress legislation to control and regulate the dumping of wastes at sea. We succeeded in getting the issue before the 1972 Stockholm Conference on the Human Environment, and a convention to control the disposal of wastes at sea was adopted in London later that year. Press coverage of the convention debates was extensive, including a front-page article in the *New York Times*. Congress then took up the legislation, commonly referred to as the Ocean Dumping Act, and passed it—an interesting example of international activity helping trigger domestic U.S. action.

I have to add that during my eight years in the Nixon and Ford administrations, I was always treated fairly by the press. I do not recall a single instance when I felt I had been misled or misreported or that any interview guidelines had been violated. At the same time, I believe I always tried to be square with the press, even when that might have been politically tricky for me. One example of this had to do with the passing of the Clean Air Act in 1972. Senator Edmund Muskie was unquestionably the environmental leader in the Democratic Congress and played the principal congressional role in formulating and then passing this important legislation. President Nixon held the signing ceremony at the White House, which included a number of congressional dignitaries—all except Ed Muskie, who, in an act of pure political pettiness, was not invited. When I went before the White House press after the bill-signing ceremony, I was asked by the press if the omission of Muskie was unusual. I readily agreed that it was, and made no effort to defend the omission.

In 1974, Nixon was weakened by Watergate and a national energy crisis. He wanted to relax emissions standards to make it easier for power plants to burn dirty fuels. Invited to a meeting in the cabinet room with Nixon and others to thrash out an agreement, I made clear that I would agree to nothing more than providing power plants a temporary variance from legal emission levels on a case-by-case basis, but without any overall lowering of standards (actually, this flexibility was already authorized by the Clean Air Act). After our meeting, however, the president went before the White House press and announced a general lowering of standards. Asked whether I had agreed, the president said I had. When the press called me afterward to find out whether that was true, I told them it was not. (It was fortunate, in any event, that Congress never acted on the presidential proposal.)[2]

Overall, the press was integral to our success in advancing the environmental agenda during those years of the 1970s. The extensive and prominent press coverage helped educate the public and heighten public awareness of environmental issues. In so doing, the press helped build and sustain congressional support. Moreover, I believe that, on the whole, such environmental reporting by the principal media was performed objectively and not in a spirit of advocacy. Of course, as political attention shifted in the mid-1970s to the energy crisis and then generally away from the environment, press coverage diminished. Today, with the growing scientific and public concern over global warming, the pendulum may be swinging back again.

Sadly, the public visibility of the EPA has almost disappeared during the George W. Bush administration. The EPA administrator seldom appears in the press, and public statements on environmental policy are routinely made by the CEQ chairman, who is, of course, speaking for the White House rather than for the responsible agency. All of this presumably means tighter control by White House political operatives, but it also greatly diminishes the public's trust and confidence in the EPA. The unfortunate fact is that there is little or no environmental leadership in the administration today. I hope that a more proactive environmental press will help reverse that situation.

As Professor Neuzil's narrative so ably demonstrates, the historical context of the interrelation of journalism and the environmental movement is a very important one. It is also a history that is still being written. As the current climate change crisis continues to unfold, I am convinced that the interrelation of the environment with energy and economic policy, with problems of political instability abroad, and with threats to our own national security will become increasingly apparent.

And it is certainly my hope that the press will play an ever more active role in informing the American public about not only these complex problems, but also their solution.

In the race to get today's news first, few journalists are interested in history. Almost nothing hurts a journalist more than having one of his or her stories insulted as "old news."

Not many of today's environmentalists are interested in the past, either—there's no looking back for these folks. "Nostalgia for the golden past is only intermittently discernable in this new case for greater simplicity," is how philosopher Peter Hay put it.[1] One of the differences between the first great wave of environmentalism in the United States—represented by Emerson, Thoreau, and the other transcendentalists starting in the 1830s—and the post–World War II movement is the yearning for a return to the primitive in the former while the latter is "oriented firmly to the future."[2]

Would it follow that modern environmental journalists are not interested in history? Not given the nature of their subject matter. Stories about humans and their interaction with the environment are incomplete without a historical context—scientists work for years on a problem, pollution accumulates over time, and today's subdivision was yesterday's soybean field. Environmental journalism, too, has a past. It has been influenced by nature writers, farmers, adventurers, mystics, and big-game hunters. This book attempts to draw those sources and others into a coherent story about today's environmental journalists. How did they come to be? What were their main influences? Who were some of their forerunners? What issues were written about? Why?

Mainstream environmental journalists in the twenty-first century are, for the most part, journalists who cover the environment, rather than environmentalists who practice journalism. It is an important distinction. There is another distinction in these pages: this book deals with news media, and it mostly leaves out entertainment media. I make this point because the average reader or viewer does not often think about the inexact usage of the general term *media;* Oprah Winfrey is in the media business, but not the news media business. The blurring of the line between entertainment and news is a subject for another day.

This book is written for anyone interested in the environment in the United States, and I figure that includes just about everyone. Who isn't interested in clear air and clean water? Or photogenic megafauna? Of course, how the water gets clean or the moose stays alive is often the point of some contention—and that's part of what makes the environment so newsworthy.

Many of the country's leading environmental journalists are close personal friends of mine (as the old saying goes), and I've had enough conversations with them over the years to know that they are interested in their profession and how it got to be where it is. This book is also for them.

My own interest in the environment began when I was a kid, passionate about fishing and hunting, in Iowa.[3] Environmental degradation was not visible to me in the late 1960s and early 1970s; I was too young to see it. If the fish in "my" lake had all died because of a spill, or the cottontails had disappeared because of a disease, I might have noticed.

At the same time, I think it was my love for fishing and hunting that brought me to an interest in history. Of the authors who influence those who cover the environment—outdoor writers, science writers, nature writers—outdoor writers perhaps most often express a yearning for days gone by, when ducks blackened the sky, pheasants cackled at dogs, trout rose to the fly, and grouse drummed thick on the ground. Today's best outdoor writers still flavor their work with appeals to nostalgia, even if it is a desire to return to days that never were.

Anyone who knows me knows I like to tell stories. (Every fisherman does.) I have tried to treat this work like a series of stories within a framework that could serve a classroom as well as a den. In the course of my research, I was delighted to dig up some interesting stories from the archives and present them to a new audience. One of my favorites is the story of the "Nature Man," Joseph Knowles (from chapter 7), the charlatan who claimed to live on his own in the Maine woods in 1913 and entertained the reading public for several weeks with his made-up exploits.

Before I began this project, I had never heard of a reporter and editor named Sam J. Shelton, who was hired by the *St. Louis Post-Dispatch* in 1913. He deserves credit not only as a solid and versatile reporter but also as a proto-environmental journalist. Besides covering crime, Shelton specialized in writing about utilities, particularly coal and electric, as well as many other conservation issues. He worked at the paper for forty-four years, retiring as Joseph Pulitzer II's personal assistant.

Some stories are in this book because they have resonated with my students over the years. (And I left out others that have bored them silly.) Students are almost always interested in the infamous Cuyahoga River fire from 1969. How could water catch fire? The conflict over feathers in women's fashions from the turn of the twentieth century also gets their attention—an entire stuffed bird on a hat? What was that about? The reaction of the students is representative of what has changed in our cultural environmental consciousness over the years. For all of recorded history, rivers have been used for human effluents, and bird and animal skins have been used for ornament. The thought that there might be something improper with using rivers as sewers and animals as clothing is recent.

There is no hard-and-fast definition of environmental journalism, as opposed to, say, science journalism or agricultural journalism. It seems reasonable to assume that science journalists write about scientists and their work and agricultural journalists write about farmers and agribusiness, and so environmental journalists cover environmentalists and the environment. But it is not only environmentalists who draw attention from these journalists. Politicians are important, as are business leaders, religious figures, homeowners, and others. For this book, environmental journalism is defined as the gathering, writing, editing, and distribution of information about the interaction of people and the natural world, and issues related to that interaction.

Many people deserve thanks for reading parts of this book and commenting on it. Among them are Amy Kuebelbeck, Beth Parke, Dan Philippon, Mark Schleifstein, Mark Harvey, David Backes, Stephen Laumakis, Tom Rochon, Christopher Thompson, Jim Motavalli, and Bill Allen. More people than I have space to mention helped with research, tips, sources, and general advice. And thanks to David Abrahamson and Northwestern University Press for seeing it through to completion.

THE ENVIRONMENT AND THE PRESS

ONE

INTRODUCTION

The week between Christmas and New Year's Day is a slow one for journalists. The savvy editor knows to have several feature-length "year-in-reviews" in the hopper to fill the lull. On the other hand, the savvy public relations person knows that a story may get more attention around the holidays, perhaps receiving uncritical coverage from rookie reporters and editors who got stuck working while the veterans are on holiday.

That was the scenario two days after Christmas 2002, when a fringe scientific group connected to the Raelian religion called Clonaid claimed it had engineered the birth of the world's first cloned baby, nicknamed "Eve." Despite Clonaid's unwillingness or inability to produce any evidence of the child—not so much as a photograph—news media from all over the world carried the story, including live broadcasts from the press conference by CNN, MSNBC, and Fox News. "If you didn't know what a Raelian was on Thursday—and let's face it, you didn't," wrote one observer, "you knew practically everything about them by Monday."[1]

A CNN medical reporter reported that Clonaid had "the

capacity to clone."[2] A former science editor for ABC News stood near the Clonaid spokeswoman at the podium, and although he did not speak, his presence seemed to add gravitas to the announcement.[3] (He later said he regretted it.) Clonaid's connection to the Raelian movement, which claims that life on Earth began when extraterrestrials cloned themselves twenty-five thousand years ago, was not always mentioned in the reports.

The story had all the trappings for the environmental journalist—science, medicine, religion, and even a little agriculture and natural philosophy. Perhaps the only thing missing was an outdoor adventure, although the Raelians' practices of public nudity and sexual freedom might qualify.[4]

As we used to say in the newsroom, it had all the makings of a good story, except it wasn't true. Eventually word leaked to reporters that members of the Raelian movement were mocking the news media for their coverage of the announcement.[5] "For an investment of $3,000 in U.S. funds, it got us media coverage worth more than $15 million," said the head of the Raelian church. "I am still laughing."[6] Criticism of the news media's performance was as intense as it was deserved. "As soon as I heard about the Raelians' cloning claim, I knew it was nonsense," said Arthur Caplan, a bioethicist at the University of Pennsylvania. "The media have shown themselves incapable of covering the key social and intellectual phenomena of the 21st century, namely the revolution in genetics and biology."[7] The former head of the National Institutes of Health said, "The smell of deception, fraud, and Barnum & Bailey circusism is everywhere in the air."[8]

Environmental journalists and their colleagues who cover medicine, science, public health, and religion chattered about the story on electronic discussion lists and Web sites. Mea culpas were issued, bad jokes abounded, and the usual promises of doing better next time were proclaimed. Many of the reporters who specialize in covering the environment were unhappy with their colleagues who failed to check the story out or did not have the training to know what to ask.

News media coverage of issues related to the environment—even when they turn out to be hoaxes—is not new, but those reporters who were chagrined at the uncritical cloning stories are part of a more recent phenomenon. That phenomenon is called environmental journalism. How environmental journalism became a regular journalistic practice, how it functioned, and how it may affect journalism in the future are the main subjects of this book.

This work draws on several categories of mass communication scholarship. Among the subjects scholars have addressed is the relationship between the news media and environmental issues in specific historical times and places. For example, in *Making a Real Killing,* Len Ackland examined the circumstances surrounding the controversial Rocky Flats Nuclear Arsenal in Colorado.[9] And David Backes looked at the role of the media and other institutions in the creation of the Boundary Waters Canoe Area Wilderness in northern Minnesota.[10] Another category of scholarship is the examination of the mass media and particular issues, including nuclear power, biotechnology, and endangered species. Environmental risk, for example, is an important subject for investigation and has been examined in numerous books.[11] A third category of scholarship is social and cultural criticism of the way the news media report on environmental issues.[12] Rhetoricians and other experts in communication studies have examined discourse, symbolism, language use, and popular culture.[13] And finally, there are the handbooks and guides for working reporters, broadcast news directors, and editors.[14]

THE PERSPECTIVE OF THIS BOOK

This book takes the position that throughout history, various power groups have interacted on many levels to induce social change. These groups control the direction of change in a society, more or less. Conflicts arise as these actors struggle for control, and change often occurs when the members of the power structure agree on which direction to take.

Social problems need to be recognized, defined, and legitimized by society in order to evolve. One of the ways a particular problem gains the attention of society's power groups is by its being brought into the public arena by the mass media. In the environmental arena, groups struggling for control include environmentalists, various governments, business interests, nonprofit organizations, scientists and universities, organized religion, farmers, outdoor lovers, and many others.

Although in the United States the news media's traditional, self-defined role is as an independent entity (commonly known as the Fourth Estate), it is more accurate to say that newspapers, magazines, and other journalistic forms exist as one of a series of interdependent circles along with their sources, readers, advertisers, community elites, government officials, and others. The news media function, in part, by defining some environmental issues as social problems and ignoring others. Historical eras, with all their differences, can come up with alternative answers to the question of what is news. For example, when the last pair of great auks in the world was killed off the coast of Iceland in June 1844, the deaths of the birds brought very little media coverage.[15] When the spotted owl, listed as an endangered species, got in the way of the timber industry in the Pacific Northwest about 150 years later, it became an issue in a U.S. presidential campaign.[16]

While groups in society operate to influence media coverage to their benefit, the news media can and do function independently as a powerful social agent. Social change, including public opinion, government regulation, industry and labor effects, and ecological transformation can be brought about or hurried along by media attention. Books, magazines, newspapers, television, and the Internet help define issues; communities of environmental awareness are created and influenced by media coverage. "Environment journalism has . . . played a role of mobilizing civic action," wrote Guy Berger. "Thus many stories are framed as a drama of choice: Save the planet or go under!"[17]

A couple of generations ago, sociologist Neil Smelzer recognized that two conditions are necessary for the emergence and development of a social movement such as environmentalism. One is social conduciveness and the other is structural strain.[18] What does social conduciveness mean in the development of environmentalism in the United States? The short answer is, it depends on the historical period. In the Progressive Era (1898–1920), the familiar trio of urbanization, industrialization, and immigration led to a kind of nostalgia for a more agrarian, or at least less citified, past and the creation of groups like the Boy Scouts, the Audubon Society, and others in what historian David Shi called a quest for the simple life.[19] Fredrick Jackson Turner's 1893 claim of the taming of the frontier added to the mix. Structural strains happen when arguments break out over how social problems are recognized, such as the proper "use" of a tamed frontier: National park? Cattle ranch? Copper mine? Water resource?

There is a complex relationship between media coverage and the strength of any social movement. Among other things, social movements need the media in order to communicate, recruit new members, solidify bonds with current members, raise funds, and compete with other groups for scarce resources. The media do not always work for progress; sometimes their function is more about social control than social change. The media usually reflect the dominant values of the day.[20] Complaints about their "bad press" from various "fringe" groups in society agitating for change probably have existed since shortly after Gutenberg's invention of movable metal type. Although one popular image of the news media is as a sentinel (for example, the "watchdog function" of the press), a more interesting concept related to social control is of the media as "guard dogs" who protect the interests of the power structure.[21] The guard dog works for its owner as the media protect the dominant members of society; if a squabble breaks out, the media may side against the weakest group in the fight. Thus the messages of the more radical environmental groups, such as EarthFirst! or the Sea Shepherds, get marginalized in news coverage.[22]

Journalistic routines or competitive pressures sometimes override any social control functions of the mass media. A common competitive situation in environmental reporting is in the coverage of a natural disaster. When CNN, MSNBC, and the other television networks rushed to the Gulf Coast in the wake of Hurricane Katrina in 2005, their coverage was highly critical of the powers that be (including President George W. Bush, and the federal response to the disaster).[23] The poor and powerless, stranded at the Superdome or on their roofs or floating dead in the muck, were reported on without fear or favor. At least one commentator said that the news media were "essential again" in providing accurate and crucial information. Journalists were sticking up for the little guy.

For the little guy, it seemed to be about time. Katrina had been preceded by a long stretch of journalistic misdeeds, sagging public confidence, and heavy criticism of the industry.[24] After the intensely competitive and hard-hitting news stories in the wake of the Katrina disaster, one response from the federal government was to tighten controls on information available to the news media, including materials related to the handling of the crisis by the Federal Emergency Management Agency.[25]

THE ORGANIZATION OF THIS BOOK

This book is meant to be a general survey of the tributaries and main currents that flow through the history of American environmental reporting; it includes materials from specific case studies and time periods, but it is organized thematically.[26]

Environmental journalism grew out of older, more established forms of writing about the environment, and these forms can be found in today's stories.[27] Part 1 of this book, comprising chapters 2 through 5, is titled "Tributaries." The themes discussed in part 1 exist, in one form or another, in the modern currents of environmental journalism. Chapter 2 discusses the prophetic voice of environmental journalists and the enduring myth of the Great Flood. It interprets ancient texts, looks at Aldo Leopold's essay on the prophets, and notes how often the label of false prophet is applied to journalists and their sources. These strains are tied together and exemplified in the coverage of Hurricane Katrina in 2005.

Chapter 3 looks at early writing about science and agriculture and the relationship of farm publications and journalism education. It studies the reappearance of themes that occur in ancient texts from writers on agriculture and science—like Pliny the Elder, Cato the Elder, and Columella—in modern stories, and it examines the development of journalism schools at land-grant colleges across the country as spurred by the need for agricultural journalists.

Chapter 4 traces the influence of outdoor adventure writing, beginning with Izaak Walton. His classic book, *The Compleat Angler,* was the standard by which such writers were judged for hundreds of years. The issues he raised, like exotic species and catch-and-release angling, still appear in news stories, columns, and books in the twenty-first century. The political involvement of outdoor adventure writers, including their important role in the passage of game laws in the United States, and the formation of pressure groups like the Izaak Walton League are significant parts of the story.

Chapter 5 outlines a general history of nature writing, including examples of the craft that environmental journalists have called influential in their work. Familiar figures like Henry David Thoreau, John Burroughs, John Muir, Leopold, and Sigurd Olson are examined.

Part 2 of this book, titled "Main Currents," addresses the primary forms of environmental journalism in recent times: persuasive writing, twentieth-century mainstream journalism practices, and broadcast media. Chapter 6, on persuasive communication, looks at the touchy subject of advocacy in environmental journalism. Historical examples of journalistic techniques used to advocate a cause, including Benjamin Franklin and the tanners in Philadelphia, the trade in bird feathers, and the debate over the creation of Dinosaur National Monument, are highlighted.

Chapter 7 looks at early mainstream environmental journalism in the United States, examining reoccurring themes in stories from the early twentieth century to the 1960s. Such journalism included the Alaskan land fraud story of the muckraking period, the "Nature Man" and the back-to-nature movement, and workplace accidents in mines and tunnels.

Chapter 8 picks up in the 1960s with the publication of *Silent Spring* and moves into the early 1970s with the environment established as a beat at mainstream newspapers around the United States. The influence and circumstances of Rachel Carson, the Cuyahoga River fire, and the development of the Society of Environmental Journalists are explored.

Broadcast environmental news, particularly the importance of media mogul Ted Turner and his extensive cable operations, are the focus of chapter 9. The National Public Radio show *Living on Earth,* the importance of the Discovery Channel, and professional training for television and radio reporters are discussed.

The final section, "On the Horizon," and the last chapter contemporize the issue. It looks at twenty-first-century practices of environmental journalism in the light of the field's historical development, discusses trends in the digital era, and speculates on the future of the craft, including the precarious position of the objectivity standard in North American journalism.

PART I

TRIBUTARIES

TWO

JOURNALISM'S PROPHETIC VOICE

Journalists, particularly those covering environmental issues, serve a prophetic function in modern times that can be seen as analogous to prophets from ancient texts. The Hebrew word for prophet, *navi,* is closely related to an Arabic word that means to proclaim or to carry out a mandate.[1] The root meaning of the Hebrew word signifies that a prophet, like a journalist, is the deliverer of a message. In his examination of the religious roots of the secular press, Doug Underwood coined the phrase "prophetic journalism"—by which he meant "a journalism of passion, polemic, and moral opinion that has come to exist alongside the modern ethic of objectivity and the commercial elements of profit taking that dictate so much of what journalism constitutes today."[2] Underwood suggested a journalistic link from the Hebrew prophets to modern columnists, investigative reporters, and editorialists. Further, most journalists do not recognize the prophetic voice in their work, he wrote, but it exists in stories of social justice and reform, albeit in a diluted and secularized way.[3]

In ancient texts, prophets spoke of hope and accountability as common themes. Certainly journalists would see themselves as writing about accountability; Underwood recalled the old directive to journalists to "afflict the comfortable and comfort the afflicted." The phrase is reminiscent of Ezekiel: "I will seek the lost, and I will bring back the strayed, and I will bind up the injured, and I will strengthen the weak, but the fat and the strong I will destroy. I will feed them with justice."[4] And accountability is evident in journalistically inspired phrases such as "Remember the *Maine!*"

The reform impulse, often hopeful in tone among editors such as James Gordon Bennett, S. S. McClure, and E. W. Scripps, featured oratory recognized by any preacher. "In a land of freedom and equal rights," thundered one Bennett article on the sorry state of New York City's nineteenth-century debtor prisons, "that such a thing should be tolerated but for an instant, is monstrous—wicked—blasphemous."[5] More recently, hope is a common theme in stories about medical breakthroughs, for example, and order restoration themes are frequently employed after conflicts or natural disasters.

Other journalists have been explicitly compared to prophets. The new journalism author Tom Wolfe was called an "American Jeremiah" for his use of religious themes as he covered cultural movements in the 1960s and later, and his writing often stressed repentance and the opportunity for renewal.[6] Gonzo journalist Hunter S. Thompson, of the same era, was described as having a "strident apocalyptic invective" in his political and moral critiques of American society.[7]

Scholars James Ettema and Theodore Glasser drew a distinction between those who are moral arbiters of a community (like the ancient prophets could be) and those who engage the public's sense of right and wrong (like modern-day journalists). Reporters interviewed by the two scholars described their work in terms of news judgments—defined by the standards of the craft rather than by moral judgments or what society views as "right behavior."[8] In this way the reporters defended the objectivity standard in journalism, while at the same time, Ettema and Glasser said, their stories seemed to "help define the boundaries of the moral order."[9]

If the meaning of "moral" considers the rightness or wrongness of human behavior, or the goodness or badness of the human character, there is an implied similarity of journalism to religious thought. The link between moral reformers, religion, and journalists was perhaps most evident in U.S. history in the Progressive Era, when the Protestant and Social Gospel-influenced muckrakers were at their peak. "The socially responsible reporter-reformer" was historian Richard Hofstadter's memorable phrase, and it was lived out in the works of Ray Stannard Baker, who campaigned for civil rights; Ida Tarbell, who fought the Standard Oil monopoly; and Lincoln Steffens, who tried to clean up civic corruption.[10]

The prophetic impulse among journalists is an implied link between religion and mass media in the United States, but there are other more direct connections as well. David Paul Nord has identified the beginnings of mass media in the United States in the printing and distribution systems of the New England tract and Bible societies, which took full advantage of new technologies and sent tens of thousands of religious books and papers across the country in the early nineteenth century.[11] Paul C. Gutjahr has described how the printers and marketers of the Bible were central to the growth of the American publishing industry during the same period.[12] By the late nineteenth century, evangelicals were firmly established in the American media marketplace with Bibles, sermons, songbooks, children's books, missionary tracts, magazines, and Sunday school materials.[13] Perhaps the best-known newspaper with a religious affiliation became a full-scale daily, the *Christian Science Monitor,* started by Mary Baker Eddy in 1908 as an alternative to the sensationalistic press of the period.[14] All Christian publishers were following the advice of Mark: "Go ye into the world, and preach the gospel to every creature."[15] Most translations of the word *gospel* take it to mean *good news.*[16]

PREDICTING THE FUTURE

A modern-day environmental journalist, perhaps as much as any reporter, is called on to write stories about what might happen in the future. Nowhere is this more prevalent than in the number of words filed on the subject of climate change. Scientists, the journalists' primary sources on these stories, are in agreement that global warming (an increase in the planet's mean atmospheric temperatures as a result of human activity) is of major concern.

Ross Gelbspan, a former special projects editor with the *Boston Globe,* has focused on the climate change story. His 1997 book, *The Heat Is On: The High Stakes Battle over Earth's Threatened Climate,* was read by President Clinton and attacked by the fossil fuel industry. The book's opening sentences seemed to conjure ancient images of disaster: the city of New Orleans, after going through the winters of 1990 to 1995 without a killing frost, was overrun by mosquitoes, cockroaches, and termites who were biting, infecting, and chewing their way through town. Other images that recalled biblical disasters, including floods, heat waves, heavy rain, snowstorms, and droughts, were all vividly described in the first few pages.

Although Gelbspan's book described modern climatic events and the political machinations surrounding the greenhouse gas issue, some of his reporting was predictive (and still heavily sourced). For example, he wrote about what could happen in coastal communities around the world should sea levels rise (twenty-six million refugees from Bangladesh, twelve million from the Egyptian delta, twenty million from India, and as many as seventy to one hundred million from China would be forced to evacuate).[17] Many scientists quoted by the author relied on computer models to estimate what might take place. In his conclusions, Gelbspan departed from a more traditional standard of objective journalism by offering remedies to the problem ("a change in our energy technologies") and by criticizing foot-dragging politicians ("partial and inadequate measures").[18] "The pervasive denial of global warming that so frustrates the reporter in me could perhaps change with equal suddenness," he wrote.[19] One reviewer, writing in the *Los Angeles Times,* called Gelbspan "impatient."[20] At least one conservative critic called him a false prophet.[21] (Gelbspan anticipated such criticism in a forty-one-page appendix.)

In his way, Gelbspan was following a path of prophesying that has its roots in ancient texts. The prophets for whom books are named in the Bible—Isaiah, Amos, Hosea, and the others—began appearing about eight hundred years before Christ; many of them used stories about nature to get their points across.[22] Prophets often appeared during times of great social agitation, which probably helped them get more attention and get their ideas more widely dispersed. Prophets also wrote and spoke both in metaphoric and literal ways to help their audience understand the message. Isaiah is a good example. Although not much is known about him, Isaiah is considered to have been highly educated and from a prosperous if not high-status family, perhaps in Jerusalem. (Scholars debate how much of the book of Isaiah was written by the man himself—not all of it was, because although he prophesied for nearly sixty years, some of what is written in the later chapters describes political circumstances that happened 150 years after his death.) Like the other prophets, Isaiah suffered his share of criticism—the label of false prophet was often thrown at him.

Among the biblical prophets, Isaiah had much to say about the natural world. One of his most famous passages is from chapter 24, in which it is written:

> The earth dries up and withers, the world languishes and withers; the heavens languish together with the earth. The earth lies polluted under its inhabitants; for they have transgressed laws, violated the statutes, broken the everlasting covenant.[23]

Isaiah was a product of his time. It would be a mistake to think of him as a journalist, of course, but his words about pollution from 2,800 years ago seem remarkably modern. Many of the ancient writers loved the Earth and its creatures because God created them all, and one way writers would emphasize the consequences of sin was to speak in terms of the destruction of God's landscape. They could imagine little worse in the way of disaster and accountability. Most of what Isaiah wrote (and he and his followers wrote a lot: their book is one of the longest of the prophetic books of the Old Testament) covered the political turmoil of the eighth and seventh centuries B.C. The foregoing text was taken from the chapters called "Apocalypse of Isaiah," so described because of the use of themes found in later apocalyptic writings. In verses like those in chapter 24, Isaiah was painting a picture of the destruction of the Earth, not unlike the warnings of modern works like *The Heat*

Is On or *The Population Bomb,* which in 1968 predicted catastrophe for humanity because of starvation and overpopulation.

Like the job of a journalist (or an economist, or a stock trader, or a meteorologist, or other occupations that traffic in the future), the business of being a prophet was a profession in ancient times.[24] (People who asked for predictions sometimes paid for them.) Although prophecy is a special call by God, some prophets also had a sort of socialization—scholars note that they often used similar language, wore the same types of clothes, and congregated with each other, and many had a self-inflicted scar on the forehead.[25] God was their primary source, and he was quoted through visions, dreams, and other appearances. "Biblical prophets occasionally made predictions about the future course of events, but they never did it to demonstrate how insightful or divinely inspired they were," wrote theologian Barry L. Bandstra. "Their predictions were basically extrapolations from the present state of affairs into the future, based on their knowledge of what God demanded."[26] Prophets were the intermediaries between the human and the divine realms; prediction was part of their job description but not all of it.

LEOPOLD ON THE PROPHETS

The historian Thomas Dunlap called environmentalism "part of a human impulse toward religion."[27] Perhaps no twentieth-century writer other than Rachel Carson has had a greater impact on environmental journalism than Aldo Leopold, whose 1949 book *A Sand County Almanac* is considered one of the landmark texts in the field. Leopold was a young forester in New Mexico when his views of the land began to shift. He rejected the model of managing natural resources for the consumption of humans (acquired in his Yale schooling) and began to tie the notions of ecology and ethics; humans, Leopold argued, had moral obligations to the natural world. An action of a human is "right when [it] tend[s] to preserve the integrity, stability, and beauty of the biotic community. It is wrong when it tends otherwise," he wrote.[28]

Moral obligations, of course, often have religious overtones. Leopold had explored this idea in a 1920 article for the *Journal of Forestry* called "Forestry and the Prophets." In his article, Leopold connected biblical prophets to modern figures like Theodore Roosevelt and John Muir. A biblical scholar might find fault with his analysis of the ecological awareness of the prophets (Leopold admitted his effort was "amateurish"), but his audience of foresters, ranchers, farmers, hunters, and government agents in the Southwest would have appreciated his conversational voice and storytelling style.

As a thirty-four-year-old forester in 1920, Leopold was looking for the beginnings of ancient forestry practices. He recognized that the Israelites did not practice forestry as he knew it, but out of necessity they understood a great deal about wood and silviculture. "Isaiah was the Roosevelt of the Holy Land," Leopold wrote. "He knew a lot about everything, including forests, and told what he knew in no uncertain terms. He constantly used the forest to illustrate his teachings, and in doing so calls trees by their first names."[29] Leopold was referring to Isaiah's technique of adding detail to his work: "Unlike Solomon and Daniel and Ecclesiasticus, [Isaiah] is not given to calling a tree just 'a tree.'"[30] Trees are cedars of Lebanon, oaks of Bashan, holm oak, boxwood, sycamore, cypress, olive, terebinth (cashew), acacia, pine, myrtle, fir, and fig. (Here Isaiah exemplifies the advice from many a writing coach: "Be specific.")

In 1920 Leopold was well aware of the reputation of John Muir, who had died only seven years earlier, as the prophet of the mountains. He cleverly flips this image on the writer of the book of Job, whom he called "the John Muir of Judah, author of . . . one of the most magnificent essays on the wonders of nature so far produced by the human race."[31] In chapter 12, Job said:

> "But ask the animals, and they will teach you; the birds of the air, and they will tell you; ask the plants of the earth, and they will teach you; and the fish of the sea, and they will declare to you."[32]

From Ezekiel, Leopold quoted the following:

> "Seemeth it a small thing unto you to have fed upon the good pasture, but ye must tread down with your feet the residue of your pasture? And to have drunk of the clear waters, but ye must foul the residue with your feet?"[33]

That, Leopold wrote, is "the doctrine of conservation, from its subjective side, as aptly put as by any forester of this generation."[34] Leopold also wrote about forest fires in the Holy Land; the fires appealed to the early writers' sense of imagery and need for simile and allegory. In the conclusion of the essay, Leopold said he hoped to write on the subject of game and fish in the Old Testament, but he never did.

FALSE PROPHETS

The denigratory label of false prophet has been applied to environmental journalists and their subjects. Those who are critical of or oppose environmentalists politically or economically use that pejorative term; for example, *Reason* magazine correspondent Ronald Bailey's 1993 book was titled *Eco-Scam: The False Prophets of Ecological Apocalypse.*[35] "The most recent apocalypse [global warming] fits the classic pattern for millenarian doomsaying," Bailey wrote. "Humanity has brought impending doom down upon itself. Some might escape if we repent and sacrifice. A small self-appointed vanguard of volunteers offer to lead us to the promised land in a post-crisis egalitarian utopia."[36] One early 1970s eco-bashing book was called *The Disaster Lobby: Prophets of Ecological Doom and Other Absurdities.*[37]

The prophetic voice of journalists is related to and dependent on its sources; it cannot be understood without them. When sources are not accurate or journalists are not sufficiently skeptical, claims of false prophecy may follow. For example, on March 23, 1989, electrochemists Martin Fleischmann of Southampton University and B. Stanley Pons of the University of Utah announced at a press conference that they had observed cold fusion—a way to produce energy cheaply and simply from nuclear fusion, one of the enduring conundrums in modern science. A University of Utah vice president told the news media: "If indeed this scientific discovery proves to be as practical as it appears to be, not only does the world's population get a promise of virtually unlimited energy, it gets the elimination of acid rain, reduces the greenhouse effect and allows us to use fossil fuels in a way which is more important than simply lighting a match to them."[38] Print and broadcast outlets from around the world, functioning more as stenographers than journalists, trumpeted their findings, adding sidebars on the end of oil dependence and the dawning of an era of cheap, limitless energy. A *Wall Street Journal* headline read: IF VERIFIED, THEIR EXPERIMENT PROMISES TO POINT THE WAY TO A VAST SOURCE OF POWER.[39]

In one of those head-shaking historical happenstances, a few hours after the *Journal* and other newspapers around the world repeated the story of the startling experiments, the oil tanker *Exxon Valdez* ran aground in Prince William Sound in Alaska. More than eleven million gallons of crude oil (and perhaps as much as thirty million gallons) oozed into the harbor, one of the largest single oil spills in history. Issues of oil, energy dependence, and ecology came together in two major stories over the days ahead. Images of oil-soaked beaches, otters, birds, and fishing boats dominated the news. Stories of the Utah-based scientists and a photograph of them and their simple experiment—jackets and ties, electrolytic cells, palladium electrodes, and heavy water—and the images of the oil spill were "suddenly juxtaposed with millenarian speculations about the impending energy revolution."[40] A few stories noted that the Utah findings had not been peer-reviewed—that is, subject to the scrutiny of their colleagues and published in a reputable journal. Many scientists were skeptical of the news reports, but that did not stop them from rushing to their laboratories to try to replicate the results.[41]

By the end of 1990, cold fusion was in trouble. A string of negative outcomes cast doubt on the Utah findings; others could not duplicate their experiment. Critics piled on, disparaging Fleischmann and Pons's techniques, measurements, data analysis, and ability to draw press attention. "Funding for cold fusion research dried up, journals declined to referee their papers, graduate students were warned off the field," wrote Jon Turney in *New Scientist*.[42] A fresh round of news media criticism began. A physicist writing in the *Washington Post* denounced "lazy journalists who had accepted every press release at face value."[43] In 1998 the University of Utah announced that it would allow its patents on cold fusion to lapse, after spending more than $1 million defending its intellectual property.[44]

Some journalists were indeed indolent stenographers on the cold fusion story. The prophetic vision of a future of cheap, safe energy trumped their usual skepticism. Or perhaps it was incomprehension of physics and the science of cold fusion that left them and their editors more accepting of the claims. And did a constant stream of photographs and video from oil-soaked Alaska beaches also affect news judgments?

In the case of Iben Browning and his inaccurate New Madrid earthquake prediction of 1990, the false prophet was the man himself. It may be arguable whether journalists were more skeptical of Browning than they were of the Utah scientists, but the actions of government officials and the general public in Missouri were not to be ignored; they made news, and journalists succumbed to the temptation of the pack. Newspapers from *USA Today* to the *Wynne* (Ark.) *Shopper* and television stations from local markets to CNN trekked to the boot heel of Missouri. Browning's prediction was amplified through the mass media over the course of several months.

The New Madrid fault, which runs about 120 miles through Missouri, Arkansas, Tennessee, and Kentucky, has the potential to be one of the most dangerous in the world. Three of the largest earthquakes ever to hit the continental United States occurred near the Mississippi River hamlet of New Madrid, Missouri, in 1811–12. They struck with such force, legend has it, as to change the course of the great river and cause entire islands to disappear. Against this background, Browning was a self-proclaimed climatologist from New Mexico (as it turned out, his degree was in zoology) who predicted that there was a fifty-fifty chance that an earthquake measuring between 6.5 and 7.5 on the Richter scale would rip through the New Madrid fault on either December 3, 4, or 5, 1990. Browning claimed to have predicted the San Francisco Bay Area earthquake of 1989 a week before it happened and the eruption of Mount Saint Helens in 1980—claims that were challenged in some but not all news reports.[45] For example, Associated Press reports on November 29, 1989, and March 19, 1990, flatly stated that Browning had accurately predicted the California quake.[46]

The *Wall Street Journal* was the first major news outlet to report on Browning's New Madrid forecast. Its story set in motion a familiar scene in American newsrooms: the local news media had to write about the same subject, or feel as if they were "beaten" on the story. In St. Louis, editors at the *Post-Dispatch,* the largest daily in Missouri, assigned its own science, medicine, and environment writer, William Allen, to match the *Wall Street Journal* story. In many ways, it was a no-brainer assignment; earthquakes and predictions were hot topics for the *Post-Dispatch.* Allen had authored a series in September 1989 on St. Louis's preparedness for a major earthquake; less than one month later, the Loma Prieta earthquake struck the San Francisco area and Allen was dispatched to cover that disaster. Then came Browning's predictions. "The story had unusualness, had that drama, had the prophecy—no doubt about it," Allen recalled.[47] And it also had the competitive pressure of a national newspaper, the *Wall Street Journal,* reporting from a location only 165 miles away from the home-state newsroom.

About 500 people—many of them from the media—poured into the town of 3,200 to await the Big One, while hundreds of others left "in Thurberish scenes."[48] Local authorities closed schools; many citizens bought earthquake insurance; county courthouse workers were sent home early. With the news media in tow, U.S. senator Christopher Bond and Missouri governor John Ashcroft toured the area, looking at earthquake preparations and getting themselves on TV. Parents brought their children home from local colleges; stores did a brisk business in camping and survival gear. One St. Louis radio station broadcast from the New Madrid Historical Museum, while another station staked a claim at a local watering hole called Hap's Bar. (At about that point, Ashcroft said he feared some weren't taking earthquake preparations seriously.)[49] The prediction window came and went and the quake did not happen. Apparently the only injury was minor; a woman was struck by a television truck while crossing the street in downtown New Madrid.[50]

There was nothing minor about the media criticism to come. Amid charges of hype, the *Post-Dispatch* investigated itself. Browning's prediction had "eased its way, through the back door," into St. Louis via other news reports, including those from the Associated Press that treated his views superficially, the paper's ombudsman wrote.[51] Early on, the paper did not examine Browning's methods or record of prediction closely enough, he wrote. The *Post-Dispatch* was not the only paper fooled. At another nearby metro newspaper, the *Memphis Commercial Appeal,* only three articles out of forty-seven mentioned that Browning was not a trained seismologist or geologist.[52]

In many stories, other scientists were critical of Browning; only one scientist was found to take him seriously. Unfortunately, that one scientist (later discredited) who supported Browning's forecast was the official earthquake adviser to the state of Missouri and as such was treated as a credible news source. But the coverage, including a special twenty-page color tabloid section in the *Post-Dispatch* complete with earthquake survival instructions, had a cumulative effect, whether it supported Browning or questioned him. By one count, at least 350 articles about the prediction had appeared in forty-five publications, plus numerous broadcast reports.[53] The National Earthquake Prediction Evaluation Council felt compelled to hold a press conference in St.

Louis to issue a sixty-six-page report that said that the odds of such a quake as described by Browning were not 1 in 2 but more like 1 in 100,000.[54] By then the scare was well under way. Certainly a *Post-Dispatch* editorial on July 25 added to the general unease. Browning "has a good track record of accurate predictions—good enough to be taken with a great deal of caution. That means he should be heeded," it said.[55] In fact, Browning's track record as a prophet was unclear and his credentials as a scientist were suspect.

The publication of the special section on earthquakes was a controversial decision in the St. Louis newsroom. Would it add to the hysteria or inform a nervous public? The newspaper decided the section was a public service. Allen recalled the debate: "Yes, there is a chance we will look like we are backing Browning's prediction. But there is a lot of anxiety in the public, and we were providing them important information when they wanted it."[56] There is no doubt that the threat of an earthquake on that fault line is real; on May 3, 1991, a 4.6 tremor hit ten miles east of New Madrid. But standard journalistic practices—worries about competition, deadline pressures, staying on a "hot story," following the pack, reliance on expert sources, balancing quotes from all sides regardless of their credibility—led the news media to give Browning's notions more credence than they deserved. Associated Press members in Illinois picked the nonearthquake as the third-biggest story in the state for the year 1990; in the Show-Me State of Missouri, the Browning story was voted number one.[57]

THE FLOOD MYTH

The prophet, as an enduring character, has enjoyed a long run in civilization's written and oral traditions. Another hallmark of journalism is the recurring use of common metaphors, myths, and story structures. Some myths date back to ancient texts. Journalism scholar Jack Lule explored these persistent stories in journalism history and came up with a list of "seven master myths in the news," one of which was "The Flood."[58] Lule noted that cultures around the world repeat the story of the flood, especially if the flood story is seen to represent other types of tragedy. "The disaster humbles and reminds humans of forces greater than themselves," he wrote.[59]

The historian Hayden White, writing about narratives in history, said:

> The content of the discourse consists as much of its form as it does of whatever information might be extracted from a reading of it. When the reader recognizes the story being told in a historical narrative as a specific kind of story—for example, as an epic, romance, tragedy, or farce—he can be said to have comprehended the meaning produced by the discourse. This comprehension is nothing other than the recognition of the form of the narrative.[60]

In early times, as today, people paid attention to their physical surroundings and used stories about nature to tell stories about themselves. Allusions, allegories, and references to these ancient texts have appeared throughout the history of writing about the environment. In the Western world, where Christianity became the dominant religion, many historical comparisons are biblical.[61] The subject matter of today's environmental stories often reads like snippets from the Old Testament—floods, plagues, droughts, crop failures, and great storms. These are familiar stories.

The Hebrew scriptures are full of environmental disasters. Part of this may have to do with the severe climate fluctuations in the lands of the prophets. For example, almost no rain falls in Palestine between May and October; rains come in the winter, but they can be very localized. In an agricultural economy, weather is going to be in the forefront of nearly everyone's mind, as are occasional plagues of locusts and other sources of crop failure. And just like in modern news stories, spectacular "acts of God" tend to trump everyday occurrences in ancient writings. Jeremiah suggested that prophets delivering disaster oracles were more likely to be true prophets than those prophesying peace.[62] These prophets took enormous personal risks—imprisonment, torture, death—in telling people what they did not want to hear, rather than delivering banal platitudes and commonplace praise.

The flood of Noah, recounted in the book of Genesis, is probably the most famous of the biblical disasters and is one of the early flood myths. God is bent on destroying everything on Earth except those whom Noah saves on his ark; God establishes a covenant (perhaps the "everlasting covenant" referred to by Isaiah) with Noah to keep the ark's passengers, both man and beast, safe. Biblical scholars note that the covenant is universal in scope, and that it is also an ecological covenant, for it is made with "every living creature," including birds and animals, as well as with the Earth itself.[63] The end of the story is that God sends the rainbow as a sign that he will never again destroy the world with a flood. The environmental historian Thomas Dunlap asked if those who relayed the story of Noah's journey in the ark could have been considered the first environmental journalists.[64] If so, their story struck a nerve.

Perhaps it is obvious to consider journalists as prophets who sometimes repeat the flood myth. As we have seen, within the current practices of environmental journalism, the prophets are sometimes the sources of news stories; at other times, the prophets are the journalists themselves, who go out and find imperfections in the moral order where no one had thought to look. Still other stories are about dramatic occurrences that may or may not have been predicted. Jack Lule asked, "Do U.S. journalists make decisions regarding coverage of disastrous events guided by stories as old as humankind?"[65] For him, the answer was yes, and he used the example of the coverage of Hurricane Mitch in 1998. In the next section I will incorporate the prophetic voice of journalism with the flood myth in the story of Hurricane Katrina. Journalists surely saw this storm coming.

PROPHETS AND THE FLOOD MYTH IN NEW ORLEANS

Few prophesied, dramatic, and near-apocalyptic events in the United States received as much attention as Hurricane Katrina (and three weeks later, Hurricane Rita). On Monday, August 29, 2005, the city of New Orleans and other areas along the Gulf Coast were smashed by a major hurricane that killed at least 1,300 people and left hundreds of others missing and presumed dead. On the Mississippi coast, the storm surge was twenty-eight feet. Lake Pontchartrain rose eleven feet in nine hours. In Pascagoula, Mississippi, winds reached 124 miles per hour. Within a day, 80 percent of New Orleans was underwater. Mass media from all over the world focused their attention on the U.S. Gulf Coast and told gripping stories of tragedy, despair, and death. In the days that followed, attention fell on the local newspaper, the *New Orleans Times-Picayune.* Notably, the newspaper continued to publish, online, for two days even while its journalists were forced to evacuate their offices due to the rising waters. (The newspaper reported thirty million hits on its Web site per day for four days after the hurricane hit, and that was with its popular "Bourbon Street Webcam" inoperable.) After publishing online only, the paper set up shop in Baton Rouge and trucked papers around the region from a printing plant in Houma. It never missed a publication day. The newspaper won Pulitzer Prizes for public service and breaking news.

Amid the attention paid to Louisiana's largest newspaper was the prophetic work that reporters John McQuaid and Mark Schleifstein had done three years earlier, in 2002. In a five-part series of fifty thousand words entitled "Washing Away: How South Louisiana Is Growing More Vulnerable to a Catastrophic Hurricane," the journalists eerily predicted much of what would happen to the city if it was struck by a powerful storm. "Hurricanes are a common heritage for Louisiana residents, who until the past few decades had little choice in facing a hurricane but to ride it out and pray," they wrote.[66] Some people paid attention to only parts of the story (a common result for a prophet), other people ignored the message altogether, and some probably prayed. (Their editor jokingly called their investigative work "disaster porn.") The series estimated that, should a storm of a Category 3 or higher magnitude hit, levees would fail, numerous deaths would occur, evacuation would be difficult, and that as a result of human actions, the effects of a storm would make the area more vulnerable, not less. "We knew it was going to happen. They knew it was going to happen," Schleifstein said later.[67] McQuaid and Schleifstein are veteran journalists who shared a Pulitzer in 1997; they often work in the "moral order" investigative tradition as described by Glasser and Ettema.[68] (Theologians also understand the work of the prophets as a form of moral discourse.)[69]

Hurricane Katrina may have been "the most comprehensively predicted catastrophe in American history."[70] In February 2005, *National Geographic News* reported that the ongoing loss of wetlands along Louisiana's Gulf Coast would make the region more vulnerable to hurricanes and flooding. The story included comments from scientists. "With the rapidly depleting wetlands, people that have lived in south Louisiana can tell that, over the last 30 years, large storms now come in faster, and the water rises faster, which gives less time to respond and less time to evacuate," said Denise Reed, a professor of geology and geophysics at the University of New Orleans. "In the next few years it's going to get worse."[71] Reed was right—except that it got worse in the next few months. Other media, including *Scientific American,* National Public Radio's *All Things Considered* news show, *Civil Engineering* magazine, and the *New York Times,* also reported on the potential danger.

The *Times-Picayune's* analysis by McQuaid and Schleifstein suggested that St. Bernard Parish and eastern New Orleans, to name two areas, were much more at risk in a storm than the U.S. Army Corps of Engineers had predicted. Among the accurate forecasts was this: "Evacuation is the most certain route to safety, but it may be a nightmare. And 100,000 without transportation will be left behind."[72] And this: "Hundreds of thousands would be left homeless, and it would take months to dry out the area and begin to make it livable. But there wouldn't be much for residents to come home to. The local economy would be in ruins." In an unfortunate twist, Schleifstein lost his home to more than ten feet of water and, months later, herniated a disk in his back while moving garden bricks. For weeks, some of his journalism awards lay in his backyard amid the ruins, thrown out in hopes they might dry in the sun.[73] One blog labeled Schleifstein a "Jewish environmental journalist as Jonah" and said "prophesy was not [his] intent," but it praised his accuracy.[74]

In invoking Jonah, the blog writer took note of Schleifstein's reluctance to assume the mantle of preacher, rather than the outcome of his prophecy. The story of Jonah, who lived sometime in the fourth or fifth century B.C. (or earlier), is of someone called by God to preach repentance to the citizens of Nineveh. He refused and fled on a ship that was sailing as far away as he could get.[75] A great storm hammered the craft, throwing the crew into a panic. When the men found out Jonah was on board, running from his duty to his God, they—at his suggestion—threw the reluctant missionary overboard. God sent a giant fish to swallow him, and, after three days, the fish spat Jonah safely on shore, from where he sped to Nineveh and commenced preaching. Nineveh repented in the nick of time, God spared it, and Jonah's prophecy of doom did not come true. He became a prophet of God in spite of himself.

Understandably, the myth of Jonah and the big fish (often represented as a whale) has resonated through the ages. The seventeenth-century English author Izaak Walton, whom we will hear more from later, wove Jonah into *The Compleat Angler,* his treatise on fish and fishing: "I might tell you that Almighty God is said to have spoken to a fish, but never to a beast; that he hath made a whale a ship, to carry and send his prophet, Jonah, safe on the appointed shore."[76] Herman Melville[77] and George Orwell[78] made use of the story, as did Aldous Huxley[79] and many other producers of cultural messages, including American minstrel singers of the late nineteenth and twentieth centuries, such as Grandpa Jones and Mike Seeger.[80] Clarence Darrow mockingly used his opponent's literal reading of the story of Jonah in his questioning of William Jennings Bryan at the Scopes Monkey Trial in 1925.

It may be more accurate to compare McQuaid and Schleifstein

to the Greek mythological figure of Cassandra. The daughter of the king and queen of Troy, Cassandra was granted the ability to see into the future after she caught the eye of Apollo. She did not return Apollo's love, so Apollo placed a curse on her that resulted in no one believing her predictions.[81] Schleifstein said he had heard such comparisons; he said he'd also been called Nostradamus.[82] A sixteenth-century French prophet who has resonated in popular culture as supposedly predicting the rise of Hitler, 9/11, the French Revolution, and the atomic bomb, Nostradamus in fact did not mention any of those disasters in his vague and handily dateless writings. (And on several occasions he denied claiming to be a prophet.)

The prophetic impulse and the myth of the flood came together in the coverage of a major environmental disaster along the Gulf Coast of North America in 2005. There is a well-known phrase about a "prophet being without honor in his own land" that would sometimes apply to reporters. Journalists do not think of themselves as prophets, nor do they think of themselves as telling and retelling ancient myths. "Yet like myth tellers of every age, journalists draw from archetypal stories to make sense of events," Lule wrote. "They draw from sacred, societal stories that celebrate shared values, counsel with lessons and themes, instruct and inform with exemplary models."[83] Some of these stories were told by prophets.

THREE

SCIENCE, AGRICULTURE, AND JOURNALISM EDUCATION

The Hebrew scriptures are not the only influential works in which ancient peoples recorded stories of the natural world. Hellenistic encyclopedias, Roman how-to manuals, and even carefully guarded "books of secrets"—handbooks of the occult, alchemy, and astrology—became part of the emerging textual tradition of the West. Some of these books discussed themes, such as science and agriculture, which reappear in environmental journalism.

One of the earliest books on scientific subjects came from ancient Rome. In the first century A.D., Pliny the Elder wrote *Historia Naturalis* (*Natural History*). It was the magnum opus of the Roman writer, who died in the year 79 as he went to investigate the volcanic eruption at Vesuvius. His thirty-seven-book encyclopedia covers subjects including geography, anthropology, botany, zoology, plant pathology (including the medicinal uses of plants), and mineralogy. There is one long section on curatives obtained from animals and another on the physical nature of the universe. Included in the text is a history of ancient art that is still used today as a rare surviving account of that discipline.

As a journalism forerunner, Pliny demonstrated an awareness of both environmental damage and its causes. For example, on erosion: "Destructive torrents are generally formed when hills are stripped of trees which formerly confined and absorbed their rains."[1] He was a keen observer of weather, noticing that rainbows occur only opposite the sun, at a place high in the sky when the sun is low or low in the sky when the sun is high. His practical advice on making glue from ox hides, raising bees, cultivating grapes and figs, preserving food, and using flax to make linen had value for hundreds of years. Pliny could also be a social critic:

> All other living creatures pass their time worthily among their own species: We see them herd together and stand firm against other kinds of animals—fierce lions do not fight among themselves, the serpent's bite attacks not serpents, even the monsters of the seas and the fishes are only cruel against different species; whereas to man, I vow, most of his evils come from his fellow-man.[2]

Pliny was among the pioneers in writing about exotic species, a popular subject among science and environmental writers of the modern period. Unlike most ecologists, however, Pliny was quite enthusiastic about the movement of plants via the pathways of the Roman Empire, including the usefulness of licorice (Russian), water dock (an English perennial), a species of sage (Ethiopian), and spiny euphorbia (North African), and their transport around the world.[3]

Impressive as Pliny's accomplishment was, a good deal of *Historia Naturalis* has not withstood the test of time. Pliny gets credit (or blame) for starting several "scientific" myths. Among his claims: porcupines shoot their quills; ears ring when their owners are gossiped about; hair and fingernails grow on a corpse; and snakes steal milk from cows' udders at night. Some of his material is grist for the science fiction writer: people with feet so large they could serve as a sun shield in hot weather; a race of humans without mouths who took nutrition by smelling plants; headless and neckless people with their eyes on their shoulders; dog-headed, human-bodied creatures who communicated by—what else?—barking; and the manticore, a meat-eating animal with a human face, lion's body, and spiked tail. When attentive, Pliny's elephants could climb ropes and write in Greek.

A fantasist tendency aside, Pliny was more of an encyclopedist than a naturalist. His sources for the book were secondhand. In his preface, Pliny claimed twenty thousand facts were gathered from two thousand books and one hundred authors. His was an important early moment in the recording and transmission of observations of the natural world.

Pliny's way of writing about nature was new for his time in Rome. (The work on natural history is the only one of his writings to survive to the present.) His text was one of the most popular books of the Renaissance, with nearly sixty editions published.[4] To be sure, scholars working in the history of science or literature may not have taken Pliny's writings as seriously as the everyday reader. One called it a "literary monstrosity" and another "among the worst works we have, from the point of view of style."[5] There is no doubting his influence, however. One author said Pliny's book was the equivalent of a "runaway bestseller," and in the Middle Ages he was "undisputed as an authority on science, nature, mankind, and the cosmos."[6] Pliny's book was most likely part of the libraries of Marco Polo, Michel de Montaigne, Shakespeare, John Milton, and Edward Gibbon.[7]

AGRICULTURAL WRITING

Writers in ancient Rome and elsewhere tackled the subject of food—growing it, transplanting it, preserving it, modifying it—in animal and plant husbandry manuals, books of advice, and recipes. Not many of the early works on agriculture survived, but enough of them were saved and republished to get an idea of their content.

Agriculture is one of the world's oldest professions, and thus it was a common subject among early writers. Cato the Elder, who lived from 234 to 149 B.C., authored a popular work on agriculture in Latin, *De Agricultura*—how to operate a farm, feed livestock, plant trees, prepare food, and treat the hired help. Cato may have been the first farm writer. (Or medical writer: one chapter roughly translates into "In Praise of Cabbage" and lauds the hearty vegetable as a cure for dysentery, urinary troubles, runny sores, cancer, and gout.) His writing style is fact-based, if not dry, and has the "tone of farmer speaking to farmer," in the words of one critic.[8] ("As for figs, plant the marisca fig on clayey, open ground.")[9] As an instruction manual, Cato's advice was limited to his region around Rome; it is hard to know whether he did not expect his book to be widely distributed or he was simply writing from personal experience and did not know of farming methods elsewhere. He wrote of fertilizer, irrigation, timber cutting, vine grafting, curing ham, and making hay. These farming methods, perhaps spread by Cato's book, were "known and recommended in Roman and early modern times."[10]

Several suggestions mentioned by Cato remained as popular fodder for agricultural writers to emulate. For example, Cato established a set of rules for the adaptation of crops to certain types of soil: "Sow wheat on dry soil that is not inclined to be weedy and where the ground is unshaded."[11] Beans should be planted on "gravelly soils" and barley on fallow ground, while turnips and radishes need a heavy dose of manure.[12] And Cato was particular about his fertilizer. Manure from pigeons was to be used for grains; olive oil dregs should be used to fertilize olive trees. And in his list of what makes for good farming, Cato emphasized (1) plowing, (2) plowing, and (3) manure.[13] Cato also gave what some scholars believe to be the oldest written account of the making of concrete, to be used for the foundation of his olive presses.[14] There is no explicit mention of crop rotation, but in Cato's time ground was cultivated one year and then lay fallow in the next.

All in all, the farming described by Cato is remarkably similar to a modern commercial, capitalistic agribusiness. Cato establishes a fairly detailed three-season calendar of events and activities. (It lacked a summer, which was often in drought where he lived.) Livestock, equipment, slaves, and land were bought in the open market. The sowing of fields was carefully planned, based on soil, sun, and water; and farm storage buildings and food-processing facilities were built. The major cash crops were olive oil and wine, with lesser income derived from grain and livestock. In addition to slaves, seasonal and year-round free workers provided labor. Landowners often lived in cities, away from their farms, which were managed by foremen. And, perhaps presaging views widely held by modern farmers, Cato recommended that farmers get out of the business and complained about bankers, all in one sentence: "It is true that it would sometimes be better to seek a fortune in trade . . . or . . . to lend money at interest, if it were an honorable occupation."[15]

Following Cato's footsteps was Columella, whose twelve-book *De Re Rustica* (*On Agriculture*) survives as an important reference work on agriculture in the first century A.D. Columella, who came from southern Spain, authored chapters on soil, fruit trees, wild animals, domestic animals, gardens, and fish and fowl, and his *De Re Rustica* is "the most comprehensive and systematic of all treatises of Roman writers on agricultural affairs."[16] He unintentionally foreshadowed the debate on corporate farming versus small family farms by quoting an unnamed poet: "Admire large farms, but yet a small one till."[17]

Columella, who was credited with devising the first soil test, was particularly insightful on the health problems of stagnant water. "Worst of all is swamp-water, which creeps along with sluggish flow; and water that always remains stagnant in a swamp is laden with death."[18] This was written about 1,850 years before the connection between mosquitoes and malaria became generally accepted scientific wisdom; about 1,889 years before DDT was found to have insecticidal effects and began to be sprayed on swamp water; and about 1,912 years before Rachel Carson cemented her legacy with the book *Silent Spring,* which traced the toxic effects of DDT. Like Cato, Columella had his hits and misses; among the notable misses was his notion that the docking of a dog's tail forty days after birth would prevent rabies.

The works of Columella influenced farmers and writers on agricultural issues, particularly in the ages before the Western invention of the printing press. Pliny cites Columella for his work on natural history, and the veterinarians Pelagonius and Eumelus quote him extensively. The fifth-century author Palladius, the sixth-century author Cassiodorus, and the seventh-century author Isidore all mention him as one of the outstanding writers on agriculture.[19] Beginning in about A.D. 809 or so, English authors use Columella as a resource on gardening, starting with Walafrid Strabo writing the *Hortulus.* In the seventeenth century John Milton, in his brief work *On Education,* ranked Columella alongside the Hebrew texts as important for students to study "after evening repast until bed-time"; students should first go to the scriptures and then to "the authors of agriculture, Cato, Varro, and Columella, for the matter is easy; and if the language is difficult, so much the better." Milton added: "Here, will be an occasion of inciting and enabling them hereafter to improve the tillage of their country, to recover bad soil."[20] Charles Darwin quoted Columella on domestic fowl in 1868.[21] By the time of Darwin, agricultural manuals had become established as popular, marketable commodities with a lineage that eventually ran from Cato to *American Agriculturalist, Wallace's Farmer,* and *Better Homes and Gardens.* I will return to the chronology that I have been mapping here later in the chapter; the important role of journalism education needs to be mentioned first.

JOURNALISM EDUCATION AND AGRICULTURE

Agricultural communication became intertwined with journalism education in the United States after many of the early journalism schools were created in land-grant colleges. Prior to the Civil War, journalists were trained on the job through what amounted to an apprenticeship, although calls for the college-level education of journalists date at least as far back as John Ward Fenno's *Gazette of the United States* in 1799.[22] In 1834 Duff Green, editor of the *United States Telegraph,* proposed a school for boys aged eleven to fourteen to learn languages and arts for five hours a day and to work as printer's devils for eight hours a day, but the local union threatened to boycott his shop and he scrapped the plan.[23]

In 1857 the board of directors of Farmers' High School (now Pennsylvania State University) asked the state legislature to establish a journalism curriculum, but the legislature did not act.[24] The official connection between journalism education and colleges of agriculture began with the Morrill Land-Grant Act (1862), which established the land-grant colleges. Under provisions of the act, states received large plots of federal land for colleges that would teach agriculture, engineering, and military science. One idea that existed within the land-grant model was serving the community, which was often translated into disseminating knowledge about practical subjects into the local culture. The Hatch Act of 1887 established agricultural experiment stations for research; and the publication of scientific farming methods began in earnest.

Robert E. Lee, then president of Washington College (later Washington and Lee University) in Virginia, incorporated many aspects of the land-grant model into his school as he sought to revitalize the South in the aftermath of the great national conflict. "War is over and I am trying to forget it," he wrote. "The South has a still greater conflict before her. We must do something to train her sons to fight her battles, not with the sword, but with the pen."[25] Lee added science, mechanical arts, and other professional programs to the classics curriculum at his school; in 1869, among his ideas was a cooperative program merging on-the-job training at a newspaper office (one hour per day) with a college education. About fifty students received scholarships under the plan, but Lee died in 1870 and the program lost momentum before ending in 1878.[26]

Nineteenth-century newspaper editors sometimes debated the merits of a college education, with Joseph Pulitzer of the *New York World,* Whitelaw Reid of the *New York Tribune,* and George W. Curtis of *Harper's Weekly* in favor and Horace Greeley of the *Tribune,* Frederic Hudson of the *New York Herald,* and E. L. Godkin of the *New York Evening Post* opposed.[27] Typical of the comments of the opposition was this from Hudson: "The only place where one can be a journalist is a great newspaper office."[28] Greeley was of a similar mind: "Of all horned cattle, I want least to see in my office a college graduate."[29] Pulitzer had originally opposed the idea of journalism education, saying there was "no sense in the suggestion," but he came around to think that journalism schools could be "made beneficial."[30]

Pulitzer (who endowed Columbia University's School of Journalism with $2 million) and Harvard president Charles Eliot, who pioneered the use of elective courses in the liberal arts, pursued somewhat different models of journalism education. Pulitzer viewed the gathering and dissemination of news through the lens of the burgeoning social science fields of the early twentieth century; Eliot was more interested in the business of journalism, including administration and production. Eliot's ideas, ironically, were not put in place at Harvard but most famously at the University of Missouri.

Meanwhile, the land-grant schools were fulfilling their own practically oriented mission. The pragmatism of the new schools was noted by the president of Iowa State College, who said that "knowledge should be taught for its uses; . . . culture is an incidental result."[31] Ralph Casey, the longtime head of the journalism program at the University of Minnesota, said the Morrill Act was "the stimulus, in my opinion, that later promoted the entry of journalism into the programs at state-supported universities and colleges."[32] The U.S. Department of Agriculture had tight relationships with the land-grant schools; extension services at schools such as Iowa State, Kansas State, Wisconsin, and elsewhere distributed information to farm papers, rural weeklies, and small daily newspapers that would have included many farmers among their readers. Scholar Janice Wood has noted that a common characteristic of the new professional schools, including those in journalism, was autonomy from the university but "more answerability to professional societies and the state."[33]

The program at Kansas State Agricultural College (now Kansas State University) was fairly typical of early college education in journalism. It focused on vocational training for printers, and a department of printing was established there in 1874. Journalism courses were added in 1910. The college's board of administration instructed the faculty to commit to training students for "work especially related to farm life."[34] One of the department heads later said that the purpose of his program was "to train people for serving rural and small city newspapers, the ag press, etc."[35] The same year Kansas State began to train printers, Cornell University started a series of lectures co-taught by a professor and the university's printing supervisor. Students labored in the university printing office, learned to set type, read proofs, and work off of forms.[36]

Educators at these schools and others also brought in students who could be employed to write press releases (at one university, students were required to prepare university public relations materials)[37] and trained to work as farm journalists for newspapers and the burgeoning agricultural magazine industry. The schools then looked to industry for financial support. At Iowa State, journalism instruction emerged out of a chance conversation at a 1904 livestock show. Iowa farmer and writer John Clay spoke at the event; in the audience was C. F. Curtiss, the dean of agriculture at Iowa State. The two men spoke of "the tremendous part that agricultural journals play in the making of a better agriculture."[38] Curtiss worked up a curriculum, and Clay's money provided the financial pillars to get it started. Clay, in an address to students in 1905 called "The Plough and the Book," argued that the two "must be more closely associated. We need [agricultural journalism] in our daily press. We can improve it in our agricultural papers. It is almost absent in our magazine literature . . . They tell us with great truth that they can find few practical writers of ability, that there is a dearth of experts in this line."[39]

At the same time that land-grant schools were attempting to establish themselves, the country was undergoing a profound period of industrialization. As factories and foundries sprang up where prairie grass once grew, farmers were worried about being left behind. Prices seemed to be controlled by the railroad men, the banks, and the industrialists in the cities. Pro-farm movements like the Grange, the National Farmers' Alliance, the Farmers' National Congress, and to a lesser degree the Populist Party began to organize in response to industrialization. Along with these social movement groups came periodicals to promote their causes and unite their members. In *Farm Journal,* for example, a department called "Pulling Together" (later called "Farmers' Problems") gave voice to the Grange, Farmers' Alliance, and other groups.[40] "Uncle" Henry Wallace, the first of three Henry Wallaces to edit *Wallace's Farmer,* did not join the Greenbacks, Grangers, or Populists, but was sympathetic to their causes and urged legislation on their behalf.[41] One Department of Agriculture survey, in 1913, concluded that the "agricultural press shows up in this survey as one of the dominating influences in American agriculture."[42]

Farm periodicals grew rapidly. There were 70 farm magazines in 1870, and by 1908 one source listed 458 agricultural publications, with a combined circulation—no doubt exaggerated—exceeding fifteen million.[43]

The *Farm Journal* was fairly typical of the early farm periodicals. Founded near Philadelphia in 1877 by a former Quaker schoolmaster named Wilmer Atkinson, *Farm Journal* took advantage of reduced postal rates for magazines and improvements in printing technology to grow to fifteen thousand in national circulation by 1881.[44] Already in the field were the *Country Gentleman* and the venerable *American Agriculturalist,* founded in 1845. Atkinson left the scientific farming stories to his competitors; he focused on more conservative, tried-and-true measures, and he became successful.

In the thirteen midwestern states, the circulation of farm publications increased 15 percent from 1910 to 1920 while the rural population actually declined.[45] After a merger with *Iowa Homestead* in 1929, *Wallace's Farmer* sold 250,000 copies per issue.[46]

Those who published the agricultural journals needed professionally trained reporters and editors to run them. The obvious place to organize the training was in the colleges of agriculture in the land-grant schools. At the University of Minnesota, one of the leaders of the push for a journalism school was William P. Kirkwood, the publications director of the university's College of Agriculture; money from William J. Murphy, the publisher of the widely circulated *Minneapolis Tribune,* seeded the program.[47]

The historian Stephen A. Banning has argued that professional journalism education did not begin with Joseph Pulitzer, as historians typically assert, but with the Missouri agricultural editor Norman J. Colman, publisher of *Colman's Rural World* and, in 1885, the first U.S. commissioner of agriculture to sit in the president's cabinet.[48] (Four other farm journalists have served as what is now called the secretary of agriculture.) Colman was one of the founders of the Missouri Press Association, which began its push for professional training for journalists shortly after the Civil War. Partly at his urging, the University of Missouri offered a lecture series in journalism in 1873 and a regular course a few years later. In 1898 the three men appointed to establish a journalism curriculum for the university were the college president, the publisher of a local paper in Columbia, Missouri, and H. J. Waters, dean of the College of Agriculture.[49] Ex-newsman Walter Williams became the first dean of the University of Missouri School of Journalism in 1908.

In the early twentieth century at the University of Wisconsin, Willard Bleyer, who came from a Milwaukee newspaper family and had earned a Ph.D. in English, built a journalism curriculum with a strong agricultural component. By 1912 Wisconsin students could take courses in the College of Letters and Science or in the College of Agriculture. Among the courses in the agricultural school were Agricultural Journalism ("the details of preparing articles for farm papers"), Agricultural Editing (with special reference to *Wisconsin Country Magazine*), Methods of Farm Advertising, and Advanced Agricultural Journalism (which added the teaching of photography and drawing).[50] Another course required working two hours per week in the business office of *Wisconsin Country Magazine*.

A Texas journalist named Laura Lane represented a typical career path. Lane's first job was on the staff of her hometown newspaper in Vernon, Texas, before she joined the Texas A&M extension service as an editor in 1939. In 1947 she moved to the staff of *Country Gentleman* magazine in Philadelphia; and then she went to *Farm Journal* in 1955 when *Country Gentleman* closed.[51]

By 1912 there were thirty-three schools offering journalism instruction—enough to form an association of faculty, the American Association for the Teachers of Journalism. Many of the schools were located in the Midwest, South, and Far West; few were near the major media centers of the East Coast. By the time Pulitzer's journalism school at Columbia University opened (that same year), "the center of journalism education had passed to the state universities," according to media scholar James Carey.[52] "The intellectual center of journalism shifted to the Middle West," wrote Everette E. Dennis, "where the land-grant colleges formed their own traditions, cut off from the Northeastern centers of the media industry."[53] When journalism education started to drift into social science methods in the 1930s, editors of small newspapers decried the shift and urged more vocational training for journalism students.[54] At about the same time, colleges that sponsored radio programs aimed at a farm audience began using students as broadcast journalists.

The American Agricultural Editors' Association, formed in 1921, supported the field as its first professional association, as did the International Federation of Farm Journalists, founded in 1946. In 1928 Charles E. Rogers, head of the Department of Industrial Journalism at Kansas State, toured his state with one of his alumni who worked as a farm reporter for William Allen White at the *Emporia Gazette*. The reporter tackled subjects such as the spread of bindweed around the county (to the protests of the local chamber of commerce, which was worried that real estate values would suffer from negative publicity). One farmer, scheduled to be interviewed about his fattened steers, declined comment: "Most of the farm stuff you saw in the papers," the farmer was reported as saying, "was about men who exaggerated their success, and he wasn't going to have people think he was a failure."[55]

FARM JOURNALISM IN DECLINE

After World War II, farm periodicals in the United States became more specialized even as mainstream newspapers cut back on agricultural coverage; the rural population continued to stream into the cities, and factory farms supplanted more and more small landowners. "Food production," wrote critic Murray Bookchin in 1976, "is reduced to mere industrial technique."[56] Only 1.84 percent of the U.S. population was engaged in farm production by 2002.[57] Farm subjects were still written about, but eventually only daily newspapers in heavily agricultural areas like the Dakotas and Iowa kept full-time farm editors and reporters on staff. Meanwhile, venerable farm periodicals such as *Country Gentleman, Capper's Farmer, Farm Quarterly,* and *Farm and Ranch* merged or folded. Others lost circulation but remained in business; *Successful Farming's* circulation in 1927 was more than 1,000,000; by 2005 its total paid circulation was down to 344,584.[58] From 1980 to 1994, *Farm Journal's* paid circulation dropped 73 percent.[59] Like the rest of the magazine industry, many general-interest farm magazines found the loss of readers and the competition for advertising revenue too great to overcome.

Membership in the American Agricultural Editors' Association peaked in the 1970s but had fallen off by more than 25 percent a generation later, to around 330.[60] Thomas F. Pawlick, in his book *The Invisible Farm,* noted that even in farming-rich Iowa, the number of daily newspapers listing a full-time farm writer declined by 62 percent between 1975 and 1995.[61] Additionally, the number of U.S. radio stations that called their format "agriculture and farm" fell from 3.4 percent of the whole in 1976 to 0.8 percent by 1994.[62] Both the mainstream media and specialized farm publications came in for heavy criticism in a 1994 survey of farm journalists by researchers at the University of Illinois. The general-interest news media covered agriculture, when they did at all, in "superficial, event-oriented, and often too cute or folksy" ways.[63] The specialized farm press too often took a pro-industry point of view, served the interests of advertisers at the expense of readers, failed to investigate scandals, and mostly ignored environmental problems.[64] Journalism education had shifted as well, so that by 1995 only 7 schools offered courses in agricultural journalism out of the 510 listed in the directory of the Association for Education in Journalism and Mass Communication.[65]

In some cases, environmental journalists have moved into the space left by their agricultural counterparts. Many writers who specialize in the environment and science consider agriculture an important part of their beat. For example, science writer and editor Paul Raeburn wrote one of the important farm books of the 1990s, *The Last Harvest: The Genetic Gamble That Threatens to Destroy American Agriculture*.[66] His book examined genetically modified crops and the risks to the nation's food supply because of the genetic uniformity of those products, particularly what he called "billion-dollar corn." His thesis was familiar to any biologist: as the gene pool shrinks, its vulnerability to disease grows. Raeburn framed the issue of the lack of genetic diversity in our food supply as a widely ignored environmental crisis. Critics, including Barry Commoner, called it "science journalism at its best," and it was not marketed as a "farm book," perhaps unintentionally highlighting how far agricultural reporting had fallen in the public mind as a journalistic form.[67]

Journalism about the farm and the environment remained common in Iowa, where the *Des Moines Register* continued to report on rural issues. Its longtime environmental reporter, Perry Beeman, authored an award-winning series in 2003 on agricultural issues affecting his state. One of his most attention-grabbing stories exposed the efforts of agribusiness to suppress the research findings of scientists at Iowa State University that were critical of the industry. Another story detailed the overuse of antibiotics that leads to the development of drug-resistant "superbugs"—

an agricultural spin on the antibiotic resistance story. Corporate farming issues were a big part of Beeman's job, and one common topic was waste from large industrial farms. As many authors have pointed out, farming through most of its history was rather environmentally benign—the wise farmer relied on local conditions, soil types, rainfall, sunlight, and so on. Industrial production of any type, not just farming, means industrial pollution, and so manure spills, fertilizer runoff, and collateral damage from pesticides and herbicides became a part of the environmental reporter's beat.

WRITING ABOUT SCIENCE

It is difficult to distinguish where writing about agriculture and writing about science divide; agriculture was often seen as a practical application of science and was treated as such. And it was not so different in the ancient world, where Pliny and his successors wrote often about science, nature, and scientific experiments as a piece. By the ninth and tenth centuries, many of the classic Greek encyclopedias had been translated into Latin and Arabic, and numerous commentaries on the original texts were published to help the reader decipher the intent of the authors.

A transitional figure in the history of science writing was Georgius Agricola, the author of the metallurgy manual *De Re Metallica* in 1556. In Agricola's time, science was not clearly defined from other scholarly efforts like the arts or philosophy. Much scientific work, if it could be called that, was carried out in secret for fear of running afoul of the church, which sought to maintain control over religious and other knowledge. The historian Bernadette Longo has shown that Agricola drew on both the

Hellenistic encyclopedic and the "book of secrets" textual traditions; Agricola, who is considered the founder of the field of geology, differed from his predecessors by distinguishing technology from the occult.[68] For example, he considered and rejected the use of divining rods to find ores in favor of surveying, digging, assaying, and smelting. With the spread of Gutenberg's printing presses, books like *De Re Metallica* were produced in increasing numbers and distributed widely.

As the works of Agricola, Copernicus, Newton, Galileo, Kepler, Bacon, van Leeuwenhoek, Boyle, and others swept across Europe in the sixteenth and seventeenth centuries, the discipline of science entered into the period known as the scientific revolution; university science curricula and scientific societies sprang up across the continent, and periodicals and other publications began to appear regularly. Many of the important, foundational books on mathematics, astronomy, and other fields were published during the eighteenth century as empirical methods came to dominate the sciences. Among the most influential of the new scientists was Alexander von Humboldt, whose prodigious output of books and monographs became required reading for Charles Darwin, as well as the writers Ralph Waldo Emerson and Henry David Thoreau. The first edition of volume 1 of Humboldt's 1845 work *Cosmos* sold twenty-two thousand copies in two months in Europe, and three translations into English followed immediately.[69] At least twenty-five places on maps and atlases were named after Humboldt.[70]

In the United States the development of the periodical press, the maturation of newspapers, and the rise of scientific associations all influenced science journalism, which became an accepted practice. In the first newspaper printed in the American colonies (which lasted only one issue), there were two paragraphs of news with a science angle. Benjamin Harris, in his *Publick Occurrences* of September 25, 1690, wrote about the "Fever and Ague" sweeping through his readership; he also commented on the latest smallpox outbreak in Boston, which by his count had killed 320 persons. One scholar noted that the newspaper's accounts had many of the ingredients of a modern science story—public health and medicine, a local angle, "progress" in reaction to the problem, and a tie to the military (reflecting the funding imperatives of much modern research).[71]

Scientists and journalists both contributed to periodicals in the nineteenth century. Bylines from journalists could be seen alongside those of scientists such as David Starr Jordan or Louis Agassiz. "Frequently newspapers published verbatim transcriptions of entire lecture series, or, at the least, executive summaries," wrote one historian.[72] Many in the field saw popularizing science as part of their job. In some ways science journalism was a complement to agricultural journalism; significantly, it became a forerunner to the environmental journalism of the last quarter of the twentieth century. Science, agriculture, and nature were covered in general-interest as well as specialty publications. One of the more popular features was the reproduction of etchings and woodcuts to illustrate the articles. "Agricultural subjects were well-treated in the scientific magazines," wrote magazine historian Frank Luther Mott, "and in the periodicals of general interest. They had been staple material from the beginning."[73]

The importance of science in the colonies was highlighted by the founding of the American Philosophical Society, by Benjamin Franklin, in Philadelphia in 1743. Doctors, clergy, lawyers, and merchants joined other citizens interested in science to investigate "all philosophical Experiments that let Light into the Nature of Things, tend to increase the Power of Man over Matter, and multiply the Conveniencies or Pleasures of Life."[74] The society became internationally known for its astronomical observations in the 1760s and the publication of Lewis and Clark's journals into the Louisiana Territory. Scientific periodicals had started in Europe after about 1665, and the first scientific journal in America was the *Medical Repository,* a quarterly out of New York City edited by Professor Samuel Latham Mitchill, who was on the faculty at Columbia and later became a U.S. senator.[75] It ran from 1797 until 1824. The *American Journal of Science* began in 1818 and was credited by Mott with popularizing geology and chemistry in the period before the Civil War.[76] This was also the time of the establishment of the Association of American Geologists (1840) and the American Association for the Advancement of Science (1847), among other organizations. *Scientific American,* profitably owned and operated by A. E. Beach, son of *New York Sun* publisher Moses Beach, was founded in 1845 and featured stories on new inventions: Thomas Edison, as a boy, walked three miles to get his weekly copy, or so he said.[77]

Science and social reform were two of the most popular subjects in general-interest periodicals during the mid-nineteenth century (along with commenting on Darwin and natural selection). Monthly magazines such as the *North American Review* (founded in 1815), the *Independent* (1848), *Harper's New Monthly Magazine* (1850), *Atlantic Monthly* (1857), and *Scribner's Monthly* (1870) often featured coverage of the latest scientific advances in their pages. *Harper's* founding editorial stated: "Scientific discovery, mechanical inventions, the creation of Fine Art, the Orations of Statesmen, all the varied intellectual movements of this most stirring and productive age" would be topics of coverage.[78]

One way science was treated by the periodical press was in the book review. Magazines like the *North American Review* published long commentaries on the latest scientific treatises. Much space in general-interest magazines was devoted to the science-religion debate. Typical was an article in *Knickerbocker* titled "The Connection Between Geology and the Pentateuch," by Thomas Cooper, president of the College of South Carolina.[79] Pseudosciences like phrenology, hypnotism, and mesmerism also received attention.

Circulation was never higher than a few thousand copies for most of the pre–Civil War monthlies (*Harper's* being an exception), but their readerships reached into the New England elites, and newspaper editors perused their editorial content looking for ideas. Henry Adams, editor of the *North American Review* (*NAR*) from 1870 to 1876, wrote that the journal "was a source of suggestion to cheaper workers; it reached far into societies that never knew its existence."[80] In 1868 the thirty-year-old Adams wrote a long *NAR* review of the tenth edition of Charles Lyell's *Principles of Geology* at the urging of that scientist. Adams ran his anti-Darwinian ideas past the true Darwinian Lyell before they were published. "Youth risks such encounters with the universe before one succumbs to it, yet even he was surprised at Sir Charles's ready assent, and still more so at finding himself, after half an hour's conversation, sitting down to clear the minds of American geologists about the principles of their profession," Adams wrote in his autobiography.[81] Adams moved to Washington, D.C., to work as a freelance journalist, and eventually he was hired as *NAR* editor.

The American media industry underwent tremendous change in the 1880s. In 1865 there were approximately 700 magazines in the United States; by 1885 the number was 3,300.[82] Congress changed the postal laws in 1879 and reduced distribution costs for magazine publishers, and an increase in leisure time among a growing middle class provided a wider market for the

magazines and their advertisers. Improvements in printing technology (wood-pulp paper production, web-perfecting presses, Li-
notype machines) made production cheaper and more efficient; a
class of professional writers emerged to staff the periodicals and
newspapers. The mass readership that had eluded most pre–Civil
War magazines and newspapers was about to appear.

General-interest magazines such as *Collier's* and *Cosmopolitan*
carried articles on popular science subjects, but much of the important science writing was published in more specialized journals,
which became more popular (and profitable) with production and
distribution improvements and other cost savings. Indeed, there
were only two magazines devoted to science that survived any
length of time before the Civil War; but a flurry of them followed
the war, among them *American Naturalist, Science, Popular Science
Monthly,* and the *Western Review of Science and Industry. Popular Science Monthly's* first press run, in 1872, numbered five thousand copies; two years later its circulation was more than eleven thousand
and growing fast.[83] Nearly each scientific field got its own periodical: the *American Chemical Journal* and the *Botanical Gazette* were
typical. "People have a wonderful appetite for science just now,"
said the *Chicago Advance* in 1873.[84]

THE SCIENCE SERVICE

As science became more significant to American editors, amplified by the horrors of "the first modern war" in Europe and the
increasing specialization and complexity of the work of scientists,
the newspaper publisher E. W. Scripps saw an opening for a news
syndicate devoted to the subject. The Science Service, formed in
1921, aimed to popularize science for the average newspaper read-

er while respecting the work and remaining credible to the scientist. There was also the leftover problem, one scientist told *Literary Digest* in 1922, of the exaggerated and sometimes outlandish coverage of science during the yellow journalism period. "We do not mind being popularized, but we do mind being made ridiculous!" he said.[85] (For example, a *New York Journal* headline from 1898 read: A MAN WITHOUT A STOMACH WHO LIVES WITHOUT EATING.)[86] In the wake of World War I, more scientists looked to the federal government to fund their work and saw publicity as part of that effort, but many scientists wanted nothing to do with publicity or journalists at that point. "Apart from the occasional practical reports on new farming or household discoveries, the science journalism of the early twentieth century seemed to be doing neither the scientific community nor the reading public any real good," said magazine historian James C. Foust.[87] For example, the Harvard physiologist Walter B. Cannon presented research findings to the American Physiological Society that showed "strong emotion, such as rage, is attended by an increase in sugar in the blood." A reporter was in the audience; the next day, headlines over an Associated Press story carried around the country said MAN IS SWEETEST WHEN ANGRY.[88]

Scripps was a millionaire by 1921, having made his fortune with a chain of daily papers in the industrial cities of the Midwest. One of Scripps's closest friends was William Ritter, a zoologist and director of what would become the Scripps Institution of Oceanography in San Diego, which was endowed with the publisher's money. Although only in his fifties, Scripps had retired from daily journalism and lived in southern California on his ranch and yacht, where he pursued science as an avocation. "I am allowed to play with science as much as I choose," he wrote a friend.[89] Another correspondence, with a Yale economics professor named Irving Fisher, got

Scripps thinking seriously about communicating science in every-day language. He arranged a meeting between Fisher and Gilson Gardner, the journalist in charge of the Washington, D.C., bureau of Scripps's Newspaper Enterprise Association. The publisher also pledged $500,000 to fund the news service he envisioned.[90]

Scripps soon became unhappy with Fisher, who seemed more interested in promoting himself than anything else, and margin-alized him in the business. By 1919 a prospectus existed, describ-ing a group of ten scientists and a journalist to provide content. The venture needed to pay for itself, which contributed to the easy readability of articles designed to appeal to even the dim-mest editor. It was up and running by 1921 in Washington, with scientist-turned-journalist Edwin Slosson in charge. Slosson had earned a Ph.D. in organic chemistry from the University of Chi-cago in 1902; he had freelanced several articles for *The Indepen-dent,* a highbrow magazine of social commentary, before being hired as its editor in 1903. Slosson maintained a prodigious out-put in science writing, authoring eighteen books and nearly two thousand articles and editorials for various periodicals.[91] Scripps, in fact, thought Slosson too technical and somewhat dry in his writing. "He is a clear enough and lucid enough writer, but he has not got that catchy style," Scripps wrote.[92] He hired a jour-nalist to work with Slosson and continuously impressed upon the Science Service the need to write for the common person, even if it tended to be a bit sensational. (HOW THE CHEMIST MOVES THE WORLD, read one headline. PUPILS KEPT IN IGNORANCE OF FACTS OF LIFE SCIENCES was another.)[93] The service also produced a weekly publication, called *Science News Letter,* which could be purchased by individuals for five dollars per year. Photographs were added to the service in 1926. In 1939 the Science Service reported that sixty editors and reporters worked as science journalists for American newspapers, magazines, and syndicates.[94] "In a sense the essential effort to put science into the American press has been successful," said the director of the service in 1937.[95]

One researcher in the 1930s claimed that the Science Service was responsible for a twentyfold increase in the amount of science coverage in American newspapers in the decade of the 1920s.[96] By the 1940s, about one hundred clients subscribed to the *Science News Letter* with a total potential readership of about ten million.[97] The service supplied eight hundred words per day to its clients, which included twenty-six papers of the Scripps chain. The service continued to supply newspapers with science content until 1970; it remained the publisher of *Science News* (the renamed *Science News Letter*), which became the lone weekly science newsmagazine produced in the United States. (By 2006, Science Service was a nonprofit organization concerned with educational programs, science fairs, and scholarships. *Science News* editor Janet Raloff became an important figure in the founding of the Society of Environmental Journalists.) Foust noted that at the time of the demise of the newspaper service, some employees thought they had done their job too well; a mass audience for science news had been created with the help of the Science Service, and newspapers now hired their own science writers and editors to supply it, making the service superfluous.[98]

MATURATION

Science writers for newspapers and magazines began talking about forming an association as early as 1934 at a meeting in New York, when twelve journalists founded the National Association of Science Writers (NASW), which was formally incorporated in 1955 to "foster the dissemination of accurate information regarding science through all media normally devoted to informing the public." The World Federation of Science Journalists came together in 2002 in Brazil, the heirs to Pliny and Agricola.

In 1940, a young professor and former United Press science writer named Hillier Krieghbaum, who would go on to a career as a highly respected mass communication scholar and administrator, surveyed the field. He found that one out of every fifty newspapers employed a science writer or editor; 74 percent of them were college graduates (compared to 47 percent of the Washington, D.C., correspondents), and most of them were newsroom veterans.[99] World War II would accelerate the development of the science beat. The atomic bomb and other scientific initiatives in the war effort focused the news media's attention on government-sponsored research; the previous world war had seen the development of tanks and poison gas. "The world wars were catalysts for greater mass media coverage of science," according to one scholarly review.[100]

At the University of Wisconsin, two fellowships were established in 1948 for science writers, in partnership with the university's news service.[101] By 1953 the NASW claimed 182 members. After the Soviet Union's launch of the *Sputnik* spacecraft in 1957, interest in science and technology in the United States—from government, universities, and corporations, as well as mass media consumers—increased dramatically. As an example, federal government expenditures on science had grown from $9 billion in 1940 to more than $97 billion twenty-five years later.[102] An NASW survey in 1958 found that 66 percent of newspaper readers were willing to have some other news cut from the paper in order to provide more space for science stories.[103] Krieghbaum reported in 1963 that "science news reporting is probably the most rapidly expanding segment in the communications of the early 1960s."[104]

Soon the NASW began admitting public information officers from government labs, universities, and other institutions into its ranks. Seventy percent of NASW members had college degrees in 1957; debates about colleges and universities training students to be specialized science journalists (rather than providing them with a general liberal arts background) intensified.[105] In 1960 the NASW set up a nonprofit organization, the Council for the Advancement of Science Writers (CASW), to raise money for educational programs for science writers. Independent from the NASW, the CASW had a limited membership and included writers, scientists, and university information officers.

Scientists, with the exception of a few like the television personality Carl Sagan, had long since left the popularizing of their work to science journalists. Perhaps inevitably, employment in the field started to level off, if not decline, by the mid-1970s, after the man-on-the-moon and Cold War glory years. Victor K. McElheny, a member of the *New York Times* science reporting staff, in 1974 lamented what he saw: "Nobody questions that the bloom is off science reporting, even if that statement really should be translated as: Science reporting will always appear to be in decline because its subject matter always changes."[106] McElheny blamed television for some of his field's problems, but acknowledged that his beat was becoming so broadly defined as to distract him from his original work. Three primary areas of "distraction" were the space program, medicine, and the environment.[107] It was no coincidence that in the next two decades two of these three "distractions"—environment and health/medicine—developed into their own journalistic specialties, with supportive professional associations, newsletters, annual meetings, professional staff, and even commemorative coffee mugs.

FOUR

OUTDOOR ADVENTURE WRITING

Reporters and editors who attend the annual conference of the Society of Environmental Journalists (SEJ) have the opportunity to take an extended field trip for several days after the close of the formal meeting. The postconference trips tend to be for the adventurous, whether it is trekking across a desert, hiking a mountain, or visiting a large body of water. In October 2006, for example, SEJers spent four days and three nights kayaking, hiking, conversing, and writing about the environment in New York State's 5.8-million-acre Adirondack Park. Enjoying the wilderness in a vigorous way is a nod to the outdoor writing roots of environmental journalism; a more explicit connection was made earlier at the same conference when the outdoor editor from the Burlington (Vt.) newspaper, Matt Crawford, and I organized a tour highlighting the connections between hunters, anglers, and environmentalists. We spent time at the Missisquoi National Wildlife Refuge at Lake Champlain, where shooters and anglers coexist with bird-watchers, and we shotgunned our way through several boxes of shells at a trapshooting range.

The trip was set up to help environmental writers better connect with issues that their outdoor-writing colleagues deal with every day. That there was even a need for such a field trip (attendance jumped after Vice President Dick Cheney accidentally shot another hunter and some news media could not tell a rifle from a shotgun) said something about the increased specialization of journalism in the twenty-first century. It was not too long ago that the outdoor editor at the typical daily newspaper, for example, was called upon to write what might later be thought of as environmental stories. The "hook-and-bullet" reporter, as they have been called, would wax eloquent in the Saturday newspaper about a goose hunt with Uncle Joe, complete with a large photograph of a smiling hunter clutching a brace of stone-dead Canada honkers. Sunday would bring a story from the same reporter about the sighting of an endangered bobcat in a nearby state park.

IZAAK WALTON

The ties that bind outdoor writers and environmental journalists stretch back several hundred years. The most important writer in that shared history is the Englishman Izaak Walton, whose book *The Compleat Angler, or The Contemplative Man's Recreation,* first published in 1653, has influenced journalists and fishermen up to the present day. More than four hundred editions of this book have been published, including five editions in Walton's own lifetime. It has not been out of print since 1750. Perhaps only the Bible or John Bunyan's *Pilgrim's Progress* have gone through as many editions, reprints, and translations as Walton's work.[1] The book seems to get more popular as time goes on—by one count there were 10 editions of the book in the eighteenth century, 159 editions in the nineteenth century, another hundred by 1950, and many more since.[2]

The Compleat Angler first appeared in a U.S. edition in 1837 (although that edition was printed in London and Edinburgh as well as Philadelphia). The first all-American edition came out in 1847 under the guidance of the Dutch Reformed minister George Washington Bethune, although Bethune published it anonymously, perhaps because of a clergyman's natural reluctance to promote a leisure-time activity.[3] German, Japanese, French, Dutch, Swedish, and Finnish editions followed. Walton's name and image were also appropriated by one of the most important and politically connected environmental groups of the twentieth century, the Izaak Walton League of America, which at its height had the largest membership of any such organization in the United States.[4]

Walton certainly was not the first author to write about fishing as a pastime, but his work struck a nerve with the reading public, partly because it could be appreciated on several levels. It is a story of nostalgia, of slow-moving English streams and countryside cottages; rolling landscapes and lightly populated, friendly villages; handmade fishing gear, firm handshakes, and grandfatherly advice. It is a book for the religiously minded, of Anglican ways, ecclesiastical themes, Moses, Job, Isaiah, Amos, and a few apostles. It is a work of subtle sociopolitical commentary, of kings, royalists, Cromwellians, civil wars and revolution, peace and exile. It is a guide for serious anglers, of fly-tying and night crawlers, notes on the weather, habits of fish, preferences in tackle, recipes, and the lives of insects. And what fish! Walton discussed almost every fish an angler could catch in England: chub, cheven, trout, grayling, cuttlefish, pike, carp, bream, tench, perch, eel, barbel, gudgeon, roach, dace, penke, loach, bleak, ruffe, salmon, herring, bullhead, and others.

The book has journalistic elements, but it is not journalism as we know it, or perhaps even as it was considered in the seventeenth century, if it was thought of as such at all. John R. Cooper was among the scholars who noted that *The Compleat Angler* does not fit "into any of the more familiar critical categories."[5] The book is not a novel, or a short story, or an essay: "It is at once an imaginative work describing a journey into the countryside around London and a textbook on angling, giving detailed and largely accurate information about fish, fishing, and related matters of natural history."[6]

Perhaps the most familiar modern form to Walton readers would be the outdoor adventure column in a newspaper or magazine. Walton's work has the travel-writing element that most outdoor writers employ, along with the inclusion of a fishing pal, useful tips on gear and fish behavior, flowery language, some soft-sell political commentary, and a successful conclusion (topped by a hearty meal) at the end of the sporting day. Walton does profess a clear preference for fishing over hunting, which few modern outdoor writers would admit to in order not to alienate readers or advertisers.

Most scholars agree that Walton must have worked slowly and carefully; his original manuscripts are filled with edits, notes, cross-outs, and other marginalia. The frequent editions of all his books are testaments to his fussiness: each of the five biographies he wrote were reissued more than once in his lifetime, and his book on the Anglican theologian Richard Hooker came out six times. After all that editing practice, his spelling remained abysmal, even by seventeenth-century standards. His last will and testament included a bequest of money "to buie coles for some pore people, that shall most neide them in the said towne; the said coles to be delivered in the last weike in Janewary, or in every first weike in Febrewary; I say then, because I take that time to be the hardest and most pinching times with pore people."[7] But a dedicated writer and editor he was. In subsequent editions of his books, place-names and dates are often added or changed, and short stories are used to flesh out existing characters. Other sections are revised, added, or deleted entirely.

In the first edition of *The Compleat Angler,* for example, Walton included this quote from the Gospel of John in the frontispiece: "Simon Peter said, I go a fishing: and they said, We also wil go with thee."[8] Two years later, in the second edition (called "Much Enlarged"), Walton edits the Gospel of John excerpt to "Simon Peter saith unto them, I go a fishing, they say unto him, We also go with thee."[9] It appears that Walton took the first version from the Geneva Bible, a translation written by Englishmen in exile in Switzerland in the sixteenth century. (The Geneva Bible was at its core an update of the scholar-translator William Tyndale's Bible of 1525.) But even as Walton prepared his work, the Geneva Bible was falling out of favor—it was the book used by the Puritans, among other marginalized groups—and in its place came the King James Bible, first published in 1611 and becoming more available and accepted among Anglicans. Walton's second edition uses the King James translation of John 21:3 verbatim. Then, in the third and all subsequent editions, Walton dropped the quote from the frontispiece altogether. Here was a man operating from a perspective familiar to exacting journalists—that of never being quite happy with one's work.

Walton was born in 1593 near Stafford. His father, Gervase, an alehouse keeper, died when Izaak was four. His mother, Anne, was remarried the following year to a man who ran an inn and bakery. The young Walton had two siblings who survived to adulthood, a brother and a sister. Anne Walton, his sister, married Thomas

Grinsell of London around 1608 and Izaak moved in with them. He was apprenticed to Grinsell as a linen draper, and in 1618 he was admitted to the Ironmongers Company (a workmen's guild, where he rose to prominence though he was never employed as an ironmonger).[10]

Although he lacked the usual British class advantages of birth and extended formal schooling, the congenial and witty Walton began hanging around with writers, clergymen, and social commentators in London. He married the well-connected Rachel Floud in 1626. The couple had seven children, all of whom died young. Rachel herself died in 1640, shortly after giving birth to their last child, who lived only twenty-two months. In 1647, at age fifty-four, Walton married Anne Ken, who was nineteen years younger. The couple had three children, two of whom survived their father. They also reared Anne's half brother, Thomas Ken, who went on to become a bishop and hymn writer, perhaps most remembered for the work "Praise God, From Whom All Blessings Flow," which is still sung as a doxology in many churches today. Anne Walton died in 1662. Walton lived another twenty-one years, to age ninety.

His literary career took flight with a biography of John Donne (1572–1631), who was vicar of Walton's church. (Some scholars have guessed that Walton edited the first collection of Donne's poetry, called *Poems,* published posthumously in 1633.) With his *Life of Donne,* which came out in 1640, Walton's literary reputation was established. It was, in the words of one scholar, a new kind of biography that "combined hagiography, true-to-life detail, colorful anecdote, informal dialog, and historical interpretation."[11] The author clearly knew Donne and his circle of friends well, but he remained fair and impartial in a journalistic sense while persuading the reader of the worth of his subject. More than one scholar has called Walton an "objective" writer.[12] The book was also un-usual for its time in that Walton for the most part leaves himself out of the manuscript. Walton went on to write significant biographies of Sir Henry Wotton, George Herbert, Richard Hooker, and Robert Sanderson. He could be called England's foremost biographer of his day. "Happy old man, whose worth all mankind knows," wrote the poet Thomas Flatman on the occasion of Walton's ninetieth birthday.[13]

The first version of *The Compleat Angler* hit the streets in 1653. Two short notices in the newspapers that spring announced its publication. Over the next twenty-three years, Walton continued to make extensive updates, including the final edition of his life-time at age eighty-three.

Walton was a dedicated royalist, and that thread winds subtly throughout all his work. Though the times during his middle age were turbulent (Charles I was dead, the court was in exile, the Anglican clergy were dispersed, and the *Book of Common Prayer* was banned), Walton does not confront the troubles head-on in his fishing book. The countryside is quiet, the rain showers are gentle, his companions are amiable, songs are sung, poems are re-cited, grace is said before supping, and the fish are biting. "No life, my honest scholar, no life so happy and so pleasant as the life of a well-governed angler; for when the lawyer is swallowed up with business, and the statesman is preventing or contriving plots, then we sit on the cowslip-banks, hear the birds sing, and possess our-selves in as much quietness as these silent silver streams, which we now see glide so quietly by us," he wrote.[14] The Walton biographer Paul Stanwood noted: "Walton is providing a general book of wisdom for hard times in the shape of a fishing manual."[15]

Walton's book is pastoral and georgic—in the tradition of Virgil and John Milton—rather than escapist. In its fifth edition, it is presented in the form of a dialogue among three men—an angler, a huntsman, and a falconer. The falconer (Auceps) soon exits the scene after saying his piece, and the huntsman (Venator) apprentices himself to the fisherman (Piscator) and the two set out on their springtime journey of several days. They begin by traveling from Tottenham to Ware. Dialogue, often in a question-and-answer format, is interrupted by lengthy instructions on the art of angling. Minor characters come and go; poems and songs are introduced; and tobacco is smoked. *The Compleat Angler's* popularity was analyzed by the writer William Hazlitt: "The minute descriptions of fishing-tackle, of baits and flies . . . make that work a great favourite with sportsmen: the alloy of an amiable humanity, and the modest but touching descriptions of familiar incidents and rural objects scattered through it, have made it an equal favourite with every reader of taste and feeling."[16] Peter Oliver, writing on the brink of World War II, said: "Our troubled world could use another Izaak Walton."[17]

The work could be classified as pastoral if the reader replaces Walton's fisherman with the traditional shepherd. The country is idealized, a place for spiritual refreshment, where leisure and love are hallmarks and innocence abounds. And the book is georgic in that there is plenty of instruction in a (rural) pursuit; the agrarian myth is in full force—fields are fertile, labor has dignity and moral superiority, and the countryside is tranquil. The action and skills of the georgic meet the contemplation and introspection of the pastoral.[18]

Walton must have been an avid reader because *The Compleat Angler* is heavily sourced. A partial list of authors he consulted includes Pliny, Bacon, Claudius Aelianus, Plutarch, Edward Topsell, Conrad Gesner, William Camden, George Hakewill, Gervase Markham, Leonard Mascall, William Samuel, and Jan Dubravius.

Five works on fish and fishing were major sources, including a volume by Mascall and Thomas Barker's *The Art of Angling.* Barker appeared to be the more experienced angler of the two, and he was a professional cook, but his leaden writing and dull commentary lacked Walton's deft touch (although Barker's recipes are better). By the fifth edition, Walton cited by title or author more than sixty works of poetry or prose in its 334 pages.[19]

The first edition is a slender thirteen chapters; the second edition adds eight chapters and the character Auceps. The English monarchy was restored before the third edition was published, and it contains a number of minor edits. The fourth edition looked like a reprint of the third. The fifth issue bundled *The Compleat Angler* with a supplement on fly-fishing written by Charles Cotton and Robert Venable's *Experienced Angler.* All three were bound and sold as *The Universal Angler.*

ENDURING ISSUES

Walton confronted issues that are still written about by modern-day journalists. For example, since the time of the first angler, poor fishing has often been blamed on competition for the fish from avian, reptilian, or mammalian sources—nearly everything but the angler's own ability or lack thereof. In Walton's time the blame was spread around, but the river otter comes in for a large share of it. Early on, Piscator and Venator come across hunters and dogs that have gotten on the scent of an otter. The otter had eaten a part of a trout and was after more fish when the dogs started tracking it. One of the hunters tells Piscator, "I am sure the Otter devours much fish, and kills and spoils much more than he eats."[20] The dogs corner the otter, which turns out to be female. It had recently given birth. The men find five young ones and want to slaughter them all. Piscator convinces the hunters to give him one to raise and make tame. They destroy the rest. Piscator says: "I am glad these Otters were killed; and I am sorry there are no more Otter-killers; for I know that the want of Otter-killers, and the not keeping the fence-months [spring] for the preservation of fish, will, in time prove the destruction of all rivers."[21] In this he manages to blame the otters for ruining the fishing while at the same time he lobbies for a closing of the fishing season during spring spawning months ("a sin so against nature" he later calls fishing during the spawn).[22] Piscator bids farewell to the hunters the next day with the admonition: "God keep you all, Gentlemen, and send you meet this day with another *bitch* Otter, and kill her merrily, and all her young ones too."[23] Though Piscator, by his own admission, will kill nothing but fish, he lists the enemies of the fish (and hopes they will be killed by others) as otters, cormorants, ospreys, seagulls, and kingfishers.

By the twenty-first century, cormorants had moved to the top of the list of those creatures to be blamed by anglers for poor fishing. Journalists in England reported that the government granted licenses to kill up to three thousand of the birds in September 2005 "to prevent damage to fish in lakes and rivers," despite protests from conservation advisers and birding and environmental groups.[24] In America, cormorants were protected by the federal government under amendment to the Migratory Bird Act in the 1970s after their numbers became depleted because of hunting and pesticides. They rebounded with an impressive intensity, and soon cormorants were once again attracting blame for declining fish populations. In 1998 nine men, some of them professional fishing guides, pleaded guilty to shooting and killing more than one thousand cormorants on an island in Lake Ontario in one of the largest mass killings of a federally protected species on record. The *New York Times* reported: "The birds' ability to take over islands for use as nesting colonies where they can ruin the habitat for other birds and down tremendous amounts of fish has raised alarms among anglers, state environmental officials and wildlife biologists."[25] Federal sharpshooters in Minnesota killed more than two thousand birds on Leech Lake in May 2005 "because of concerns that they are hurting the walleye population," according to one outdoor writer.[26] Plans were in place to kill another one thousand to two thousand of them. In Michigan, state officials oiled the eggs in 3,220 cormorant nests to prevent them from hatching.[27] "Cormorants," said one graduate research assistant at the University of Vermont, "have a long history of people not liking them."[28]

The effects of fishing on the health of fish populations and the idea of catch-and-release angling are other subjects Walton shares with modern outdoor and environment writers. At one point Venator worries about a trout that has swallowed his hook and broken his line: "But, Master, will this *Trout* die, for it is like he has the hook in his belly?" Piscator assures him that unless the hook is caught in his throat, time and the river water will erode the hook and leave the fish healthy.[29] A similar debate has continued in modern times. Most outdoor writers uncritically support catch-and-release fishing, for example, but there are a few exceptions. A story in a Tampa newspaper reported that the mortality rates of red snapper were as high as 66 percent after being caught and released.[30] When a California fisherman caught and released a potential world record largemouth bass in March 2006, at least one outdoor writer criticized him and decried the culture of catch-and-release fishing, calling it an "unhealthy obsession" and "partly to blame for disease outbreaks."[31]

Walton also touched on such popular modern topics as tagging fish for research purposes ("tying a Ribon in the tail of some number of the young *Salmons*"),[32] adding scent to bait to attract more strikes ("a drop, or two, or three of the Oil of *Ivy-berries*"),[33] and the introduction of exotic species into English waters. In the latter example, Walton devoted a chapter in his first edition to the carp, which according to him was brought to Britain by the author Leonard Mascall of Sussex a few years earlier.[34]

SPORTSMEN AND JOURNALISTS IN THE MID-NINETEENTH CENTURY

American authors were slow to pick up on the tradition of Izaak Walton. An Englishman, writing in 1835, described this exchange between two fishermen:

> Simpson: "Have you ever seen any American books on angling, Fisher?"
> Fisher: "No. I do not think there are any published. Brother Jonathan is not yet sufficiently civilized to produce anything original on the gentle art. There is good trout-fishing in America, and the streams, which are all free, are much less fished than in our Island, 'from the small number of gentlemen,' as an American writer says, 'who are at leisure to give their time to it.'"[35]

In fact, America had not produced much in the way of *any* mass media until the 1820s or 1830s, when the first economically viable magazines got going and glimmerings of regional markets for advertised goods began. Two men who helped bring outdoor subjects to the periodical world were John Skinner and

William Trotter Porter. Perhaps the first regular publication on outdoor subjects in America was the *American Turf Register and Sporting Magazine,* founded by Skinner in 1829. Skinner, postmaster general from 1841 to 1845 and also the editor of a humor magazine, ran the sporting periodical for several years until selling it to Gideon B. Smith, who in turn sold it to Porter in 1839.[36] Skinner went on to edit an important farm periodical, *Turf, Field and Farm.*[37]

Porter, who was said to have printed the first baseball box score, was already in charge of a sporting journal called the *Spirit of the Times,* which he had founded in 1831.[38] A tall, genial man, Porter owned and edited both of young America's leading sporting journals for nine years. Stories on hunting, fishing, horse racing, boxing, and other sports filled the pages of both magazines. He recruited authors such as Thomas Bangs Thorpe, Albert Pike, and Henry William Herbert to his cause.

Porter closed *American Turf Register* in 1844 and sold *Spirit of the Times* in 1856 but stayed on as editor until his death two years later. "In his own way," wrote the *Mirror,* "Porter had no rival in the press of our country. Inimitable pen, playful fancy, heart all kindness and sincerity, an able and skilfull [*sic*] caterer to public taste."[39] *Spirit of the Times* ran in one form or another until 1912. Pike, writing Porter's obituary, said: "Where in all the world was there so pure, so manly, so unselfish, so loving a soul . . . true, generous, unselfish gentleman."[40]

One of Porter's authors, Henry Herbert, made a lasting mark on outdoor writing that brought the inevitable comparisons to Walton. The English-born Herbert, writing under the pseudonym of Frank Forester, produced a series of how-to sporting books in America in the 1840s and 1850s that far outstripped his romance novels in popularity. His writing style was elegant, literary, and to-the-manor-born British. For example, on fishing for carp, he wrote: "This, I confess, I regard as very miserable sport, for though the fish is shy and wary, the difficulty in taking him arises only from his timidity and unwillingness to bite, and he is as lazy when hooked as he is slow to bite."[41] He occasionally employed a fishing guide, and he recognized "Old Izaak" as the "last authority" on fly-fishing.[42]

Herbert could be called America's first professional writer on field sports. One historian said he was "the first nationally famous sports writer" and a "legend to sportsmen of later generations."[43] He also dabbled in magazine publishing and contributed articles to newspapers and periodicals on political topics of the day. His high-class upbringing may have led him to write his sporting treatises under the pseudonym, although this practice was not uncommon.

Porter convinced Herbert to submit a series of stories to the *American Turf Register* that were well received and published in 1845 as a sporting book titled *The Warwick Woodlands*.[44] The success of his first outdoor work spurred Herbert to write three more books in the same genre and cemented his reputation as a successful writer of field sports. His nonfiction book *Fish and Fishing of the United States and British Provinces,* first published in 1850, influenced Thaddeus Norris and many others. This and other works "by the general consent of the sporting world are second to none in their department, in any of the qualities which should distinguish this sort of writing," wrote *International Magazine* in 1851.[45] Other titles included *My Shooting Box* and *Field Sports of the United States and British Provinces.* A man of much vanity and ego ("priding himself upon killing as much if not more game than any other gentleman" in New York) yet dissolute in his habits, Herbert committed suicide at age fifty-one in 1858 in New York after being snubbed at his own dinner party.[46]

References to Forester show up in hook-and-bullet writing for the rest of the century. For example, in an 1873 article for *Harper's,* Porte Crayon (the artist David Hunter Strother) described an outing in which a group of rambunctious children outfished some serious adults that he called "our scientific sportsmen, who read Frank Forester, and go out armed with joined rods, reels, horse-hair lines, and books of cunningly designed flies."[47] A writer from *Macmillan's Magazine* credited Forester with changing the public perception of the American sportsman from an "almost despicable position" and "first cousins to drunkenness and dissipation" to something more respectable.[48] The memory of Forester became "exceedingly dear to American sportsmen, who now fish and shoot with impunity."[49]

Nearly equaling Herbert in significance and exceeding him in misty-eyed public adoration was the Pennsylvanian Thaddeus Norris, who became known as the American Walton after the publication of his *American Angler's Book* in 1864.[50] Unlike Walton, whose fishing comments were usually restricted to the countryside around London, Norris attempted to describe the American piscatorial scene from Canada to the Gulf of Mexico. Like Walton, "Uncle Thad" Norris wrote in a friendly, accessible manner that visited the cultural touchstones of nostalgia, extended family, and the agrarian myth. In a eulogy that was included in the front of Norris's magnum opus, Joseph Townsend wrote that his friend held "some of the characteristics of an angler whom Walton would have loved as a kindred spirit."[51]

Norris was born in Virginia in 1811 and at an early age moved to Philadelphia, where he lived the rest of his sixty-six years. He took up fishing as a boy, and eventually he built his own rods and tied his own flies. His debt to Walton was such that in the first edition of his book, published in 1864, Walton's poetry was included at the beginning of some chapters. Norris created several ideal types of anglers, including a True Angler "thoroughly imbued with the spirit of gentle old Izaak" who fished with no affectation or expectation of success and was modest and true.[52] There is more than a touch of the rural utopia in Norris: "How pleasingly rough everything looks after leaving the prim city! How pure and wholesome the air! How beautiful the clumps of sugar-maples and the veteran hemlocks jutting out over the stream; the laurel, the ivy; the moss-covered rocks; the lengthening shadows of evening."[53] No doubt the air was cleaner in the woods than in industrial-age Philadelphia.

Like modern-day outdoor writers, Norris worried about overfishing. In particular, he was aware of the potential damage that extensive news media exposure could do to a fishery. To wit: Bethune's American edition of Walton was very familiar to him, as was Forester's *Fish and Fishing*. The publication of both books caused "sporting fish [to] have decreased in some parts of the country where they were once abundant," Norris wrote.[54] Highlighting the best fishing holes and exposing them to overuse did not stop Norris from doing so, much like his modern hook-and-bullet descendants.

Roads in areas where there had been none, a hot topic among modern environmentalists, were on the mind of Norris, as were fish-limiting high dams, poison runoff from mines, sawdust from mills, tannic acid from leather makers and their factories, and other industrial pollutants. Fishing with nets or spears were bugaboos for him (as they are for most of his modern counterparts); he thought those who recreated in such a way were not true anglers. One favored solution for Norris was fish breeding and stocking; he wrote an entire three-hundred-page book on the subject.[55] None of these stories would seem unfamiliar to the modern reader of a newspaper's outdoor page or a subscriber to a twenty-first-century sporting magazine.

POLITICAL INVOLVEMENT

Among those influenced by Norris and Forester was Charles Hallock, a founder of the magazine *Forest and Stream* and one of the most high-profile and politically active of America's nineteenth-century outdoor writers. And it seems unavoidable that Hallock was compared to the original angling author: upon the publication of his guidebook *The Fishing Tourist, Scientific American* said Hallock was "one of the most charming of all spring-time companions since the days of Izaak Walton."[56]

Hallock founded *Forest and Stream* magazine in New York in 1873 and edited it until he was forced out in 1885, when he sold it to George Bird Grinnell, who was a regular columnist. Hallock went on to edit *Nature's Realm,* another sporting magazine. Under the editorships of Hallock and Grinnell, *Forest and Stream* became the leading voice in America calling for the creation and enforcement of fish and game laws. At the forefront of a tradition of political involvement by outdoor writers that continued through the twentieth century, their participation did not fit with the journalistic standards of objectivity held by some of the rest of the news media.

Sportsmen-editors were agitating for fish and game laws because they'd had firsthand experience of the decline of animal populations from their days in the field. Many of them blamed market hunters and game dealers for the collapse of some species, and they could immediately point to the remaining few American bison or passenger pigeons as examples of how indiscriminate killing could cause ecological havoc. The causes of the exhaustion of these and other species had many roots (including the fencing of the open range), but the gunners who shot game for eastern restaurants and butcher shops took the blame. An increase in leisure time and improvements in firearms technology also played roles in intensifying the pressure on game populations.

The editors aggressively formed and supported the creation of activist groups such as the Audubon Society, the Boone and Crockett Club, and the American Ornithologists' Union, many of which became adept at lobbying Washington and state governments for the passage of game laws. There was an elite eastern cast in the organization of these groups; conversely, the game dealers and market hunters who were the focus of their ire often were immigrants or first-generation Americans from the South or Midwest. In this conflict rest some of the roots of the class tensions in the environmental movement of one hundred years later. The editors of the magazines and their influential friends succeeded in restricting the occupations of the professional hunters while codifying their own behavior in the field. Examples included closing seasons, requiring licenses, daily bag limits, shooting males only, and restricting the interstate transportation of game.

Grinnell, who grew up on John James Audubon's former estate and was tutored by his widow, founded a forerunner of the Audubon Society in 1886 with members of New York's social elite such as Oliver Wendell Holmes, John Greenleaf Whittier, and Henry Ward Beecher. The following year, Grinnell and Theodore Roosevelt cofounded the Boone and Crockett Club, along with J. P. Morgan, Henry Cabot Lodge, Elihu Root, and Madison Grant. This partnership of editor, politician, and environmental organization continued into the next century.

The National Geographic Society (1888), Sierra Club (1892),

American Scenic and Historic Preservation Society (1895), and Campfire Club of America (1897; also cofounded by an outdoor journalist) followed Grinnell's lead.[57] Most of these groups communicated with the public through the pages of their specialized publications. By 1885, twenty journals considered outdoor sports as their main subject, and four years later that number had nearly tripled. *Fur, Fin and Feather* (1868), *Game Fanciers' Journal* (1870), *American Sportsman* (1872), *Forest and Stream* (1873), *Chicago Field* (1874), *Appalachia* (1876), *American Angler* (1881), and *Outing* (1882) were some of the early titles.[58] Subscription discounting, the printing of event calendars, and other incentives encouraged the formation of the clubs and the sale of magazines.[59] *Outing,* for example, had reached a circulation of more than eighty-eight thousand by the mid-1880s.[60]

Forest and Stream campaigned long and hard for English-style game laws, restricted access to wildlife, and a "refined taste for nature objects."[61] When market hunters reported massive game kills, the magazine would print the results and mock the hunters.[62] In 1879 the magazine offered a model piece of legislation entitled "Simplified Plan for Uniformity of Closed Season—Legislation Made Easy," and called for states to adopt it.[63] Beginning with Iowa in 1878, states began passing legislation that required possession limits, hunting and fishing seasons, licensing, limits to resale and transport, and other measures sought by the editors. Market hunters were legislated out of existence.

Hunters have often existed in a cultural place somewhere between noble saviors of wildlife and it-flies-it-dies killers of all they see. Beginning about the time of Hallock and Grinnell, the prevailing hunting ethic was to kill the large adult male animals and leave the females alone; governments institutionalized this ethic in state and federal game laws. A single male can reproduce with several females, so such a policy made biological sense. The media, according to one hunting history, helped "transform this biological tenet into a cultural one by featuring large-antlered deer, giant-horned sheep, and enormous, threatening bears on the covers of periodicals."[64] Trophy hunting replaced hunting for food for many shooters. Whether hunting or fishing qualifies as a "sport" or is some other pursuit, such as a ritual, is a common argument among hook-and-bullet journalists.[65]

Magazines, more than books, were critical to the diffusion of sporting information in the nineteenth century; there were no other nationally circulated mass media. Newspapers did not reach beyond their local or regional area and tended not to print the longer stories of outdoor adventure that the magazines favored. "The whole tendency of the age is magazineward," wrote Edgar Allen Poe, who perhaps not coincidentally was editing a magazine at the time. "We now demand the light artillery of the intellect; we need the curt, the condensed, the readily diffused, in place of the verbose, the detailed, the voluminous, the inaccessible."[66] It was common, as in the case of Forester, for books to be created out of several magazine articles. That trend continued well into the future, notably in the *New Yorker* serialization of Rachel Carson's *Silent Spring* in the early 1960s.

THEODORE ROOSEVELT

Norris, Grinnell, Theodore S. Van Dyke, and Robert Barnwell Roosevelt were among America's most famous native sporting writers at the time of the settlement of the West. Grinnell's obituary in the *Times* called him "the father of American conservation."[67] But Grinnell's good friend and Robert Barnwell Roosevelt's nephew, Theodore, became the most influential sporting writer of them all. "His influence on American outdoor writing was never surpassed," wrote one author.[68] Much of Teddy Roosevelt's early writing on the outdoors appeared in *Outing* magazine, including his treatise on ranch life and the country lifestyle in the Dakota Territory in 1886. Roosevelt irritated the publisher of the struggling magazine by sending him a bill for $100 after the story was published.[69]

Roosevelt wrote and cowrote stories, magazine pieces, and books on the outdoor life almost all his adult life. He was a skilled hunter and angler, a naturalist of some renown, a taxidermist, and an important critic. Roosevelt often said that good writing was the sportsman's obligation but that he did not see much of it: "There have been many American hunting books; but too often they have been very worthless, even when the writers possessed the necessary first hand knowledge, and the rare capacity for seeing the truth."[70] Roosevelt appreciated Forester in a way, but said of his predecessor: "Unfortunately, he was a true cockney, who cared little for really wild sports, and he was afflicted with the dreadful pedantry which pays more heed to ceremonial and terminology than it does to the thing itself."[71] His taste ran more to Herman Melville and James Fenimore Cooper, and his favorite contemporary author was John Burroughs, "foremost of all American writers on outdoor life."[72]

The popular Dakota Territory trilogy penned by Roosevelt included two books called *Hunting Trips of a Ranchman* (1885) and *The Wilderness Hunter* (1893), both of which dealt with all matters of science and nature in the American West for East Coast audiences. "One of the chief attractions of the life of the wilderness," he wrote in *The Wilderness Hunter,* "is its rugged and stalwart democracy; there every man stands for what he actually is, and can show himself to be."[73] The British magazine *Spectator* said the first book "could claim an honorable place on the same shelf as Walton's *Compleat Angler.*"[74] Three American editions and one British edition were in print within a year.[75] The *Atlantic Monthly* said the latter book had "the air of solid, substantial record of a manner of life which will one day be historic."[76] In between those works Roosevelt authored *Ranch Life and the Hunting Trail* (1888). *The Nation* said of *Ranch Life:* "Mr. Roosevelt's observations on the natural history and the game of the region are thoroughly trustworthy, and consequently possess a considerable scientific importance."[77]

It was Grinnell's not completely favorable review of *Hunting Trips* that brought the two men together when Roosevelt went to *Forest and Stream*'s offices to complain.[78] Roosevelt wound up as Grinnell's coeditor on three books published by the Boone and Crockett Club: *American Big-Game Hunting* (1893), *Hunting in Many Lands* (1895), and *Trail and Camp-Fire* (1897). Roosevelt paid for their publication and Forest and Stream Publishing Company printed them at cost and advertised them for free.[79] More space was allotted to conservation issues as the series went on.

Roosevelt, of course, continued his interest in and championing of the outdoors as president; working with the forester Gifford Pinchot, his chief adviser; establishing national parks, monuments, and refuges at a record pace; building dams and irrigation systems; involving himself in the nature faker controversy; and engaging in many other conservation activities. He continued to write on hunting and the wilderness while president, and his earlier books were reprinted.

The Boone and Crockett Club lobbied successfully for the passage of the National Wildlife Refuge System (1903), the Weeks-MacLean Migratory Bird Act (1913), the National Park Service

(1916), and the Federal Duck Stamp Program (1934).[80] "The results accomplished by the Boone and Crockett Club bear testimony to the alertness and energy of its members, and to the success of the methods which they have pursued," Grinnell wrote
in his history of the group.[81] Although the Boone and Crockett Club continued its lobbying activities in the ensuing years,
it became better known as a keeper of records for trophy kills.
The other path-setting nineteenth-century pressure groups, the
American Ornithologists' Union (AOU) and the Audubon Society, also ended up in different places. The AOU became a primary home for professional ornithologists; the Audubon Society
retained a focus on counting and protecting birds while keeping
an influential presence in Washington, D.C.

THE IZAAK WALTON LEAGUE OF AMERICA

Though somewhat late to the table in terms of mobilization, the
Izaak Walton League of America (IWLA) became an influential
force in American conservation shortly after its founding in Chicago in 1922. The group's reputation has been one of fairness and
deliberateness (a "tradition of avoiding purely political stances"
was how one writer put it).[82] For example, the group established
a program in the late 1990s to mediate the stormy relationship between hunters and landowners over access to private lands.[83]

The connection between the Ikes, as they were nicknamed,
and journalists dates from the creation of the organization. Stories differ about the exact sequence of events, but one version has
the Ikes organized by Dan Starkey, publisher of *Outers-Recreation*
magazine (soon to be merged with *Outdoor Life*).[84] One of Starkey's regular contributors was an advertising man and obsessive

angler named Will Dilg, who issued an invitation for all interested in forming a "Walton Club" to meet at the Chicago Athletic Club on a cold January day. Dilg's signature appeared under the letter, which was actually composed by *Chicago Daily News* outdoor writer L. J. Boughner. Fifty-four men attended the meeting, including four professional outdoor writers. Among the audience was a thirty-one-year-old minister named Preston Bradley. The title "Walton Club" was not impressive enough for Bradley, who had fished at Walton's favored Dove River in England and preached at Winchester Cathedral, where his hero was buried. At least call it the Izaak Walton Club, he said, and soon the debaters settled on the Izaak Walton League of America.[85] The IWLA incorporated a bust of Izaak Walton in its official seal, letterhead, and logo.

Two of the leading sporting journals of the day, *Field and Stream* and *Outdoor Life,* offered to publicize the Izaak Walton League and even provided financial help. Both magazines were already partially underwriting the American Game Protective Association and wanted something similar on the fishing side.[86] The IWLA's goals were as follows: to limit the take of the "fish hog"; to outlaw shooting or dynamiting of fish; to put government in charge of pollution abatement; to add more hatcheries; and to create biological experiment stations for aquatic life. Dilg would work without respite for the league for four years; in 1927 throat cancer took his life not long after he was forced out as director. Dilg started the group's monthly magazine with his own money. "His belief in what he was doing and saying bordered on fanaticism," Bradley said.[87] The magazine, which reached one hundred thousand readers by 1925, attracted well-known contributors, including Theodore Dreiser, MacKinlay Kantor, Zane Grey, Aldo Leopold, Henry Van Dyke, Gene Stratton-Porter, Irvin S. Cobb,

Jay N. "Ding" Darling, Albert Bigelow Paine, and David Starr Jordan. By the end of the IWLA's first year, chapters had been organized in thirty-four states. Although the media-savvy Sierra Club may have been the first nationally famous conservation group and the elite Boone and Crockett Club was more politically powerful, the Ikes were, in the words of historian John Opie, the first environmental organization with a mass membership.[88]

In the years to follow, the Ikes, along with their journalistic compatriots in the sporting press, fought against pollution, overfishing and overgrazing, and supported fish stocking and game protection laws. The Ikes' most famous member was secretary of commerce and future president Herbert Hoover, an avid fly-fisherman who helped successfully lobby for more federal wildlife refuges in the 1920s. Writers took marketing and public relations jobs with the Ikes, returned to the periodical press or industry, and then came back again.

OUTDOOR WRITERS ORGANIZE

The advocacy that modern outdoor writers routinely express has roots as deep as the conservation organizations they helped establish. In 1927 journalists took a cue from the success of the Ikes and founded an organization for writers and editors. The Outdoor Writers Association of America (OWAA) became the largest and most important trade association for hook-and-bullet journalists. Like the Izaak Walton League, the OWAA was created in Chicago. In fact, the OWAA was dreamed up at an Izaak Walton League annual convention in that city on April 9, 1927. It was the beginning of a long and complicated connection between the two groups.

Perhaps nothing could highlight the link between outdoor journalists and outdoor organizations more than the OWAA's creation; several writers were seated together at an IWLA banquet discussing the pressing conservation issues of the day—fish, wildlife, water, forests, soil—when one of them had an idea. Morris Ackerman, a lawyer-turned-outdoor-editor of the *Cleveland Daily News,* wrote the idea down on the nearest piece of paper, which was the back of the menu for the IWLA banquet. It read:

> Bill of Organization
>
> We the undersigned, being agreed that an organization of recognized outdoor writers should be formed in America, for the purpose of bettering our profession, to give more stability and standing to the same, and to eliminate untruths from stories of the outdoors, do hereby form the Outdoor Writers Association of America.[89]

Signatories included Ackerman, Peter P. Carney, Cal Johnson, Buell A. Patterson, Ed G. Taylor, Jack Miner, "El Comancho" (W. L. Phillips), and Mrs. Hal Kane Clements. No affiliations were listed on the signatures except for Clements, who was identified as being with *Water Motoring* magazine. (Johnson edited the *Sporting Goods Journal,* Patterson was with the *Chicago Herald-Examiner,* Taylor was from the *Chicago Tribune,* and Phillips was from the *American Lumberman* and *The Whole World.* The affiliation of Carney remains a mystery. Miner had founded a Canadian bird sanctuary in 1904.) During the remainder of the IWLA conference, at least eleven more names were added to the OWAA list and a professional association was born. But the new members were not all professional writers: among them were an official with the Western Cartridge Co., of Alton, Illinois, and an operator of a Canadian big-game hunting and fishing camp.[90]

The cozy connections between the OWAA and industry, government, and the nongovernmental organizations its members were supposed to cover dogged the association for years. Several annual meetings of the group were held in conjunction with the Izaak Walton League's annual conferences. At one get-together, Henry Baldwin Ward, IWLA president and a zoology professor at the University of Illinois, urged the writers to join the conservationist cause. He saw "a great future for outdoor writers in their efforts to interest many readers who had given no serious thought to conservation of natural resources and wildlife."[91] The relationship between the writers and magazines and their biggest advertisers, outdoor equipment manufacturers, increased the potential for conflicts of interest.

The OWAA attempted to maintain a public image of impartiality, but at the same time it did not apologize for its advocacy of conservation programs. "Discussion by the writers present [at a workshop] clearly pointed out that partisan politics had no place in conservation programs, and that partisan politics had done more than any one thing to block conservation programs. The writers were unanimous in their opinion," read the minutes of one meeting in 1929.[92] Many members of the OWAA, including Ding Darling, were present at the formation of what would become the National Wildlife Federation in 1936.[93] By 1941 the OWAA's membership had reached two hundred, of whom ten worked for the federal government, thirty-two for state governments, and twenty-four for conservation "with various organizations."[94] Thirty-three percent of the group was thus not primarily engaged in journalism. Political activity proceeded through the pages of *Outdoors Unlimited,* the group's magazine: "Keep hammering away at Senate Bill 1030, which would permit public grazing on our National Forest areas . . . Make your senator and congressmen see how vicious this bill really is," read one article.[95] By the late 1940s, some OWAA members were grumbling that writers were being shunted aside in favor of "a pressure-type group" that had been built by the leadership.[96]

In the mid-1950s the OWAA considered the "Are we journalists or lobbyists?" conflict important enough to call for the adoption of a new constitution under which, its president said, the OWAA "ceased being a policy making, lobbying or conservation group."[97] This brought a storm of criticism from some members who wanted to continue jumping into the important environmental issues of the day, and led the leadership to retreat from its no-politics stance. In 1970 the OWAA passed a resolution in favor of what would become known as the Clean Water Act of 1972.[98]

More than clean water, gun control (and hunting in general) remained a hot-button issue for the group. Efforts at removing the organization from overt political involvement in this issue led to a series of actions, including tighter membership guidelines, a code of ethics, and a "Position on Hunting" that included the statement: "An organization of professional communicators, the Outdoor Writers Association of America (OWAA) avoids advocacy within issues not related to journalism." The same statement said that the "OWAA recognizes legal hunting as an appropriate use of natural resources."[99] In 2004 the OWAA and the National Rifle Association feuded over support of an effort by the Sierra Club to join with hunting groups to protect wildlife habitats.[100]

MODERN TRENDS

What of the post-1960s state of outdoor adventure writing? Paul Schullery, writing in the *New York Times* in 1985, attempted to assess the differences among outdoor, nature, and environment writing. In nature writing, Schullery noted, "the writer hardly ever kills anything." In environmental writing, the author "hardly ever has any fun." Outdoor writing, he claimed, "seems an odd mixture of corny rhetoric and commitment to frontier values long ago discarded by urban America."[101] Schullery credited (or blamed) Walton, the poet Odell Shepard, and a few others with the inclination "to puff themselves up about the classiness of their vocation."[102] The American tradition of outdoor writing, he said, has been an "uneven combination of rare brilliant contributions and a massive production of the mediocre."[103]

The future of outdoor writing is perhaps less clear than other tributaries in environmental journalism. In 2005 the *Los Angeles Times* announced it was killing its hefty weekly outdoor section and offering buyouts or reassignments to its ten full-time journalists. The paper's editor said the section had failed to consistently attract advertising and a high percentage of habitual readers (only 28 percent read it regularly, he said).[104] The controversial move provoked two reactions in the industry: one side said the *Times*'s coverage was too much "dogs catching Frisbees in Griffith Park," and the other side said the newspaper relied too heavily on hook-and-bullet stories.[105] So the solution was either more or fewer outdoor adventure stories. What would Izaak Walton do? Probably go fishing: "And upon all that hate contentions, and love *quietesse,* and *vertue,* and *Angling.*"[106]

---◇---

FIVE

NATURE WRITING

The essayist Hamilton Wright Mabie, writing in the late nine-teenth century, noted that the three great themes of literature are God, Man, and Nature.[1] "To Nature, therefore, we turn as to the oldest and most influential teacher of our race," he wrote. "From one point of view once our task-master, now our servant; from another point of view, our constant friend, instructor, and inspir-er."[2] And yet Mabie knew well the difficulty in acquiring an ap-preciation of nature through reading alone. "It is not to be gotten out of text-books of any kind; it is not to be found in botanies or geologies or works on zoology; it is to be gotten only out of familiarity with Nature herself," he noted in *Books and Culture.* "Daily fellowship with landscapes, trees, skies, birds, with an open mind and in a receptive mood, soon develops in one a kind of spiritual sense which takes cognizance of things not seen before and adds a new joy and resource to life."[3]

The experiential component in Mabie's concept of nature writing fits well with environmental journalism, the best of which has included strong scene-setting images as part of the narrative. For example, the *New Yorker* writer Diane Ackerman included in her adventurous search for penguins this paragraph: "Nowhere, yet, had we seen king penguins, the species I helped raise at Sea World, the most gaudily colored of all. To find them, we had to sail again across galloping seas, and when we last dropped anchor at Cooper Island, at the tip of South Georgia, and climbed into our Zodiacs, we realized that we had arrived at one of the most astonishing places on earth."[4]

No tributary of the river that is environmental journalism has had more attention from scholars than nature writing; and rather than attempt a comprehensive examination in these pages, this chapter briefly reviews a few principal figures in American nature writing—Henry David Thoreau, John Burroughs, John Muir, Aldo Leopold, and Sigurd Olson. Almost all of them got their start writing for newspapers or periodicals. None of them worked as a full-time journalist per se, but their works influenced generations of nature writers and others, including environmental journalists. These authors all achieved a high degree of popularity, either in their working lifetimes or posthumously, and in scholarly or popular reassessments. Thoreau and Leopold were not widely read among the general public while they lived; Burroughs, Muir, and Olson were very popular authors during their lifetimes.

Nature writing has been defined in a rather broad way; there is no general agreement among scholars about a canon for the genre. Some would have a field guide qualify as nature writing; others might include a travel memoir. The scholar Thomas J. Lyon wrote that "nature writing in truth is not a neat and orderly field."[5] Lyon's taxonomy includes three main dimensions to nature writing: natural history information, personal responses to nature, and philosophical interpretations of nature.

What is it about Olson and Leopold and the others that make them different from ecologists and poets who went off into the woods and felt the need to describe it? Peter A. Fritzell suggested that it was, in part, their knowledge and use of "scientific catalogues, descriptions, or explications."[6] When Burroughs wrote about birds or Olson wrote about canoe country, their expertise and long experience in the field were evident. On the other hand, poets like Walt Whitman or William Cullen Bryant knew less of science, and scientists like Louis Agassiz or John Wesley Powell did not write enough personal philosophy to qualify their work as nature writing.

Furthermore, American readers like first-person narratives, which as we have seen marks favored writers with a scientific bent such as Izaak Walton and Theodore Roosevelt. In nature writing, Thoreau dubbed this method "the ramble." The author hikes into the woods or desert, often near home, or interacts with nature in another way, and writes about the experience. John Burroughs was the master of this style from his earliest work. "It is a significant fact in Mr. Burroughs's early history that he tapped the maple-trees, and secured the earliest market for his sugar, in order that he might buy text-books," Mabie wrote.[7] Burroughs noted in 1912: "When I have dwelt in cities the country was always nearby, and I used to get a bite out of country soil at least once a week to keep my system normal."[8] Ironically, it was Burroughs's preference for the quiet local ramble in the hills and farms of the Hudson River Valley that may have cost him some twentieth-century popularity, as other more popular writers focused on the sublime. Bill McKibben titled an essay on Burroughs (and why his reputation may have declined) as "The Call of the Not So Wild."[9]

When the ramble takes the writer into dangerous, hostile, or forbidding territory—none of which applies to Burroughs's best work—the writing becomes a tale of adventure. Peter Matthiessen's *The Snow Leopard* is a good example. Matthiessen's ramble took him, a scientist, and several sherpas and porters to the Tibetan Plateau in search of the rare and elusive snow leopard. His hikes were somewhat more spine-tingling than those of Burroughs: "The Suli Gorge is so precipitous that the path must climb high above the Bheri [River] before rounding the steep mountainside above the confluence and entering this canyon, and even here, one thousand feet or more above the water, the incline is such that the path is scarcely two feet wide in places, sometimes less; where the path has slid away or been blotted by slides, we scrabble across loose rocks as best we can."[10]

The combination of a first-person narrative and scientific expertise is "distinct and peculiar to the best American nature writing," according to Fritzell.[11] This type of work contains the research and reporting familiar to the modern newspaper or magazine reader, but also includes a personal touch—the self-doubt, the inner discovery, the enthusiasm, or the ego that sets it apart from the mainstream media's environmental journalism.

For our purposes, Lyon's taxonomy and Fritzell's refinement of it include a lineage of writers that influenced journalists covering the environment. These writers' works were widely circulated and thus known to journalists; they have been the subjects of many books, collections, edited volumes, and other scholarly examinations. Many of these writers were involved in political battles surrounding the environment, and they found themselves becoming the subjects of newspaper and magazine stories or serving as sources for journalists. Their work is taught in journalism schools as well as in departments of English. Most have been familiar names to devoted readers of nature writing over the last several decades.

There have been attempts by critics to describe, define, and catalog nature writing since at least 1902, when Francis Halsey authored "The Rise of Nature Writing" for the *American Monthly Review of Reviews.*[12] Even before Halsey wrote this article, Burroughs had commented on his craft many times in essays for popular periodicals like *Century, Lippincott's,* and *Atlantic Monthly,* and his efforts included pieces on Thoreau and the English essayist Gilbert White.[13] (Burroughs was sometimes credited with reintroducing the public to Thoreau.) After almost twenty-five years of working out his thoughts on the genre in print, Burroughs concluded that the term *literary naturalist* would describe what he did. In opposition was the "nature faker" who sought to personify, humanize, and anthropomorphize nature; by contrast, the literary naturalist was grounded in science, rational thought, and empiricism. Thoreau was about as far as Burroughs was willing to go in the personification arena and still count him as a member of the nature writers' club. "He had no self-abandonment, no self-forgetfulness; he could not give himself to the birds and animals; they must surrender to him," Burroughs wrote of Thoreau in 1882.[14]

One of the first important anthologies of American nature writing appeared in 1950, and the field has been a popular subject for book publishers ever since. Joseph Wood Krutch's *Great American Nature Writing* was a serious attempt by a well-known literary critic and nature writer to define a genre and list a few notable contributors to it, including himself. The book's long prologue established Krutch's standards; he included Thoreau, Muir, and Burroughs—Thoreauists, he called them—as his first three authors and quoted Leopold in the frontispiece.[15] A historiographer of nature writing would undoubtedly find Krutch's concepts (if not all his writers) alive in many recent formulations, edited volumes, and reviews of the field. For Krutch, nature writing was defined not just by a writer's desire to get away from it all, or by an author writing a work of natural history. Krutch called the key feature in his definition of nature writing "a sense of oneness."[16]

Krutch acknowledged Walton's *The Compleat Angler,* Gilbert White's *The Natural History of Selborne,* and Alexander Pope's *An Essay on Man* among important older works, but he said that nature writing as he understood it began with Thoreau, "the most original of modern nature writers" from whom "everyone who has come after has learned something."[17] Although Krutch did not have much use for pre-Thoreauvian authors, later scholars such as Michael Branch have rectified his omission.[18]

One of the distinctive features of Thoreau is that he examined nature not as humans' dominion, but from "some point of view common to all its creatures . . . [a] sense of oneness, this conviction that we are all, as it were, in the same boat."[19] Modern nature writers often share Thoreau's sense of wonder, his direct observations as an amateur naturalist, and a genuine live-and-let-live love for fellow creatures that a fisherman like Walton or a big-game hunter like Roosevelt did not have.

HENRY DAVID THOREAU

Krutch began his seminal nature-writing anthology with Thoreau, which may seem inevitable to us today but perhaps was less clear-cut to an essayist in 1950. Krutch wanted to include writers who proceeded "on the assumption that nature is to be learned *from* as well as *about*."[20] He did not want a simple, fact-based retelling of a scientific expedition or exploration; his authors would "exhibit some sense of oneness with" nature, as we have noted.[21] Thoreau was the first American writer to consistently meet those requirements. In beginning with him, Krutch rejected candidates like Sir Walter Raleigh, Captain John Smith, William Woods, William Bartram, Alexander Wilson, and John James Audubon, all of whom wrote on natural history. Those men were more scientists or adventurers than writers; Thoreau was a top-shelf writer and a keen observer of nature.

Thoreau was influenced by Ralph Waldo Emerson, as has been well documented. Emerson's first book, *Nature,* was published in 1836 while Thoreau was studying at Harvard. *Nature* included the now-famous phrase "in the woods we return to reason and faith."[22] That sentence alone had hints of three essential ingredients in nature writing: personal experience ("we"), science ("reason"), and personal philosophy ("faith"). But nature was a means to an end for Emerson, who was more interested in writing about the human spirit than about the wood thrush.

Emerson and Thoreau were transcendentalists—a philosophical, spiritual, and literary movement of mostly New Englanders who rejected traditional Christian teachings about heaven, Earth, and hell. Transcendentalists interpreted a divine spirit in nature; neither scientific rationalism nor divine authority was sufficient to explain it. They rebelled against the machinery of environmental consumption and industrial progress; they encouraged contact with and ethical considerations of wilderness. The wild was not a place of evil, as early Christian writers often posited. Emerson and Thoreau were transcendentalism's most famous social critics, and their influence can be seen in the work of later thinkers like Whitman, Muir, Emily Dickinson, and Frederick Jackson Turner.[23] "Thoreau led the intellectual revolution that was beginning to invest wilderness with attractive rather than repulsive qualities," wrote Roderick Nash.[24]

After finishing his college work, Thoreau became friends and neighbors with Emerson, who introduced the young writer to authors such as Margaret Fuller, Bronson Alcott, and Nathaniel Hawthorne while encouraging him to put down his thoughts on paper. Fuller was the influential editor of the transcendentalist magazine *The Dial,* and after some hesitation she published Thoreau's first important essay, "Natural History of Massachusetts," in July 1842.[25] In her introductory note, Fuller compared Thoreau to the British masters: "With all thankfulness we begged our friend to lay down the oar and the fishing line, which none can handle better, and assume the pen, that Izaak Walton and White of Selborne might not want a successor, nor the fair meadows, to which we also have owed a home and the happiness of many years, their poet."[26] In his essay Thoreau wrote: "In society you will not find health, but in nature . . . Society is always diseased, and the best is the most so."[27] He went on to describe some of the 280 species of birds that spend time in Massachusetts, along with forty quadrupeds, 107 fishes, eight tortoises, twelve snakes, nine frogs and toads, nine salamanders, one lizard, and assorted vegetation. Thus began an important two-decade career that has influenced nearly every nature writer since.

Nature was Thoreau's focus, and particularly its relationship with culture. He used personal experience, science, and natural history to inform his philosophy, criticisms, and reflections. In his first sentence to "Walking," published in the *Atlantic Monthly* shortly before his early death from tuberculosis in 1862, Thoreau wrote, "I wish to speak a word for Nature, for absolute freedom and wildness, as contrasted with a freedom and culture merely civil—to regard man as an inhabitant, or a part and parcel of Nature, rather than a member of society."[28] The same essay contained his phrase, "in Wildness is the preservation of the World," which environmentalists used as a rallying cry in the 1960s.[29]

In between his essay in *The Dial* and "Walking," Thoreau's most widely remembered work, *Walden,* was published. The seeds of the book were sown in the spring of 1845, when the twenty-seven-year-old Thoreau started cutting down white pines and building a ten-by-fifteen-foot cabin on Emerson's land near Walden Pond, a few miles south of Concord. After moving in on July 4 of that year, he would live there for slightly more than two years and two months, keeping in regular touch with family and friends while working on his observations and writing *A Week on the Concord and Merrimack Rivers,* the story of a canoe trip he had taken with his beloved brother John, who had died of tetanus in 1842 after cutting himself while shaving. He began the text that would become *Walden* in 1846; he worked through seven manuscript drafts over the next few years before he was satisfied with it. The Boston publisher Ticknor and Fields produced two thousand copies of the book on August 9, 1854; most reviews were enthusiastic, including one from *New York Tribune* publisher Horace Greeley.[30]

In *Walden,* Thoreau refined his philosophy of the wilderness, using his field observations and even a little psychology. "His writing was also aesthetic, ethical, and spiritual, and this breadth is part of what made Thoreau's work distinctive, laying the groundwork for a kind of American essay striving to view the natural world in all its physical and cognitive fullness," noted Frank Stewart in *A Natural History of Nature Writing.*[31] There are sections in *Walden* about liberty, freedom, and justice, as well as flowers, birds, and the sky. In all his writings, including the well-known essay "Civil Disobedience," his observations were from firsthand experience—even his thoughts on freedom, as the abolitionist and pacifist Thoreau was jailed for a night for refusing to pay taxes as a form of social protest against the Mexican War.

Thoreau walked in the woods every day, seeking truth in nature and looking for a way to communicate it. "Sometimes I rambled to pine groves, standing like temples, or like fleets at sea, full-rigged, with wavy boughs, and rippling with light, so soft and green and shady that the Druids would have forsaken their oaks to worship in them."[32] Sometimes his walks would lead him to more metaphysical thoughts: "Time is but the stream I go a-fishing in. I drink at it; but while I drink I see the sandy bottom and detect how shallow it is."[33] His text is rich with references to ancient authors from Aeschylus to Xenophanes. Cato the Elder is present, as well as Pliny. Dickens, Shakespeare, Confucius, Aristotle, Mungo Park, and Christopher Columbus are all alluded to, as are many more. A chapter in *Walden* called "Brute Neighbors" includes a dialogue between characters named Hermit and Poet that is reminiscent of Walton's Venator and Piscator.

To say that *Walden* was highly influential in Thoreau's brief lifetime (1817–62) would be an overstatement. The book went out of print in 1859, although a second printing (of 280 copies) was in the works at the time of his death and a third printing (of another 280) came out in 1863.[34] It seems not to have gone out of print since. Thoreau's great impact was on the nature writers to follow, particularly Burroughs and Muir, and in the book's adoption by the twentieth-century environmental movement as a seminal text. "It is one of the most widely read and quoted books in American letters," wrote historian John Opie.[35] Thoreau's rebellious message of shucking commercial and industrial civilization in order to find the transcendent spirit in wilderness found a receptive audience in the 1960s in particular. His work also raised doubts about empiricism and science as the sole means of understanding life, a theme that struck home for many in the midst of the fears of the atomic age. "For no writer in the literary history of America's dominant subculture comes closer than he to standing for nature in both the scholarly and popular mind," wrote Lawrence Buell, who explored Thoreau's modern reputation in great detail.[36]

Another way to measure the influence of writers is to examine what the critics have said about him, and Thoreau did have a few critics. James Russell Lowell charged him with imitating Emerson as early as 1848, and this observation, along with Emerson's well-intentioned but not well-understood eulogy on the antisocial aspects of the author's character, morphed into conventional wisdom for many decades.[37] Emerson had the highest respect for his friend, but inadvertently emphasized the negative: "He was a protestant *à outrance,* and few lives contained so many renunciations," commented Emerson in widely reprinted remarks at the time of Thoreau's passing.[38]

The opposite view was held by Bronson Alcott, who said a few weeks before Thoreau's death: "I had never thought of knowing a man so thoroughly of the country as this friend of mine, and so purely a son of Nature," and by the *National Anti-Slavery Standard:* "If men were to follow in Mr. Thoreau's steps, by being more obedient to their loftiest instincts, there would, indeed, be a falling off in the splendor of our homes, in the richness of our furniture and dress, in the luxury of our tables, but how poor are these things in comparison with the new grandeur and beauty which would appear in the souls of men."[39]

Much of Thoreau's important work was published by his friend Ellery Channing after his death, and those publications were the occasion for more review and comment, including additional criticism by Lowell, who said the author "had not a healthy mind."[40] As the Civil War period evolved into the economically charged Gilded Age, it was probably inevitable that a free-spirited naturalist and philosopher like Thoreau would slip from public view. But as the last frontier was settled and romantic notions of wilderness were reconsidered in the 1880s, the writings of Burroughs and others spurred a new interest in Thoreau; his work was also published in anthologies. Houghton Mifflin reissued his books and cross-promoted him with Burroughs and its other nature writers. These republications of his essays focused on his more market-friendly nature writings and not on his political and social commentary; this was rectified in 1906 by the issuance, in twenty volumes, of his *Journal*. "The publication attracted wide notice," wrote one commentator, "and for the first time readers were able to see that proportionately nature lore took up comparatively little space in the *Journal*. Thoreau as a philosopher and social critic began to come into his own."[41] The back-to-nature movement, as described by Peter J. Schmitt, contributed to his popularity.[42] Thoreau's disciples read from his work, edited his papers, and wrote biographies of him.

Comments from critics continued through the early twentieth century, when writers as diverse as Burroughs, Mabie, Robert Louis Stevenson, Krutch, Alice Hubbard, Odell Shepard, Lewis Mumford, Henry Miller, and Henry Seidel Canby weighed in. Fannie Eckstrom, commenting on Thoreau's *The Maine Woods* in 1908, poked holes in the writer's reputation as a master woodsman while acknowledging his ability to find poetry in the wilderness.[43] Sinclair Lewis, writing in 1937, called *Walden* "one of the three or four unquestionable classics in American literature."[44] In perhaps the most unusual instance of commentary, the erudite heavyweight boxer Gene Tunney told of reading Thoreau during the intense training for his last championship bout and said "the spirit of Thoreau lends its luminous wisdom to man and nature wherever they meet."[45] Mahatma Gandhi used Thoreau's "Civil Disobedience" essay extensively and kept a copy with him during his stays in jail. In a 1991 survey of American professors by the Modern Language Association, *Walden* was considered the single most important work to teach in a course on nineteenth-century American literature.[46]

JOHN BURROUGHS

As Thoreau's reputation became entrenched among nature lovers and others in the twentieth century, the literary fame of his champion, John Burroughs, waned.

If Thoreau was mostly obscure during his lifetime, Burroughs was mostly famous. The author of more than two dozen books and the friend of a president (Roosevelt), scientist (Thomas Edison), and industrialists (Henry Ford, Harvey Firestone), Burroughs seemed an unlikely candidate for such grand relationships. Born in 1837, he lived nearly eighty-four years and was buried on the farm of his birth. The son of a Catskill farmer (a boyhood chum was Jay Gould), he lived a simple life not unlike Thoreau's, even as an adult earning part of his living by selling homegrown fruits and vegetables. His writing and popularity grew out of the values and simplicity of a mostly rural life and his observations of sparrows and trout, and he included thoughts on philosophy and literary criticism in his ramblings. "I have gone a-fishing, or camping, or canoeing, and new literary material has been the result," he wrote. "My corn has grown while I loitered or slept."[47]

The books *Wake-Robin* (1871) and, four years later, *Winter Sunshine* made his reputation as a nature writer. *Wake-Robin* was on its surface a book about birds (although the title undoubtedly confounded several generations of schoolchildren—wake-robin is the common name for a trillium, a woodlands flower in the lily family, which blooms about the time migrating birds return in the spring). His close friend Whitman helped Burroughs choose the title for the manuscript; Whitman was returning a favor, as Burroughs had written the first book about the poet's work, *Notes on Walt Whitman as Poet and Person,* in 1867.[48]

Wake-Robin described the return of the birds, a walk in ancient hemlocks, a trip to the Adirondacks, observations on birds' nests, and other encounters with the natural world. The reader gets a hint of what is to come from Burroughs and his conservation ethic in his description of the state of the hemlock forest: "Their history is of an heroic cast. Ravished and torn by the tanner in his thirst for bark, preyed upon by the lumberman, assaulted and beaten back by the settler, still their spirit has never been broken, their energies never paralyzed. Not many years ago a public highway passed through them, but it was at no time a tolerable road."[49] There are several mentions of Thoreau, but few mentions of other authors except for scientific references. One modern scholar called Burroughs "the nature writer-cum-ecocritic."[50]

Burroughs's friendships with Whitman and Emerson were an important influence on his work. His use of spirituality in nature reflected Emerson's transcendentalism, and his lyrical style recalled Whitman. His personal philosophy contained a touch of Thoreau, but it was almost always expressed in the context of his appreciation of natural things. "I think it is probable that my books send more people to nature than Thoreau's do," he wrote. "My enjoyment is more personal and contagious. I do not take readers to nature to give them a lesson, but to have a good time."[51]

For example, the highly publicized extinction of the passenger pigeon (the last known individual died in 1914) spurred him to describe one of the great migrations he had seen many years earlier: "In my boyhood the vast armies of the passenger pigeons were one of the most notable spring tokens. Often late in March, or early in April, the naked beechwoods would suddenly become blue with them, and vocal with their soft, childlike calls," he recalled.[52] But the nostalgia of that observation was followed with this: "The pigeons never came back. Death and destruction, in the shape of the greed and cupidity of man, were on their trail."[53] And he does not spare himself from criticism, remorsefully admitting to killing the last passenger pigeon he ever saw.

His honest expression made Burroughs popular among the reading public, and he was particularly loved among children (he had spent ten years as a teacher in a rural school). His books, of which by one count more than 1.5 million copies were in print, graced the shelves of every school library worthy of the title; in fact, several schools were named after him.[54] Burroughs Mountain, a series of three peaks in Mount Rainier National Park, was named in his honor shortly after his death. Yet though he was one of the most popular nature writers in his day, Burroughs is now perhaps the least remembered.

He did not write a single, symbolic masterpiece like *Walden, The Compleat Angler,* or *A Sand County Almanac.* And Burroughs was not a man naturally drawn to politics or social commentary like Thoreau or Muir, although he did get involved in a tiff with the "nature fakers," a group of writers who anthropomorphized wildlife for public consumption to a ridiculous extent—nesting birds knotting the end of strings to prevent them from fraying, foxes that rode on the backs of sheep to escape hunters, porcupines curling into balls to roll down hills, and in the most extreme example, a woodcock that set its own broken leg and made a cast out of mud. Burroughs attacked "sham naturalists" in a 1903 essay in *Atlantic Monthly;* Theodore Roosevelt coined the "nature faker" term in an interview published in the pages of *Everybody's Maga-*

zine in 1907.[55] Roosevelt's involvement in the accuracy of scientific observation and its retelling were not new issues for Burroughs. In fact, he had fretted about poets using nature inaccurately since at least 1879.[56] Both men were worried that, in a time of tremendous growth in the popularity of nature stories, some standards needed to be set for the field.[57] What came about was even more emphasis on scientific-style observation ("facts") as opposed to more literary conventions that might allow for some embellishment here and there.

He did not avoid political or social commentary, but it was not front and center like Thoreau. Burroughs wrote on industrialization and its effects: the Model T was a "demon on wheels" and sooty Pittsburgh was "the Devil's laboratory," but these writings are less remembered than his literary naturalism.[58] His account of a trip to Alaska in 1899 as the official historian of the Harriman Alaska Expedition, organized by the railroad tycoon E. H. Harriman, seems similarly less significant. Muir, Agassiz, and George Bird Grinnell were along on the trip, which included forty famous scientists, artists, and photographers traveling in first-class comfort. The trip's planners did not leave much time for exploring specific sites, which would have lent itself to Burroughs's special skills of observation, and the writer was clearly homesick.[59] The daunting, primal landscapes seen on that trip affected Burroughs; the familiar cycles of the farm and field in the East never looked the same to him again.[60]

The nature writer Bill McKibben speculated on the decline of Burroughs's reputation in a 1992 essay; he fell out of fashion because his subject matter was more chickadee than crevasse.[61] Burroughs's best writing—"quaint" was the term McKibben used—came after his rambles through the woods near his home. While his friend Muir and others wrote popular tomes on the sublime

scenery of the American West, Burroughs's trips to "untamed wilderness" were more limited. "As his vast popularity demonstrated,
he found a language for making others appreciate the small spec-
tacles of nature: he articulated the mute delight that people have
always taken in their surroundings," McKibben wrote.[62]

Burroughs enjoyed a small resurgence in the 1990s. Some of his
books and essays were republished; two biographies were issued
and more edited volumes appeared, as well as a master index of
his work in 1995.[63] The John Burroughs Association, which was
formed shortly after his death in 1921, helped keep his spirit alive,
particularly with the awarding of the John Burroughs Medal "to
a distinguished book of natural history," an award jointly given
with the American Museum of Natural History. Medal winners
have included a who's who of twentieth-century American nature writing: William Beebe (the first honoree), Carson, Leopold,
Matthiessen, Olson, Krutch, Paul Brooks, Roger Tory Peterson,
John McPhee, Barry Lopez, Gary Paul Nabhan, Loren Eiseley,
and Ann Zwinger, to name a few.

JOHN MUIR

While Burroughs slid from sight for several decades, John Muir,
his friend and fellow rambler, enjoyed continued popularity. The
two men had met in the mid-1880s at an editor's house, and they
reconnected several years later when Burroughs invited Muir to
his home in New York. "He is a poet and almost Seer," Burroughs
wrote. "Something ancient and faraway in the look of his eyes.
He could not sit down in the corner of a landscape, as Thoreau
did; he must have a continent for a playground."[64] Both men
knew and admired Emerson, and their relationship grew after the

Harriman Expedition. The differences in the men can be seen in their nicknames: Burroughs was "John O'Birds" and Muir was "John O'Mountains."

Muir was born in Scotland in 1838, and his family moved to Wisconsin when he was eleven. His strict, humorless father was an offshoot Calvinist, and the value of hard work was passed on to his children. John was mechanically minded, impressing his professors at the University of Wisconsin with his inquisitiveness and skill. After leaving the school without a degree, Muir rambled to Canada for two years to avoid conscription in the Union army. He returned to the United States after the war and was working in a machine shop in Indiana when a metal file pierced his right eye. He quickly lost sight in his other eye in sympathetic nervous shock and was bedridden for a month before he recovered his vision.[65] That was the end of his life in the industrial workplace and the beginning of the career of America's most famous environmentalist, who would "devote the rest of my life to studying the inventions of God."[66] He was twenty-nine years old.

Muir set off on another journey, this time a thousand-mile walk to Florida, followed by a voyage to Cuba and then to New York before his fateful steamship trip to California's northern end, where he settled in, finally feeling at home, in 1868. He farmed, cut wood, herded sheep, guided visitors, and was a general handyman for several years. Visits from famous citizens, including Emerson in 1871, buoyed his spirits, and his friends encouraged him to submit his writings to major national publications. His first attempt was an essay on his theories of glaciation, "Yosemite Glaciers," for the *New York Tribune* in 1871. The piece contained the important elements of nature writing—a first-person account, keen scientific observation, and a philosophy of nature. "As I lay on my back, feeling the presence of the trees—gleaming upon the dark, gushing with life—coming closer and closer around me, and saw the small round sky coming down with its stars to dome my trees, I said, 'Never was mountain mansion more beautiful, more spiritual; never was moral wanderer more blessedly homed.'"[67] More writing jobs followed over the next four years, including articles for the *Overland Monthly,* a West Coast version of an eastern literary magazine, and New York and San Francisco newspapers.

Muir was a slow, painstaking author with a lean, sparse style that stood out in periodicals like *Harper's* and *Scribner's,* where overwrought prose was the order of the day.[68] In "Snow-Storm on Mount Shasta," an 1877 piece for *Harper's,* he wrote: "The sky speedily darkened, and just after I had completed my observations and boxed the instruments, the storm broke in a full vigor. The cliffs were covered in a remarkable net-work of hail rills that poured and rolled adown the gray and red lava slopes like cascades of rock-beaten water."[69]

Although he found immediate success as a writer, Muir spent most of the 1880s working on the ranch of his new bride's family near the Sacramento River; his writing was set aside. That came to an end in 1889, when he met with *Century* magazine editor Robert Underwood Johnson in San Francisco. By then Muir was worried about development and water diversions encroaching on his beloved Yosemite, and he was interested in preserving as much wilderness as he could; he would use the pages of a national magazine to support his position. "Perhaps yet we may hear of an appropriation to whitewash the face of El Capitan or correct the curves of the domes," Muir wrote.[70] For his part, Johnson was looking to spruce up the magazine and cover some new subject matter.

Johnson's two-hundred-thousand-circulation magazine, which beat the drum for electoral reform, the rights of the poor, and the gold standard, would get the work of a popular, crusading author in John Muir. Over the next twenty-five years Muir worked and wrote tirelessly for conservation causes, many concerning the protection of the Yosemite region. On some issues, like the creation of Yosemite National Park, he was successful; on others, like the prevention of the dam at Hetch Hetchy, he failed. Muir was "the most exuberant lover of nature and wilderness that American writing has witnessed," Frank Stewart wrote.[71] In 1892 Muir persuaded several influential friends to form a new group for the purpose of defending Yosemite; the Sierra Club would become one of the nation's most effective environmental organizations.

Muir's writing, as seen in several books and articles, was built on the idea that humans and nature are interdependent—plants, animals, birds, reptiles, all of it. "The world, we are told, was made especially for man—a presumption not supported by all the facts," he wrote.[72] He was eloquent in his defense of the American wilderness; his work was passionate, informed, and intense. A vision of an ecological interdependence, expressed often by Muir, was developed more fully by Aldo Leopold, most famously in a series of essays that would become the book *A Sand County Almanac*.

ALDO LEOPOLD

Among the influential nature writers of mid-twentieth-century America, Leopold stands out for his development of what he called a "land ethic." Taking strands from Thoreau, Burroughs, Muir, and many others, Leopold's central idea was that a community should include not only humans but soil, animals, water, and plants: the land. Furthermore, the land does not exist solely for economic exploitation by humans, but is to be cared for as in a relationship. "That land is a community is the basic concept of ecology, but that land is to be loved and respected is an extension of ethics," he wrote.[73] An ethical responsibility of people is to protect and preserve the health of their natural surroundings. Moreover, humans need to establish a personal connection to the land in order to fulfill this ethical requirement.

Leopold differed from Thoreau, Burroughs, Muir, and many other nature writers who came before him in one critical sense: he was a highly trained scientist. His book *A Sand County Almanac* became the bible of modern conservation "because science talks," wrote J. Baird Callicott.[74] As a forester and expert in wildlife management who often published in scientific journals and conservation magazines, Leopold was well known in the scientific community before he attempted to engage the general public with his ideas in *A Sand County Almanac*. His scientific credentials gave his views legitimacy. Born in Iowa in 1887, Leopold attended Yale University and graduated with a forestry degree in 1909. He entered into a career with the newly created U.S. Forest Service in the desert Southwest, where he began his scientific studies. Leopold was nearly killed by a bout of nephritis while in the desert and spent eighteen months recovering, during which he had time to read an eleven-volume edition of Thoreau that he had been given as a wedding gift.[75]

Two significant accomplishments marked Leopold's time in New Mexico and Arizona. First, at the Carson National Forest, he was made supervisor at the young age of twenty-four, becoming a rising star in the federal system. Second, over the next few years he developed the plan for the Gila National Forest to become a wilderness area, which came to pass in 1924. It was the first such wilderness area in the country and an important development in the federal government's policies of protecting wildlands. That same year he was transferred to Wisconsin, where he published a widely used textbook on wildlife management and eventually was appointed to a faculty position at the University of Wisconsin in Madison.

In 1935 Leopold, Robert Marshall, Ernest Oberholtzer, and seven other conservationists formed the Wilderness Society, an organization intended to lobby politicians and influence public opinion on the extension and protection of the wilderness areas that Leopold had helped design. Marshall urged Leopold—who had also joined the Izaak Walton League the year before—to take the first presidency of the group, but Leopold declined.[76] He also turned down a job as chief of the U.S. Biological Survey in Washington, D.C., at about the same time.

Instead he began working on the essays that would result in *A Sand County Almanac*. The book had elements of poetry, wildlife management, wilderness preservation and philosophy, and, for its time, a radical critique of American society. "We abuse land because we regard it as a commodity belonging to us," he wrote in the foreword.[77] The book's vocabulary was often scientific, and the writing was often elegant. Leopold's goal was to reach beyond his fellow scientists and graduate students to a general audience. His language was accessible and his examples were compelling. "A thing is right when it intends to preserve the integrity, stability, and beauty of the biotic community. It is wrong when it tends otherwise," he wrote.[78] Many editors apparently found the book hard to understand, however, or thought it would not sell. Alfred A. Knopf, Macmillan, and the University of Minnesota Press were among the publishing houses to reject the book before it came out in 1949.[79]

A Sand County Almanac ranks with *Walden* and *Silent Spring* as among the most important books ever published on the environment in the United States. Two million copies were in print by

2005, and it was translated into nine languages.[80] Several branches of science have been influenced by Leopold's work, including wildlife management, conservation biology, environmental ethics, ecosystem management, and restoration ecology, to name a few. "His enduring achievement was to integrate the two strands—the scientific basis and the conservation imperative—in a compelling ethic for the first time," said one of his biographers, Susan Flader.[81]

Leopold never saw his masterwork in print, nor even knew the title. He suffered a fatal heart attack on April 21, 1948—one week after the Oxford University Press had agreed to publish the book—while fighting a brush fire on a neighbor's property. Leopold had called the manuscript "Great Possessions"; his son Luna and several colleagues did the final editing on the book and reluctantly agreed to change its title, and it was published the following year.

The twenty-five pages in the chapter near the book's end that set forth the land ethic concept "became the intellectual touchstone of the most far-reaching environmental movement in American history," Roderick Nash wrote.[82] Reaching for the same image, Scott Russell Sanders, in an introduction to other Leopold writings, said, "He is one of the touchstones in our thinking about nature and culture, one of the essential figures we reckon by."[83] Wallace Stegner called Leopold the "American Isaiah."[84] Sales of the book were not spectacular at first—perhaps twenty thousand until 1966; critics tended to read it as yet another collection of nature essays, and they missed the significance of the land ethic. But three editions, including two in paperback, were published in a four-year span starting in 1966 to more receptive, environmentally aware audiences. Leopold biographer Curt Meine credited Carson's *Silent Spring,* the Wilderness Act of 1964, and antinuclear issues as part of the metamorphosis of the conservation movement into the environmental movement that helped *A Sand County Almanac* find its audience.[85]

SIGURD OLSON

One of the men that Leopold attempted to mentor during his years at the University of Wisconsin was Sigurd Olson, who was struggling with a career as a nature writer from his home in Ely, Minnesota, where he was the dean of the junior college and a natural resources professor. Leopold tried to get Olson admitted to the graduate program at Madison to study white-tailed deer, but failed.[86] Olson, like Muir, wrote painstakingly and with great effort; after a long, slow start churning out fairly standard hook-and-bullet stories for the outdoor periodicals, Olson found his voice in late middle age. He resigned as dean in 1947 to become a professional conservationist and writer. "All I ever wanted to do was sit down and write," he wrote in his journal. "I must make good my dreams, the things I have denied."[87] His work was highly popular in the 1950s and 1960s; his first book, *The Singing Wilderness* (1956), made the *New York Times* and *Philadelphia Inquirer* best-seller lists, when Olson was fifty-seven years old.[88] Olson had worked on some of the ideas in the book for thirty years.

Modern society is too far removed from the wilderness experience, according to Olson; humans need regular contact with nature for their souls. "We sense intuitively that there must be something more, search for panaceas we hope will give us a sense of reality, fill our days and nights with such activity and our minds with such busyness that there is little time to think. When the pace stops we are often lost, and we plunge once more into the maelstrom hoping that if we move fast enough, somehow we may fill the void within us."[89] Olson, who like Leopold was trained as a scientist, promoted the idea of a "land aesthetic," in which people must use all of their faculties and fully participate in the outdoors, like art patrons experience a museum. Olson carried a Thoreau book with him on many of his wilderness travels; he was also known to pin a Bible verse to a backpack and study it for inspiration while canoeing.[90]

Olson's writing was infused with a spirituality that readers found accessible and not as dark as Leopold's. Olson biographer David Backes called Leopold an Old Testament prophet and Olson a New Testament evangelist.[91] "But *A Sand County Almanac* and *The Singing Wilderness* are no more incompatible for environmentalists than the Old and New Testaments are for Christians," Backes wrote. "Olson echoes Leopold's critique of and prescription for modern society, and Leopold echoes Olson's sense of wonder and joy."[92] Olson would go on to write eight more books, the final one appearing in the year of his death.

Perhaps because Olson's style was more readable than Leopold's, his books sold better than *A Sand County Almanac* through most of the 1960s. Some two hundred thousand copies of the hardcover versions of his work were in circulation by 1972.[93] Paperback editions and Backes's biography increased interest in him in the 1990s, while his legacy as a conservationist continued in several forms. For example, Ashland College in Wisconsin became home to the Sigurd Olson Environmental Institute, and his family established a nonprofit foundation, Listening Point, to continue his work.

Like Muir, Olson was heavily involved in politics. A controversial figure, he worked for the preservation of the Boundary Waters Canoe Area Wilderness in northern Minnesota and the passage of the Wilderness Act of 1964; for his efforts, he was hung in effigy in his hometown of Ely. He was a member of the governing council and president of the Wilderness Society and president of the National Parks Association, among many involvements. Olson was among the most political of the pre-1960s nature writers (except perhaps for Muir) in his personal life, but among the least political (except perhaps for Burroughs) in his writing.

Like Burroughs, Olson built a writing shack on his property where he could work on his essays. (The shack was in Ely; he did not write at Listening Point, his cabin on Burntside Lake and the title of one of his popular books.) Olson died while snowshoeing near his home in Ely at age eighty-two. In the typewriter in his writing shack was written one final sentence: "A New Adventure is coming up and I'm sure it will be a good one."[94]

Olson's influence on contemporary nature writers and readers was important, if sometimes overlooked. For example, Olson read and liked the first part of what would become *Pilgrim at Tinker Creek* by Annie Dillard. She wrote him in 1972: "It is an undreamed of pleasure for me that you (Sigurd Olson!) should have taken the time to read the first chapter of my book of prose, let alone that you should write me personally about it . . . Your writing has been a joy and a beacon to me for the last several years."[95] Like Olson, Dillard read widely and studied other nature writers intensely; her master's thesis was on Thoreau and *Walden*.[96]

In 2000 the editors of *Sierra* magazine, the official publication of the Sierra Club, listed twelve "classic" books in environmental literature: Leopold's *A Sand County Almanac* topped the list, and *Walden* was No. 6, followed by *Pilgrim at Tinker Creek*.[97] Terry Tempest Williams, Mary Hunter Austin, Edward Abbey, Leslie Marmon Silko, Susan Griffin, Rachel Carson, Gary Snyder, Barry Lopez, and Gretel Ehrlich were the other authors named.

It was not lost on the magazine's readers that the Sierra Club's patron saint, Muir, was nowhere in the top dozen. "This magazine may never have done anything more controversial than printing a list of the 'best' environmental books that did not include Sierra Club founder John Muir," said the editors a few months later.[98]

The magazine's editors did a new top twelve based on readers' reactions and dropped almost half the list: Austin, Silko, Griffin, Snyder, and Ehrlich. Added were Muir's *My First Summer in the Sierra* (No. 2), John McPhee, Wendell Berry, and David Quammen.

New at No. 5 was Olson's *The Singing Wilderness.*

MODERN CURRENTS

As we have seen, nature writing has been well established in the American literary marketplace for more than 150 years. It is scrutinized in academia by organizations like the Association for the Study of Literature and Environment. The important authors in the genre are almost too numerous to mention: John Elder compiled an American nature writer reference work that ran to more than 1,200 pages in two volumes in 1996.[99] By the time of *Sierra* magazine's Top Twelve list, the language and form of nature writing ranged from "the precise, technical prose of an entomologist in the tropical rainforests to the lyrical, allegorical reflections of a native American artist in the Southwest; from the field notes of an Arctic anthropologist to the personal diaries of a desert backpacker," Frank Stewart wrote.[100] In addition, blends of nature writing and other, related forms have been explored and, as we have noted, the lines can be blurry between nature, science, agricultural, and outdoor adventure writing.[101] The career of Russell Lord, author of *Behold Our Land,* is an example; he was a staff member of the *New Yorker* in its youth, wrote for farm journals, and worked for the Soil Conservation Service.[102]

Some nature writers avoid that label: John McPhee has been compared to Thoreau, but he disliked the term *nature writer* and called himself a reporter.[103] (He taught journalism at Princeton and offered a course called The Literature of Fact.) Quammen, who wrote the natural history column for *Outside* magazine for several years, called himself a science journalist and noted that "my first loyalty is to turn out interesting prose."[104] Debates over what constitute "interesting prose" have continued. John Madson, who had a long career as a journalist in the Midwest before writing *Where the Sky Began,* said: "There are all kinds of writers who want to go to Papeete or Nairobi, but who in the hell is willing to write about a vacant lot outside Des Moines?"[105]

Thoreau, Burroughs, Muir, Olson, and particularly Leopold have influenced several generations of writers; environmental journalists will refer to any of these authors when possible. One can almost randomly pull books by journalists off the shelf at the local library and see this. For example, science writer Yvonne Baskin, in her important work on invasive species called *A Plague of Rats and Rubbervines,* set up two chapters with quotes from Leopold.[106] Environmental journalist William Allen, in his book on the Costa Rican rain forest, wrote in his introduction that "the reader should know that for years I have been deeply influenced by the writings of Aldo Leopold."[107] Karen Schaefer, a reporter for the National Public Radio affiliate WCPN in Cleveland, grew up influenced by her father's love of Leopold's writing and sense of place. At his funeral, the family took the oldest of her father's four copies of *A Sand County Almanac,* let the book fall open, and read from whatever page appeared.[108] Former *Newsweek* correspondent Daniel Glick compared the musings of one of his sources on the arson at the Vail ski resort to the insights of Muir.[109] Pulitzer Prize winner Robert Cahn switched from thirty years of general assignment journalism that included subjects as varied as Marilyn Monroe and the U.S. Supreme Court to the environment after reading *A Sand County Almanac.*[110]

Scholars have noted that women authors are not as prevalent in nature writing, with explanations ranging from theories that women are less likely to enjoy the taste of solitude extolled by literary naturalists to a shortage of women in the sciences in general.[111] But there are examples of outstanding women in the field, including Marjory Stoneman Douglas, who wrote for the *Miami Herald* (founded by her father) before her landmark book *Everglades: River of Grass* was published in 1947. Like male nature writers in the nineteenth and twentieth centuries, many important female authors got their start working for newspapers or magazines and continued to do so after finding literary fame.

Journalism has been a more hospitable place for females than other professions such as medicine and law. Mary Austin, who wrote a well-received book on the Owens Valley, *Land of Little Rain,* in 1903, and Mabel Osgood Wright, one of the most prominent nature writers of pre–World War II America, are good examples. Austin's writing career began in periodicals, including the *Atlantic Monthly.* Before her death in 1934 she had completed hundreds of magazine articles, several plays, and thirty books of nonfiction and fiction on subjects ranging from literary criticism to feminism.[112] She had been warned off of a nature-writing career by her mother, whom she remembered saying that it would scare off potential suitors: "You must not quote; especially poetry and Thoreau. An occasional light reference to Burroughs was permissible, but not Thoreau."[113]

Wright was a conservationist in a literary family who wrote a series of nature stories for the *New York Evening Post* that were collated and published as *The Friendship of Nature* in 1894.[114] Her journalistic output increased as the years went on—as a contributing editor to *Bird-Lore* magazine and others, and as an author of nature books and field guides. She weighed in on the nature faker controversy in the pages of the *New York Times* and "helped broaden the argument for environmental reform and deepened the arguments used by its reformers" by appealing to suburban women in her work.[115] Journalism was part of a varied literary career for Wright and many other women nature writers, including perhaps the most famous, Rachel Carson.

PART II

MAIN CURRENTS

SIX

PERSUASIVE COMMUNICATION AND ENVIRONMENTAL ADVOCACY

A contentious issue for environmental journalists working for mainstream media is the level of advocacy that exists in (or is absent from) their work. Phil Tichenor and I have labeled environmental advocacy "the uncomfortable issue" and described in some detail the reasons why.[1] A modern journalistic standard holds that objectivity is one of the highest values in American reporting; sometimes the idea is called fairness, or balance, or detachment, or covering all sides of the story. "Leave the crusading to the Knights Templar," wrote William J. Coughlin, editor of the *Washington* (N.C.) *Daily News.* "You'd be better off if you keep in mind that your job is reporting, not crusading."[2] And when various parties perceive their interests threatened or seek some advantage from journalists' activities, the news media are often accused of bias; failure to meet the objectivity standard is the first argument often raised by critics.

At one level, one could posit that *any* news coverage of an issue is advocacy in the sense that it focuses public attention where it may not have wandered on its own. "All environmental reporting is advocacy because it raises awareness," said Teya Ryan, a senior producer for the Turner Broadcasting program *Network Earth,* in 1991.[3] In the course of daily reporting, the media advocate for themselves, their audiences, and their communities—a Houston newspaper will cover, promote, and defend the Texas coast rather than, say, the Oregon coast. And as part of writing about their communities, the news media will report on conflict. Media attention often focuses on the clash between elites—groups such as the Natural Resources Defense Council or Environmental Defense against chambers of commerce, land developers, or chemical companies, in the case of the environment.

An important question is: do reporters sometimes advocate for environmental groups or causes at the expense of business, political, religious, or other interests? In many cases, it depends on which elite group is winning the social struggle. Our suggestion was that the more powerful the environmental group involved in an issue, the more pro-environmental the coverage will be. While scholars have struggled with measuring this hypothesis, the news media themselves have taken note of the strength of the old-line environmental groups. Reporter Tom Knudson, in a five-part series in the *Sacramento Bee* in 2001, looked at fund-raising, litigation, public relations, and other measures used by movement groups and concluded that they resembled the big businesses they often fought.[4] Paul Rogers, environment writer for the San Jose *Mercury News,* told a scholar: "I used to assume that the environmentalists always have the best interest of society at heart, and they never lie to you, and they were always the good guys. And I found that environmentalists mislead, obfuscate, and lie as much as government or industry does."[5]

The perceived pro-green leanings of reporters have been cited as a reason to remove an environmental journalist from the newspaper beat more than once. Some have been high-profile writers. Philip Fradkin, credited with starting the environmental beat at the *Los Angeles Times* in 1970, was reassigned five years later by his editors for "not being objective."[6] Longtime *New York Times* reporter Phil Shabecoff quit the paper when editors, for similar reasons, shifted him to covering the Internal Revenue Service after fourteen years on the environment beat.[7]

In a major survey of environmental journalists, David Sachsman, JoAnn Valenti, and James Simon found that most of them rejected the idea that they should sometimes be advocates for the environment.[8] At the same time, in an example of the third-person effect, around 40 percent of the respondents thought their fellow environmental journalists were "too green" in favor of environmentalism.[9] This was an interesting twist on "the media does not affect me, but it sure affects my neighbor" viewpoint. In the pages of *SEJournal,* the official publication of the Society of Environmental Journalists, the title of the quarterly roundup of news from around the country was changed from "The Green Beat" to "The Beat" after members worried that "Green" in its name meant an endorsement of that position.

As the debate over mainstream media bias continued, there were alternative media that were unabashed advocates of green viewpoints. Magazines such as *Sierra, On Earth, E/The Environmental Magazine,* and *Audubon* forcefully argued over various environmental causes and represented the interests and political views of their audiences in the tradition of *Forest and Stream* and *Bird-Lore.* For example, on the issue of toxic waste in minority communities, Gerry Stover, executive director of the Environmental Consortium for Minority Outreach, noted that the issue took root in the alternative press: "The majority of public discussion of this subject has taken place in regional journals and newsletters or in the publications coming out of the social justice and civil rights communities such as *New Age Journal,* the *Utne Reader,* or *Race, Poverty and the Environment.* The mainstream media should take a lesson from their more progressive brethren."[10] Further, as Craig LaMay noted, "in environmental coverage, as in many other areas, the best sources of information are the specialized media—newsletters, trade publications, electronic bulletin boards and other services—that do not serve a mass audience."[11]

One proponent of advocacy journalism, Michael Frome, wrote in *Green Ink: An Introduction to Environmental Journalism* that for-profit media do not adequately report on environmental issues and that the inverted pyramid style of reporting (a fact-based summary lead, followed by a value-free list of details in descending order of importance) fails the reader. His book considered the case for objectivity and mentioned "objective" journalists such as Ida Tarbell, John B. Oakes, and Edward J. Meeman, who were known for their evenhandedness. But Frome urged prospective environmental journalists to follow the lead of John Muir and Rachel Carson in a "desire to advance the cause of a better world."[12] He wrote: "Advocacy writing is to the mainstream media and to many journalism schools sheer anathema."[13] In another book, he was critical of science writers and the handbook *A Field Guide to Science Writing,* a book that "shows science writing heavily influenced and employed by corporations, trade associations, educational institutions, and government agencies."[14]

A book only about the history of "objective" environmental journalism would miss an important part of the picture. "Advocacy journalism is most responsible and works best if not everyone does it (and certainly many news media do not want to do it)," Ryan wrote.[15] The fine art of journalistic persuasion shows up in several historical debates; this chapter will look at some examples.

BENJAMIN FRANKLIN AND THE TANNERS

The idea of objectivity as a journalistic standard is relatively recent, although David Mindich, in his study of its acceptance, noted that claims to some of its characteristics—fairness, detachment, nonpartisanship, and balance—existed in written accounts as far back as the first American newspaper, published in 1690. But even though nonpartisanship claims were made in colonial papers, one wonders whether printers or their readers took them seriously. It was not until the penny press period of the 1830s that some of these notions gained credibility; and by the 1890s, as Mindich showed, the main traits of objectivity as a journalistic "ethic" were all in place.[16]

Benjamin Franklin, the most famous of the early American printers, may have made claims to fairness in his columns, but journalistic objectivity was not the expectation of his day. The Philadelphian was involved in an early, publicized environmental controversy in his city and wrote as an advocate, not as an unbiased observer. The issue was water pollution in the commercial district of Philadelphia. Tanneries, breweries, distilleries, and slaughterhouses dumped waste into Dock Creek. A petition was sent to the Pennsylvania Assembly in 1739, with Franklin's editorial endorsement, to regulate the tanners. "Many offensive and unwholesome smells do arise from the Tan-Yards, much to the great Annoyance of the Neighborhood," he wrote. Franklin's *Pennsylvania Gazette* said that the waste "choaked the dock—which was formerly as navigable as high as Third Street—with the Tans, Horns, &c."[17] The petition asked that the tanneries be declared a public nuisance.

Franklin, whose shop and home were two blocks away, argued for the property rights of those along the creek who had to put up with the smell, limits to navigation because of the effluent from the factories, and the water's problematic use in fighting fires. Fire and disease were two major issues in eighteenth-century urban society, and defiled water magnified the predicaments of both.

The tanners did not dawdle, using tactics that a modern public relations firm could learn from. First, they took their case to the competing newspaper. Andrew Bradford was Franklin's rival as publisher of the *American Mercury;* he defended the property rights of the tanners against the claims of their foes.[18] In what would become a grand American tradition, the two sides argued their points on the pages of the rival newspapers. The tanners offered to wash the pavement once a day, build a fence around their grounds and a roof over part of them, and release waste into the creek only at high tide. Bradford also could not resist a shot at Franklin and his property interests near the tanning yards: "Here is the Rabit! [*sic*] Good people observe what a concern they have for the promotion of lots!"[19]

Historian Michael McMahon noted that the involvement of newspapers highlighted the power of the two sides because each had access to the printed word.[20] In the end, the assembly accepted Franklin's petition but endorsed the remedies of the tanners.[21] The factories were not moved and the tanners staged a parade through town celebrating their victory. Unfortunately, in 1741 a yellow fever epidemic swept through Philadelphia, killing five hundred residents. Thomas Bond, a local physician and mem-

ber of the city council, blamed the polluted creek for that tragedy and other outbreaks, including regular occurrences of malaria,
and asked that the waterway be filled in.[22] Franklin and others
were named to a committee to address the problem; they recommended a common sewer system, dredging, and a rebuilt dock to
accommodate larger vessels, but their proposal did not get very
far due to lack of funds. Residents debated the issue of the creek
until the 1760s, when a comprehensive plan was finally passed to
deal with water supplies and other problems.[23]

Franklin was a journalist and an entrepreneur, and he was also
taking on an important segment of the business establishment
of Philadelphia in the pages of his newspaper. Bradford's paper
represented the power elite of the city. Though Franklin was not
without influence, it seems reasonable to propose that the likely
success of an environmental advocacy campaign like his depend-
ed at least in part upon the resources, organizational ability, and
communication activities of the advocates.

PLUMAGE WARS

Women's fashion may seem an unlikely site for a nineteenth-
century environmental controversy, but the popularity of plumage
in hats led to worries about the extinction of some avian species
and ignited a movement to change how birds were regarded in
American society. And women writers, particularly the authors of
popular books on bird-watching, were at the center of the struggle. In the case of the campaigns to protect avians from killing,
groups recruited influential citizens, created media, and used other organizing and persuasive tactics to try and reach their goals.
The first attempt was a failure, the second attempt a success.

Humans have worn animal skins and the plumage of birds since the beginning. In North America, the colonies and the young United States usually followed the fashion trends of London and Paris. By the 1880s, the millinery industry in the United States was using tens of thousands of bird feathers, particularly in women's bonnets. In some cases, entire bodies of songbirds were stitched into brims and crowns in poses designed to be as lifelike as possible. One estimate had five million birds killed annually for the fashion industry, although no one knows with any precision how many were taken.[24] Herons, egrets, and other birds that resided in large colonies, including gulls and terns, were most likely to be killed because it was easier to shoot or net several at a time. Fashion designers also preferred their white feathers.

Meanwhile, birding, egg collecting, skin collecting, and taxidermy gained in popularity in late-nineteenth-century America with the onset of more leisure time, the growth of a middle class, and the wide circulation of a number of books on birds. Such works included those by the painter John James Audubon (*Birds of America*) and U.S. Army surgeon Elliott Coues, whose *Key to North American Birds* (1872) was a classic ornithology text for several decades. Those who enjoyed birds in the field, represented by writers like John Burroughs, began to worry about population declines. The example of the American bison was foremost in many minds, and avian species like the passenger pigeon, heath hen, great auk, and Carolina parakeet were extinct or about to be.

In most states, bird-protection laws were either designed for game birds only (agitated for by wealthy sportsmen and their publications, as we saw in chapter 4) or were not enforced. Partly in response, a group of ornithologists in Boston met in 1883 to form the American Ornithologists' Union (AOU), an outgrowth of the Nutthall Ornithological Club, a small Cambridge-based assembly named after the famous American ornithologist Thomas Nutthall. The AOU was meant to be larger and more proactive; by 1884, at the group's second meeting, William Brewster, curator of birds for the Boston Society of Natural History, expressed concern over the slaughter of birds for use in women's hats. The Gilded Age critic Charles Dudley Warner said of the fashion: "A dead bird does not help the appearance of an ugly woman, and a pretty woman needs no such adornment."[25] Also in 1884, the AOU's long-running journal, *The Auk,* was founded, featuring a column by Coues, who was an associate editor. The AOU formed the Committee on Protection of North American Birds, a group including publisher George Bird Grinnell and C. Hart Merriam, later director of the U.S. Biological Survey. A model state bird-protection law was drafted, which defined game birds and non-game birds.

Grinnell's *Forest and Stream* magazine announced the committee and its intentions of "collecting facts in the matter and giving them wide publicity" on January 21, 1886.[26] Grinnell donated a thousand reprints of the statement to the committee, and these and additional copies were sent around the country.

The AOU committee sought to create a new organization that would reach out to nonornithologists and encourage the formation of bird-protection societies and women's "anti-bird-wearing leagues." Grinnell volunteered the use of his magazine as a communication and organizational resource, and also named the new assembly: "We propose the formation of an association for the protection of wild birds and their eggs, which shall be called the Audubon Society," he wrote.[27] The well-connected Grinnell was a family friend of the Audubons; soon important people such as Oliver Wendell Holmes, John Greenleaf Whittier, and Henry

Ward Beecher signed up for the cause. The AOU assigned Grinnell as a committee of one to run the new association. "We shall employ every means in our power to diffuse information on the subject over the whole country," said the group's founding editorial.[28]

Publicity and persuasion go hand in hand in the social movement business. To that end, a series of articles written by committee members was published as a supplement to *Science* magazine, including a statement of purpose, a piece on bird killing for millinery use, bird destruction in the New York City area, an indictment of "eggers," birds' importance to agriculture, the need for protective laws, and the role that women could play in saving birds.[29] There were ten million women "of bird-wearing age" in the United States, an article said, and nearly every species of bird was used as a headdress. Even common birds were not exempt. T. Gilbert Pearson, an important leader in the bird-protection movement, recalled as a thirteen-year-old shooting a grackle and tacking the glossy black feathers on the wall of his room. A few days later the feathers disappeared, only to reappear on his sister's hat.[30]

Thousands of copies of the *Science* supplement, known as Bulletin No. 1, were reprinted and distributed with help from the American Humane Society.[31] By August, a committee member reported in *Science* that the publicity campaign had worked: it "far exceeded the most sanguine hopes of the committee: the press of the country took up the subject vigorously, there being scarcely a newspaper, magazine or journal of any sort . . . that did not publish copious abstracts."[32] By the end of 1886, eighteen thousand members had signed up with the association, with three thousand more interested but not yet registered; fifty thousand were on board in two years. At Smith College, Florence Merriam (later

Bailey) organized a chapter, reaching classmates by cutting "articles on bird destruction from newspapers, choosing the most graphic ones [she] could find."[33] Grinnell started a monthly periodical, the *Audubon Magazine,* in February 1887 to support the work. A subscription fee of fifty cents per year was voluntary; single issues were six cents. Prizes were given to those recruiting ten subscriptions or more.

Yet the entire endeavor collapsed around the end of 1888, without much success. Frank Graham Jr., historian of the Audubon Society, noted that the first incarnation of the group existed "wholly on paper."[34] There were no dues, the club owned no property, engaged no perpetrators, and lobbied no legislators, according to Graham. Grinnell and others claimed the Audubon Society grew too big too fast and outstripped any ability to control it. Grinnell suggested that the magazine, at the time he folded it, was not essential to the success of the movement.[35]

Money was a problem. The magazine was not self-supporting, and Grinnell refused to underwrite it after two years of effort. As the sole person in charge, he found the club and the magazine draining his and his staff's time, as well as his finances.[36] Without a national vehicle like a magazine, communication was difficult. Press attention, one organizer said, fell off to nothing.

Opponents of the group's efforts, including the powerful fashion industry, were organized and had their own communication media. Fashion journals continued to publish stories and illustrations with prominent mention of plumage or bird skins, including a *Harper's Bazar* article on "blackbirds . . . posed in pairs, with beaks meeting lovingly."[37] Other important fashion journals of the time were *Graham's Lady's and Gentlemen's Magazine* (1826–58), *Godey's Lady's Book and Magazine* (1830–98), *Peterson's Magazine* (1842–98), and *Vogue* (1892–). Perhaps the largest was *Delin-*

eator (1873–1937), which reached nearly a half million subscribers by 1892.[38]

Publications like the *Millinery Trade Review* and organizations like the Millinery Merchants' Protective Association worked against the Audubon Society. The milliners defended their industry by claiming that most hat trimmings were done with artificial feathers and that when real feathers were used, bird farms in South America and India were the suppliers. Molted feathers were picked up off the ground and shipped to the United States.[39] Some opposed the issue on biblical grounds (birds being part of man's dominion), while many taxidermists and scientists were worried that the proposed model law would hinder their collecting. In the final issue of *Audubon Magazine,* at the end of 1888, Grinnell gave up: "Fashion decrees feathers; and feathers it is."[40] The failure of the AOU's first effort reflects sociologist William Gamson's idea that a movement's choice of organization—in this case, one man in charge—significantly affects the probability of success.[41] A mismatch between strategy and tactics—a small leadership, and no dues or financial strategy, coupled with a large membership—did not help.

But the failure of the initial AOU push for legislation to protect birds was relatively short-lived. In 1896 the stirrings of a new Audubon Society began in Massachusetts, using a different organizational model founded on state associations, paid memberships, for-profit media, and state government lobbying. The first new group, the Massachusetts Audubon Society, comprised a cross section of Boston's elite and encouraged the formation of other state societies; more books on birds were published, including several for children; and ornithology gained standing in the federal government with the establishment of the Bureau of Biological Survey. Women and women's clubs played a critical role in organizing and doing the heavy lifting of volunteer work, while men like Grinnell and Theodore Roosevelt were appointed to honorary positions.[42]

The two important periodicals of the second wave of the movement were the birders' new publication, *Bird-Lore,* and the AOU's *Auk.* Both were meant for internal audiences: *Auk* was a science journal, and *Bird-Lore* was targeted to a more general audience of bird-watchers. (Other for-profit birding journals, like *Osprey,* also occasionally joined in the struggle.) A second wave of persuasive communication was meant for external audiences: pamphlets, brochures, bulletins, letters to the editor, and articles placed in the mainstream press. A highly successful system of Junior Audubon clubs was designed for schoolchildren. "Audubon Societies, organized for bird protection and the encouragement of bird study, have sprung up on every hand, and nearly every person in touch with the public press is to-day acquainted with the movement for the protection of wild birds and their exclusion from millinery," wrote *Auk* in 1900. "The matter has also extended to the schools with most encouraging results."[43] A similar movement got under way in England.

Bird-Lore was a privately run, for-profit bimonthly started in 1899 by Frank M. Chapman, curator of birds at the American Museum of Natural History and author of a number of popular books. Copies were twenty cents each (expensive for the day) or one dollar for an annual subscription. Chapman printed six thousand copies of the first issue.[44] *Bird-Lore,* which was accepted by the local societies as the "official" voice of the movement, and, to a lesser extent, *Auk* kept local organizations informed about what everyone else was doing. Mabel Osgood Wright, already a well-known author, edited the Audubon societies' section in *Bird-Lore* for eight years. She urged the local leaders to send her news, gossip, and future plans. Wright was a critical figure in mobilizing suburban women, in particular, and she pushed a dual agenda of education and legislation.[45] The community-based organizing of women was one difference in the success of the new group in the wake of the failure of Grinnell's highly centralized first effort.[46] Another was money: wealthy New Englanders stepped in with financial contributions when needed.

In an era before broadcast communication, or even regular telephone use, the Audubon societies relied on the persuasive print media of the day. "The pamphlet was the primary weapon in this campaign for hearts and minds, and the society issues a steady stream of didactic tracts," Graham wrote.[47] Among the titles were *Ostrich Feathers, How Birds Affect the Farm and Garden* (written by Florence Merriam Bailey), *Hints to Bird Students,* and, reprinted from the Grinnell magazine, *Women's Heartlessness.*[48] Celia Thaxter, author of the latter piece, wrote of her encounter with a fashionable woman who refused to give up her plumes. "It was merely a waste of breath," she recalled, "and she went on her way, a charnel house of beaks and claws and bones and feathers and glass eyes upon her fatuous head."[49] As scholar Jennifer Price noted, bird-free hats were posed as signs of moral superiority.[50] An editorial in *Osprey* tried a different tack: the plumage hats were so popular they were unfashionable, "so common no one noticed them."[51] *Bird-Lore* attempted to demote the hats to the lower classes, "to the 'real loidy' who . . . with hat cocked over one eye . . . haunts the cheaper shops, lunch[es] on beer . . . rides a man's wheel, chews gum, and expectorates with seeming relish."[52]

The campaign used several other persuasive media. Calendars with colorful images of birds sold for fifty cents each, and poster-sized bird charts were distributed. Schools were encouraged to hold "Bird Days." Signs for garment stores reading "We Do Not Sell Birds or Bird Plumage That Are in Violation of Law or Public Sentiment" were distributed. "White lists" were published, with the names of milliners who sold feather-free hats. Fashion shows were organized to specifically exclude plumage.[53]

Perhaps the best-known idea, and one that continued into the twenty-first century, was the creation by Chapman, in 1900, of the annual Christmas Bird Census. Volunteers were asked to survey their neighborhoods for birds on the holiday and report back to *Bird-Lore* on what they spotted. Twenty-seven persons responded, counting ninety species in locations from Ontario to California, although most were in the eastern United States.[54] More than a hundred years later, the bird count has become an important source of data on several species (it was extended to about a three-week period). More than fifty-two thousand observers participated in the 2005–6 count.

The Audubon societies were successful in extending their issue to general-interest publications, which occasionally joined the fracas and helped them recruit new members. Edward W. Bok, the crusading editor of the popular women's magazine *Ladies' Home Journal,* wrote more than once in opposition to the killing of birds for hats. *Living Age, Harper's, Scientific American,* and the *Independent* all commented in favor of the birds.[55] Even *Harper's Bazar* began having second thoughts by the late 1890s: "Feathers and plumes still wave from the edifices which women wear on their heads, and it really seems as though it were time a crusade were organized against this lavish use of feathers, for some of the rarest and most valuable species . . . soon will be exterminated if the present craze continues."[56] The plume craze did continue, and it should be noted that *Bazar* continued to report on the latest European fashions, feathers and all. "There is very little that women wear that does not cost life," *Millinery Trade Review* opined, setting down the nudity playing card, "and if these Audubon notions were to be carried to extremes, we blush to think of the possibilities of her future appearance."[57]

Women's complex roles in the issue cannot be underestimated. In addition to providing moral leadership against plumage in hats, women provided the primary labor supply in the millinery business; they were also the main audience for the fashion magazines and the designers who underwrote them. At least three female authors wrote popular and influential books and dozens of articles on birding that helped arouse public sympathy against the milliners. "Between 1893 and 1898, 70,000 books on birds were sold, many of which were written by women similar to Mabel Wright, with interests not only in gardening but civic organizing," wrote scholar Daniel J. Philippon.[58] Wright penned *The Friendship of Nature* (1894), *Birdcraft* (1895), and, with Coues, *Citizen Bird* (1897). Bailey wrote scores of articles and *A-Birding on a Bronco* (1896) and *Birds of Village and Field* (1898), among other titles. "Why should we expect the milliner . . . to be more moral than the woman?" Wright wrote.[59]

The highly prolific Olive Thorne Miller came to birding after a career as a popular author. "When we stop to consider that her real work did not begin until she was 54, after which 405 of her articles and 19 of her books were written, and moreover that during her later years, by remarkable self-conquest, she became a lecturer and devoted much of her time to lecturing on birds in New York, Brooklyn, Philadelphia, and other towns, we come to a realization of her tireless industry and her astonishing accomplishment," Bailey wrote of Miller upon her passing.[60] She died at age eighty-seven in Los Angeles in 1918.

As in almost all social movement communication, hyperbole

The prophet Isaiah, shown in *The Calling of Isaiah* by artist
Benjamin West (1738–1820), wrote eloquently about the natural
world. The ancient prophets often used stories about nature
to effectively communicate with their audiences. Tales about
environmental disasters were common. Library of Congress,
Prints and Photographs Division, LC-USZ62-62403.

Henry C. Wallace combined a career as a farm editor and politician.
The second of three Henry Wallaces to work in journalism and
public life, Harry, as he was called, assumed editorship of *Wallace's
Farmer* after the death of his father in 1916. He was appointed U.S.
secretary of agriculture by President Warren G. Harding in 1921
and served until his own death in 1924. Library of Congress, Prints
and Photographs Division, LC-USZ62-95943.

The English writer Izaak Walton, shown with a fly rod in action in a Louis Rhead engraving from 1900, was the author of *The Compleat Angler*. His text, first published in 1653, served as the prototype for outdoor adventure writers well into the twentieth century. His name lives on in the eponymous conservation group. Library of Congress, Prints and Photographs Division, LC-USZ62-88498.

Henry Herbert, writing under the name Frank Forester, was
America's first popular outdoor adventure writer. In the 1840s
and 1850s, he authored a series of how-to sporting books that sold
well and brought him the status that his romance novels did not.
He committed suicide in 1858 in New York after being snubbed
at his own dinner party. Photograph by Mathew Brady; Library of
Congress, Prints and Photographs Division, LC-USZ62-109950.

By the time this photograph was taken in 1910, there was nothing left of Henry David Thoreau's cabin on this site at Walden Pond near Concord, Massachusetts, except a pile of rocks. Thoreau lived in a hut for about two years, starting in 1845. His experience was recorded in perhaps the single most influential environmental book in U.S. history, *Walden; or, Life in the Woods*. Detroit Publishing Company; Library of Congress, Prints and Photographs Division, LC-USZ62-39828.

John Burroughs (1837–1921) was one of the most beloved nature writers of his day. He perfected the story experienced in a "ramble," in which he would simply stroll through the woods and fields near his home and keep close track of what he observed. His tales were particularly popular with children. This photograph was taken in 1901. Library of Congress, Prints and Photographs Division, LC-USZ62-130730.

Mary Hunter Austin (1868–1934) was a prolific author who specialized in subjects around her home in the Owens Valley of California. Her nonfiction work *The Land of Little Rain* (1903) preceded by several decades many popular books on California and its water problems. George Grantham Bain Collection; Library of Congress, Prints and Photographs Division, LC-DIG-ggbain-05744.

Fashion designers exaggerated feathers and other plumage on
women's hats, especially in the late 1800s. Sometimes the hat would
feature an entire stuffed bird. This is a "chanticleer"-style hat from
around 1912. Dramatic drops in many bird populations caused a
fashion backlash and led in part to the creation of the Audubon
Society. George Grantham Bain Collection; Library of Congress,
Prints and Photographs Division, LC-USZ62-61248.

The junction of the Yampa and Green rivers in Colorado, shown here in a Timothy O'Sullivan image from 1872, is some of the most rugged country in the lower forty-eight states. Dinosaur fossil beds were discovered near here in 1909, and the area was set aside shortly thereafter. Plans for a dam at Echo Park on the Green River in Dinosaur National Monument in the early 1950s became a national controversy. Photograph by Timothy O'Sullivan; Library of Congress, Prints and Photographs Division, LC-DIG-ppmsca-11853.

Richard Ballinger (1858–1922) was secretary of the interior under
President Taft. He became enmeshed in a public battle with Taft's
chief forester, Gifford Pinchot, and was accused of interfering
with an investigation into claims on coal lands in Alaska.
Conservationists were outraged, but a congressional investigation
cleared Ballinger. George Grantham Bain Collection; Library of
Congress, Prints and Photographs Division, LC-USZ62-97993.

African American laborers and their families lived in tar-paper
shacks such as these while working on the Hawk's Nest Tunnel
project near Gauley Bridge, West Virginia, beginning in 1927.
Hundreds of workers died of silicosis from breathing in dust silica
in the tunnel. The work was undertaken without masks or other
safety devices. Farm Security Administration; Library of Congress,
Prints and Photographs Division, LC-USF33-030255-M5.

Dinner 2½ miles underground—miners with safety lamp, in a soft coal mine—Illinois. Copyright 1903 by Underwood & Underwood.

Soft-coal miners such as these Illinois men, photographed in 1903, faced many dangers on the job, including fires. In an early example of environmental reporting, the *St. Louis Post-Dispatch* investigated the cause of an explosion at Centralia Coal Company Mine No. 5 that killed 111 miners in 1947. Photograph by Underwood and Underwood; Library of Congress, Prints and Photographs Division, LC-USZ62-97319.

was a part of the persuasive efforts, although the plug was pulled on the most egregious excesses relatively quickly. A petition written by "the songbirds of Massachusetts" to the state court (politician George F. Hoar was the author) was reprinted in *New England* magazine. "People with guns and snares lie in wait to kill us, as if the place for a bird was not in the sky, alive, but in the shop window or under a glass case," it read. "If this goes on much longer, all your songbirds will be gone."[61] There was an attempt to label egret-plumed hats as "the badge of the harlot" before cooler heads prevailed and the campaign was renamed "the white badge of cruelty." Pamphlets telling of birds being skinned alive so their feathers would not fade and containing statements such as "Connecticut has lost 75 percent of all its birds in the last 15 years" and "all species will soon be exterminated in the United States" were more the exception than the rule.[62] Compromise came from the Millinery Merchants' Protective Association, which offered to stop using birds from "civilized" countries: "this, however, will allow [the use of] the birds of China, Japan, India, Africa . . . and the islands where no white men . . . penetrate."[63]

In 1900 Congress passed the first of many federal protections for birds, the Lacey Act, which prohibited the interstate shipment of wild birds or other wild animals taken in violation of state laws. By 1905, thirty-three states had passed the ornithologists' model bird-protection law in some form.[64] During Theodore Roosevelt's presidency (1901–9), fifty-three public sanctuaries for birds were created. By 1913, trafficking in bird plumage was illegal and what was left was entirely on the black market. In 1918 Great Britain (representing Canada) and the United States signed the Migratory Bird Treaty, giving cross-border protection to the birds and additional legal muscle to their protectors.

Enforcement remained a problem for years, as did smuggling.

The Audubon societies hired and paid for wardens, and an incident in Florida turned into the type of dramatic event that can capture much press attention and ignite a movement. Guy Bradley, an Audubon warden, was killed by a poacher while making an arrest on Oyster Key in 1905. The movement now had a martyr. "Heretofore the price has been the life of the birds, now is added human blood," Chapman wrote.[65] Bradley had told Chapman he expected an attempt on his life; but after a bungled investigation by the local authorities, no one was convicted of the crime. Across the country, women's clubs foreswore the use of plumes; the Audubon societies raised funds for a new home for Bradley's widow and children. A *Collier's* magazine article was headlined BIRD PROTECTION'S FIRST MARTYR.[66] Two more Audubon wardens would be killed in the next few years and another shot in the face.

Perhaps inevitably, the Audubon movement evolved from a federation of state societies into a centralized national organization with local chapters and affiliates. Thirty-four state societies, plus the District of Columbia and the Territory of Oklahoma, incorporated into a new National Audubon Society in 1905.[67] Chapman sold *Bird-Lore* to the group in 1935, where it eventually became the magazine *Audubon*. "Inspiration and information through the printed word . . . brought the new Audubon movement together," Graham wrote.[68]

What successfully concluded the bird-protection issue? Its proponents were well-organized, dedicated, and influential citizens and their views were communicated effectively to the public, which allowed their group to grow. Jennifer Price said the phenomenon of highly organized women's clubs was the key.[69] The issue was recognized as legitimate, and legislative success followed. Of course, the new cultural appreciation of nature in a natural setting was important, but Dame Fashion is also fickle, and it could be that high hats simply became yesterday's style. World War I certainly hindered the fashion industry; it is also possible that the increased use of the horseless carriage and its breezy, topless riding favored smaller, more aerodynamic chapeaus.

DINOSAUR NATIONAL MONUMENT

Water resources have been a point of contention in societies for almost as long as humans have worn birds' feathers. In the case of the dam-building efforts of the federal government in the mid-twentieth century, a persuasive campaign as effective as the anti-plumage movement and a large coalition of conservation, regional, and government interests would be effective enough to stop the construction of one such barrier.

The story begins with John Muir's final defeat. The old preservationist and his Sierra Club spent years in what would be a losing battle to stop a dam from being thrown up in Yosemite National Park in a valley called Hetch Hetchy. The dam was finished in 1923, and its water is used to supply the San Francisco Bay Area. Many scholars have analyzed the Hetch Hetchy case and its legacy; one conclusion is that it ended in a lost-the-battle, won-the-war outcome.[70] No national park has been so encroached upon since—though in the case of the Dinosaur National Monument in the 1950s, it very nearly happened. The anti-dam forces in that case used coalitions, a persuasive campaign, and compromise to work toward their goals.

At first glance, the construction of a dam by the federal Bureau of Reclamation just below the confluence of the Green and

Yampa rivers in Dinosaur National Monument at a place called Echo Park seemed routine. The monument was established in 1915, when President Woodrow Wilson set aside an eighty-acre piece of northeast Utah to protect valuable dinosaur fossils found there; at the urging of local interests and the Interior Department, President Franklin Roosevelt expanded the site to two hundred thousand acres in 1938, including river canyons in western Colorado.[71] Both rivers were part of the massive Colorado River system, which supplied water to the fast-growing southwestern states of Colorado, Utah, Arizona, New Mexico, Nevada, and California.

Demand for power and water grew dramatically in the West in the postwar period. Dozens of water projects were planned; the Bureau of Reclamation and to a lesser extent the Army Corps of Engineers were in charge of building them. No water was more precious than the Colorado River's, which was divided among the states using a series of dams and reservoirs, the most famous of which was Hoover Dam, completed in 1935. A 1946 government report, *The Colorado River: A Comprehensive Report on the Development of Water Resources* (nicknamed "the blue book"), outlined 134 possible projects.

Bills were introduced in Congress in early 1950 to fund the Colorado River Storage Project, which would feature several dams, including one at Echo Park. But voices of dissent rose, a few at a time. Bureaucratic infighting among the Bureau of Reclamation, the National Park Service, and the Corps of Engineers intensified. The National Park Service had been in a long turf battle with the Bureau of Reclamation, which it saw as encroaching on parks and monuments with its building projects. "Construction of dams at these sites would adversely alter the dominant geological and wilderness qualities and the relatively minor archeological and wildlife values of the Canyon Unit so that it would no longer possess national monument qualifications," a park service report said.[72] Perhaps this was not persuasive speech making of a sort to make people forget Winston Churchill, but the park service was persistent: "The greatest peril to the parks from dam proposals comes from the plans and the programs of the government dam-building agencies themselves and the pressures which their activities generate in various sections of the country."[73] Interior secretary Oscar Chapman, who was in charge of both the Bureau of Reclamation and the park service, approved dams at Echo Park and Split Rock in the national monument in June 1950. Park service director Newton Drury, publicly upset about Chapman's decision, eventually resigned under pressure and became a cause célèbre.[74]

In the early stages of a social problem, there is often a struggle as to how to define it in the public arena. The western historian and social critic Bernard DeVoto offered an erudite defense of the Echo Park wilderness in the *Saturday Evening Post* (an article later condensed in *Reader's Digest*). He called the Yampa-Green confluence "one of the great scenic areas of the United States."[75] DeVoto thought that parks should be left alone, and he recognized that they were in danger: "There are, however, various ways of skinning a cat if you are good with a skinning knife. No one has ever said that the Bureau of Reclamation isn't."[76] It was DeVoto's last article for the *Post;* one journalist wrote that western water interests pressured the editors not to hire him again.[77] But DeVoto succeeded in framing the issue as one of protecting the sanctity of the park system.

As in the movement against the milliners, the formation of coalitions was critical to any success of the anti-dam forces. Southern California business interests and their congressional representatives, who were worried about receiving less Colorado River water for their region, allied with the conservation forces. An array of midwestern and eastern interests, ranging from farmers worried about crop surpluses to fiscal conservatives fretting over the project's billion-dollar-plus costs, also became involved on their side. Howard Zahniser, head of the Wilderness Society, almost immediately assembled seventeen conservation groups into a new organization eventually called the Citizens Committee on Natural Resources. Zahniser convinced Edward Mallinckrodt Jr., a wealthy St. Louis chemical manufacturer, to help bankroll the opposition to the project.[78] Two more conservation lobbies were formed. The Sierra Club was a central actor in the movement to halt the project, and in the end seventy-eight organizations, including the Wilderness Society, Izaak Walton League, National Parks Association, and National Audubon Society, joined.[79] "Never before had so many sporting, wildlife, and wilderness organizations come together in such a powerful coalition," wrote historian Mark Harvey.[80]

Local support for building the dams was high; politicians in Utah, Wyoming, and Colorado were behind the deal, as were the construction and hydropower interests that would benefit from such a big-budget undertaking. President Dwight Eisenhower toured the area by plane while on vacation and saw no reason not to dam it. Dam proponents tried a number of reasons to justify the project—power, irrigation, location, and recreation—but could not settle on one, which weakened their cause. The old "conquest of the wild" argument was used: "History ought to record that those few who have entered these areas have been principally concerned about getting out alive," wrote one supporter.[81] The Bureau of Indian Affairs was a supporter of the dam; thirty-eight thousand tribal members living in the area figured to

benefit from the water and power outputs. The Bureau of Reclamation was used to getting its way; it would build more than
six hundred dams and reservoirs in the West. In fact, it could be
argued that the bureau had not encountered serious opposition
since its establishment in 1902, and so it was not prepared for the
fierce resistance from what looked like a fairly small group of
conservationists, rafters, and skinny-legged hikers.

The Muir-like charismatic figure who led the opposition
to the project was David Brower, the leader of the Sierra Club
and a keen student of conservation history. "He seemed to hear
echoes of Muir resounding in the canyons of the Green and
Yampa rivers, calling him and the Club to act," wrote Harvey.[82]
Where Muir was a writer and wilderness philosopher, Brower
was a publicist and wilderness salesman. Brower's persuasive strategy included books, pamphlets, brochures, advertisements, lobbying, visual aids, outfitted trips to the area, and continuous letters.
One pamphlet read "Will You DAM the Scenic Wild Canyons of
Our National Park System?" and another was titled What Is Your
Stake in Dinosaur?[83] Official publications of the Sierra Club, the
Izaak Walton League, National Audubon Society, National Wildlife Federation, and the Wilderness Society urged members to
visit Dinosaur National Monument, and, perhaps more important, to write to elected officials. By January 1954, the House
Subcommittee on Irrigation and Reclamation was receiving
hundreds of letters per day.[84]

Dinosaur National Monument was not well known like Yosemite or Yellowstone and needed the exposure that intense publicity could bring. An important persuasive device for the anti-
dam forces was the extensive use of visual images. Three films and
a coffee-table book were part of the campaign. One short film,
Two Yosemites, and Harold Bradley's movie of a family trip down

the Yampa River were credited with increasing public awareness and convincing conservation groups and politicians of the rightness of the cause.[85] Brower and photographer Charles Eggert also produced a twenty-eight-minute movie on the area called *Wilderness River Trail* in 1953. "Brower's ability to captivate the public with images and descriptions of wilderness areas turned out to be his greatest gift," Harvey wrote.[86]

The seventy-three-year-old Bradley, a friend of the famed photographer Ansel Adams, was the son of one of Muir's lieutenants, and he remembered lessons from the failure at Yosemite forty years earlier. With his own sons along, Bradley filmed the canyons, cliffs, rapids, and sandbars of the Yampa for six days; should the dam be built, the scenery in the movie would be under many feet of water. The film, first shown to get Sierra Club members involved, meshed with the club's strategy of outfitting trips to the remote area. In 1950, before the issue was well covered, about thirteen thousand people visited Dinosaur National Monument and fewer than fifty rafted the rivers; in 1954, seventy-one thousand visitors appeared and more than nine hundred floated through the canyons.[87]

Two Yosemites, with eleven minutes of still photographs, contrasted the lovely valley of Hetch Hetchy before the dam with the stark, moonscape-looking mud flats of the area at low water after the dam was built. Zahniser used the film in his lobbying efforts; he carried it and a projector into the halls of Congress and showed it to legislators when he could buttonhole them.

In New York, the book publisher Alfred Knopf, chairman of the Interior Department's Advisory Board on National Parks, created a ninety-three-page coffee-table book titled *This Is Dinosaur,* edited by the historian and novelist Wallace Stegner. The book contained essays by Stegner, Knopf, Wilderness Society executive director Olaus Murie, and others; copies were sent to every member of Congress, officials at Interior, and newspaper editors throughout the West.[88] Stegner was Thoreauvian in his prose, urging that wilderness be saved not only for wildlife but also for humans squeezed by "20th century strains and smells and noises."[89] In addition, Robert Cutter's *Hetch Hetchy—Once Is Too Often* was mailed to the nine thousand members of the Sierra Club and another one thousand people.

In addition to the emotional arguments buttressed by the visual images, Brower and Zahniser used technical data in their congressional lobbying efforts, enlisting the language of science on their behalf. Walter Huber, president of the American Society of Civil Engineers, and Luna Leopold, son of Aldo and chief hydrologist with the U.S. Geological Survey, coached Brower on his technical testimony.[90] Recognizable names, including Sigurd Olson and General U. S. Grant III, an army engineer, testified for the anti-dam forces.

Government publications from the Department of the Interior offered a clue as to the views of the dam builders. For example, the blue book was subtitled *A Natural Menace Becomes a Natural Resource.* Chambers of commerce across the Southwest engaged in a letter-writing campaign of their own in support of the dam, with notes coming from Vernal, Utah; Grand Junction, Colorado; Farmington, New Mexico; Flagstaff, Arizona; and dozens of other towns.[91] Utility companies and western civic associations aided the cause. Newspapers in Salt Lake City, Denver, Cheyenne, and elsewhere editorialized in favor of the project. "California is a potential rival for this water, which rightfully belongs to the intermountain region," the *Salt Lake Tribune* said.[92] The coalition that favored the dam (sometimes called the "Aqualantes" in a twist on vigilantes) also produced a film, and it emphasized the inaccessibility of the area. However, one Utah representative admitted that they had "neither the money nor the organization to cope with the resources and mailing lists" of the anti-dam forces.[93] Pro-dam forces suspected that the conservationists were dupes of the California water interests; lobbyists from California spent $1 million opposing the project, by one count.[94]

The conservationists and their allies were guilty of hyperbole, with Brower telling congressmen that "a dam would be the tragedy of our generation," perhaps momentarily forgetting the recent World War and the Korean conflict.[95] The *Wilderness River Trail* film used sound from an ocean liner going through a heavy sea to represent the sound of the water through the canyon.[96]

Senators Paul Douglas of Illinois, John Kennedy of Massachusetts, and Hubert Humphrey of Minnesota spoke against the bill. The *New York Times,* in particular columnist John B. Oakes, editorialized against the Echo Park Dam, as did *Scientific Monthly. Time* magazine favored the dam. Eleanor Roosevelt was opposed. The *Salt Lake Tribune* published a special edition touting the project.[97] *Life, Collier's,* and *Newsweek* covered the controversy.[98]

One estimate had it that letters were running 80 to 1 against the dam in congressional offices.[99] Colorado congressman Wayne Aspinall, chair of the reclamation subcommittee, said, "If we let them knock out Echo Park, we'll hand them a tool they'll use for the next 100 years."[100] But after nearly six years of controversy, Aspinall ultimately took what he could get: he deleted the Echo Park Dam from the bill in July 1955 and settled for the rest of the Colorado River Storage Project.[101]

Several western senators held a meeting in Denver in the fall of 1955 in a last-ditch effort to restore the dam, but Zahniser got wind of it. He took out a full-page "open letter" newspaper ad in the *Denver Post* the day before the meeting, making it clear that the coalition would fight the entire Colorado River project if the Echo Park Dam was not taken off the table.[102] By this time, Bureau of Reclamation supporters knew Zahniser was not bluffing. President Eisenhower signed the Colorado River Storage Project Act on April 11, 1956; it contained a clause that no dam or reservoir would be built within any national park or monument.

The coalition opposed to the dam was willing to compromise, although in the case of Brower it was with great regret. The Bureau of Reclamation gave up its attempts at a dam in Dinosaur National Monument, but farther downstream, at Glen Canyon—which was unprotected by any federal park or monument designation—key coalition members agreed not to oppose a dam in exchange for the dropping of the Dinosaur project. Zahniser's open letter in the *Post* stressed that his group was "NOT anti-reclamationists, and . . . NOT fighting the principle of water use in the West."[103] Partly by focusing on the protection of the national monument system as the source of the problem, the anti-dam forces won. One by-product of the Echo Park debate was that the conservation coalition stayed more or less intact and went on the offensive to create the Wilderness Act of 1964, which organized a federal wilderness preservation system, and to prevent dams in the Grand Canyon a few years later.

Historian Donald Worster has argued that the Bureau of Reclamation and the control of water were central to the rise of the American West after World War II.[104] The dam at Glen Canyon became the last of the great western structures; the Bureau of Reclamation's mission shifted to water distribution and water resource management and away from new construction. And the Glen Canyon Dam did affect a national monument—water from Lake Powell backed up into Rainbow Bridge National Monument, which conservationists thought they had protected.[105] The

Sierra Club lost its tax-exempt status as a nonprofit organization in 1966 because of the intensity of its lobbying campaigns.[106]

Samuel Hays has highlighted the "advanced consumer economy" of postwar America, in which the middle class became less worried about basic living needs and more about vacations and other leisure-time activities.[107] These changes provided a foundation for the modern environmental movement. Antitechnology attitudes in the atomic era were probably a factor in the cessation of major dam projects, as well as strains on the federal budget because of the Korean War. But a major cultural shift in favor of wild places was completed by the 1960s. "The Dinosaur Battle is noted as the first time that all of the scattered interests of modern conservation—sportsmen, ecologists, wilderness preservers, park advocates, and so forth—were drawn together in a common cause," wrote John McPhee.[108] Prior to Dinosaur, conservation groups tended to focus on more narrow issues than "wilderness preservation": the Audubon Society and its birds or the Izaak Walton League and its fish.

ADVOCATING THROUGH JOURNALISM

Persuasive materials are important to the communication strategies of social movements. Such materials help keep coalitions informed and in sync; bystanders are often recruited to the cause; and the general-interest media gets wind of the issue by reading the materials. Throughout their work on topics like women's hats and concrete dams, nature lovers used communication tools old (pamphlets) and new (film) in the art of persuasion. At the turn of the twentieth century, the printed word was the only viable option for the anti-plumage groups; they started their own periodicals and helped force the issue into the mainstream news media, where it was granted legitimacy in the social system. By the 1950s, in the case of the Echo Park Dam opponents, the printed word was supplemented to great effect by newer visual forms, particularly movies. The images of the prominent features of Dinosaur National Monument became symbolic representations of wilderness to many Americans.

The importance of advocacy journalists covering environmental issues remains. Even Hetch Hetchy, given up for lost decades ago, resurfaced in 2005 when Tom Philp, an editorial writer for the *Sacramento Bee,* won the Pulitzer Prize for his editorials calling for the restoration of the valley and the destruction of the dam. On July 19, 2006, a study commissioned by California governor Arnold Schwarzenegger (whose attention to the issue started with the *Bee*'s editorials) announced that it would be technically feasible to tear down the dam.[109] Echoes of the voices of Grinnell, Bailey, Muir, Brower, and others could be heard in the debate.

SEVEN

EARLY MAINSTREAM
JOURNALISM

What is early mainstream journalism? How is *mainstream* defined?
When did mainstream journalism start? The journalism historian Mitchell Stephens used the term "journalistic method" to describe the act by which reporters obtain news via direct observation, interviewing, and other information gathering.[1] Prior to the
establishment of the journalistic method, in the colonial period
of Benjamin Franklin's *Pennsylvania Gazette,* for example, printers
traded news, gossip, and rumor by reading it in other papers. They
were less skilled at news gathering, other than occasionally hiring
a fast sloop to meet information-carrying ships sailing into a port.
Something like mainstream journalism incubated in the penny
press era, which began in the 1830s, as the first mass-circulation
media evolved and editors like James Gordon Bennett sometimes
left the office to talk to news makers. The job of a reporter (as opposed to a printer or editor) became part of the staffs in big-city
daily (or, to use a more modern term, mainstream) newsrooms by
the mid-nineteenth century as journalism became more specialized. By the time of the yellow journalism period of the 1890s,

some reporters could be expected to have a "beat"—that is, to specialize in covering crime or politics, for example, or to write about horses and boxing for the sports section. Newspapers written in English for a general audience living in a specific region became mainstream media.

In spite of the specialization, or perhaps because of it, newspapers employed men and women who could report on anything and everything. "There is little debate regarding the new prominence of the reporter," wrote historian Ted Curtis Smythe. "City dailies in 1880–1900 relied heavily on large numbers of reporters to gather and report the news."[2] Today many of those reporters would work on the general assignment desk—the special place for the nonspecialist. In 1900 they were simply called reporters, and mainstream journalism is a good way to describe what they did.

As the job of a journalist changed, so did the definition of news. The journalism historian Hazel Dicken-Garcia described this content transition as one from idea-centered (in the early nineteenth century) to event-centered (midcentury) and then to an amalgam of event and idea and, importantly, the "story" and its dramatic telling.[3] By the end of the nineteenth century, reporters wrote conservation "stories" about the slaughter of nesting shorebirds and the morality of wearing feathers, but more often their subjects were car crashes, council meetings, and church picnics. Though covering the environment via the beat system did not happen until the 1960s, there were regular reports about nature, wildlife, pollution, land use, and water from the late nineteenth century on. Many of these early-period stories were about dramatic environmental events—the Johnstown Flood in 1889, for example, or the Galveston hurricane of 1900. But a few of the early-period reports came from the combination of ideas, events, and especially storytelling that were showcased in the muckraking tradition of the Progressive Era. The muckraking stories did not involve natural disasters, but included investigation, interviewing, and the rest of the journalistic method.

PRESIDENT TAFT AND THE ALASKAN LAND FRAUD

William Howard Taft was the last president not to have a press office or regular briefings; an Alaskan land controversy, known as the Ballinger-Pinchot affair, highlighted some reasons why successive presidents have tried to control the news with public relations professionals.[4]

By the end of the presidency of Theodore Roosevelt, the journalistic method was in place at the White House and Congress with a fully staffed press corps.[5] Roosevelt understood the news media as well as any president; newspapers and magazines stationed reporters in Washington to produce regular stories, which he was (usually) happy to provide.[6] "It was a wonderful stream, and it furnished entertainment and gossip not only to Washington, but to the whole country," wrote Edward G. Lowry upon Roosevelt's exit. "Washington correspondents counted the day lost that brought from the White House no 'color story' of some new Roosevelt performance. It was gay and interesting while it lasted."[7] Taft, although Roosevelt's handpicked successor, did not court the correspondents; he "chose to ignore the routine practices of producing news," journalism historian Stephen Ponder wrote.[8] Simple actions such as supplying the press with advance texts of presidential speeches, common in Roosevelt's day, were not done by Taft.

Editors still expected stories from their correspondents at the White House, and increasingly those stories came from the president's critics, many of whom were unhappy with Taft's conservatism, which they saw as undoing the progressive policies of Roosevelt. Conservationists were among the most dissatisfied with Taft, who did not share Roosevelt's interest in the natural world. A major point of contention was Taft's favoring of the private development of public lands.[9] "Muckraking flared up at about the time when land was no longer freely available and large scale industry had begun to throw vast questions across the horizon," wrote Walter Lippmann in 1914.[10]

Taft's news media problems began with what had become a standard journalistic practice: the leak.

Among the unhappiest of Taft's administrators was chief forester Gifford Pinchot. A close friend of Roosevelt, Pinchot was as expert in manipulating the press as Taft was inept. Pinchot has been called the first American-born, professionally trained forester; by the time of his appointment to the Department of Agriculture's Division of Forestry in 1898, he had a national reputation in timber management and a flair for public relations.[11] "Nothing permanent can be accomplished in this country unless it is backed by sound public sentiment," he wrote.[12] Pinchot was operating in an era that saw a shift in institutional attitudes toward the media, from what public relations pioneer Edward Bernays called the "public be damned" Gilded Age to the "public be informed" Progressive Era.[13] Pinchot had the administrative skills to implement Roosevelt's conservation policies, including the creation of the U.S. Forest Service in 1905 and a 172-million-acre national forest system by 1908.[14]

The forest service was headquartered in the Department of Agriculture; much of the rest of the federal government's conservation policies were set at the Department of the Interior, headed by a pro-development Taft appointee named Richard Ballinger.

The usual bureaucratic turf war between the agencies partly explains the campaign of anti-Ballinger leaks that began in the summer of 1909, but the poor relationship between Pinchot and Ballinger extended beyond governmental infighting. Pinchot biographer Char Miller wrote that their dislike began as a political difference and wound up personal.[15] They were certainly different men. Pinchot was a rich, eastern, Ivy League– and Europe-educated sportsman; Ballinger was middle-class, western, and a career lawyer-politician. Further, Ballinger had replaced the popular trustbuster and Pinchot confidant James Garfield as head of the Interior Department.

The first leaks came only two months after Taft took office. In early May, the *Philadelphia Press* accused Ballinger of planning to give five million acres of public land to the private "water power trust." Follow-up stories in the *Press* and *Outlook* magazine (where Roosevelt wrote a regular column) claimed Ballinger was disloyal to the former president and that he was attempting to fire one of his division heads, Fredrick Newell, chief of the U.S. Reclamation Service. Leaks from the forest service and the reclamation service were the sources of the stories.[16] A widely circulated United Press story said Ballinger was going to turn over fifteen thousand acres of hydroelectric sites on public land in Montana to the "power trust." That leak was timed to coincide with Ballinger's appearance in Spokane, Washington, at an irrigation industry meeting; stories from Spokane were then framed in that controversy, rather than the scheduled topic.[17]

Framing big business as the bad guy was intentional. William Kovarik and I have suggested that the conservation movement gained strength in the Progressive Era because of structural strains caused by the late-nineteenth-century trusts.[18] In Samuel Hays's view, conservationists, when pushing the idea that the financiers could lock up control of the country's natural resources, aided trust-busting politicians like Roosevelt.[19] Ballinger thought of himself as a progressive—he had been reform mayor of Seattle—but he held a traditional nineteenth-century westerner's view of natural resource policy, favoring businesses and individual rights over the common good. He had supported the selling of federal coal and grazing lands to private parties, in stark conflict with the Roosevelt-Garfield policy of leasing the lands. Further, he angered Pinchot by speaking against the creation of the Chugach National Forest in Alaska, which would add thousands of acres to Pinchot's empire.

Alaska turned out to be where the line in the snow was drawn. A whistle-blower named Louis Glavis, a General Land Office investigator, suspected that Alaska coal claims filed by a miner named Clarence Cunningham were a front for an eastern syndicate making an illegal land grab. Glavis had been stonewalled as he pushed his suspicions through the proper channels at Interior. Ballinger had been Cunningham's lawyer in private practice and others in the syndicate were political associates of Ballinger, and to Glavis and his supporters, that was at minimum a conflict of interest. Glavis was removed twice from the Cunningham investigation before the frustrated investigator went to Pinchot, whom he knew disliked Ballinger.[20]

Pinchot provided Glavis with a letter of introduction to Taft, and the young man took his evidence straight to the president. Taft did not respond publicly after the Glavis visit, but Spokane and Denver newspapers wrote brief accounts of their meeting and wire services distributed the story across the country. Taft hesitated for several weeks before exonerating Ballinger of all charges, but the delay gave the impression that a conspiracy was afoot. Taft then fired Glavis, saying it was "impossible for him to continue in the service of the government."[21]

Glavis, possibly with Pinchot's help, wrote his own account and took it to Norman Hapgood, the muckraking editor of *Collier's* magazine. Glavis refused payment for the piece, even though he was offered $3,000 from another magazine.[22] The article, titled "The Whitewashing of Ballinger," was printed in October 1909. Hapgood added his own editorial comment demanding Ballinger's hide. The story of robber barons, a possible government cover-up, and the giveaway of valuable public lands was too good for other journalists to pass up; the forest service men leaked like cracked faucets, "and they had done it with remarkable effect," Pinchot recalled in his autobiography.[23]

The story shifted from a bureaucratic turf struggle to a full-blown investigation of the Taft administration. *Collier's* put veteran muckraker C. P. Connelly on it. National magazines such as *Hampton's, McClure's, Outlook,* and others joined the pack while newspapers hurried to catch up. John Mathews, reporting in *Hampton's,* claimed Taft was in on the conspiracy.[24] *Collier's* charged that Ballinger's election as Seattle mayor in 1904 was engineered by railroad magnate James J. Hill, and the magazine attempted to connect the secretary with the Morgans, Guggenheims, and Standard Oil.[25] "Are the Guggenheims in Charge of the Department of the Interior?" read a *Collier's* cover. "Apostles of vomit," Ballinger called the news media.[26]

A common theme of the stories was a call for congressional hearings, which would serve as an arena for more coverage within the news frame of alleged wrongdoing. Ballinger agreed to the hearings to clear his name; Glavis, with *Collier's* money, hired future Supreme Court justice Louis Brandeis to serve as his counsel. Taft ordered his administrators not to comment on the case, but Pinchot, after being asked for information, wrote a letter to one of the Republican insurgents in the Senate, confessing to the leaks and accusing Taft of abandoning Roosevelt's conservation policies.[27] After the letter was read on the Senate floor, Taft fired Pinchot and the cause had another very public casualty. (Pinchot was burned in effigy in Alaska.)[28]

In late 1909, Taft instructed his postmaster general to draft legislation that would rescind the favorable postage rates that magazines had enjoyed since 1879. The proposal failed, and the magazines, angrier than ever, continued to muckrake the president and his staff. At the hearings, Glavis was calm and professional while Brandeis held daily briefings for reporters. The frustrated committee chair, Senator Knute Nelson of Minnesota, said, "It might help senators to understand that counsel is trying this case for the other table, the press table, and not this one."[29] Pinchot commissioned a flyer distributed to newspapers across the country as a summary of testimony, a "handy reference guide for busy editors," as one historian called it.[30] (Pinchot's mailing list included twenty-two thousand journalists.)[31] The Taft side was damaged by testimony alleging a cover-up, including the backdating of a key letter and the burning of others. And Taft continued with his policy of public silence through the forty-five sessions of hearings.[32]

The committee voted along partisan lines 7 to 5 to exonerate Ballinger. The muckraking of Ballinger and others in the Taft administration continued for several months; finally, in March 1911, Ballinger resigned, citing poor health. His successor voided the Cunningham claims. Taft, seeking to reclaim lost political ground, wound up opening up to the press while removing more public lands from private entry than did Roosevelt in a similar amount of time. But his political reputation was too damaged to fix and he finished third in his reelection bid behind Woodrow Wilson and Roosevelt in 1912.[33] Wilson, perhaps with Taft's experience in mind, became the first president to hold regular news conferences open to all correspondents, and his secretary held daily news briefings. The issue of conservation versus exploitation of natural resources became a hardy perennial in American politics and a familiar topic for the press.

NATURE MAN

The public's appreciation of the outdoors continued unabated in the early years of the twentieth century. Newspapers tried to capitalize on this interest by telling stories about people and nature; some stories were more fact-based than others. In the case of Joseph Knowles, his nicknames included the Nude Nymph, Nature Man, Primitive Man, Forest Man, and Cave Man. He was also, with considerable evidence, called a fraud in the Boston newspapers that were engaged in a circulation war that played on the public's fascination with nature. The type of writing was called stunt journalism.

Knowles was a forty-something, pudgy, part-time newspaper illustrator and artist when, with much media fanfare, he announced that he would live alone in the Maine woods for two months without taking any equipment with him other than his breechcloth. On August 4, 1913, surrounded by newspaper reporters and photographers, Knowles stripped, sucked on a final cigarette, and ran into the forest. The *Boston Post* headline read: NAKED HE PLUNGES INTO THE MAINE WOODS TO LIVE ALONE TWO MONTHS.[34]

The *Post* sponsored the trip, and Knowles provided the newspaper with birch bark dispatches written in charcoal, left in the crotch of a tree for a trapper to collect. In the best tradition of the stunt journalism popularized by Nellie Bly and the *New York World* in the late 1880s, Knowles's exploits included building a fire by rubbing sticks together, collecting berries for food, and making clothing and utensils from strips of bark.[35] Soon Nature Man moved into more complex forms of sustenance, including catching trout and partridge by hand and wrestling a deer to the ground, killing it, and making a skirt out of its hide. Another story said the Nude Nymph lured a bear into a pit, killed it, and fashioned a coat with its skin. Print media throughout the East Coast and from as far away as Kansas City picked up the tale in syndication deals with the *Post*. Other Boston papers—there were ten dailies in that city in 1913—scrambled to respond to the *Post*'s circulation successes. Maine papers looked on with bemusement.

Knowles exited the woods in Canada on October 4, 1913, stinky and disheveled but healthy. He gave short speeches at train stops in Augusta, Lewiston, and Portland, Maine; when his train reached Boston (after extensive news coverage along the way), an estimated eight to ten thousand people turned out to hear him. Knowles's book, *Alone in the Wilderness,* sold three hundred thousand copies; he went on the vaudeville circuit and signed a contract to tour Europe with Jack London. The *Post* claimed huge increases in circulation.

In addition to understanding his adventure as part of the stunt journalism phenomenon, Knowles represented an extreme example of the breed of back-to-nature lovers and their movement. When Knowles (a former hunting guide and trapper) left civilization behind for two months, in addition to reading a rollicking good story, the public was left with the idea that if he could return in one piece, perhaps society had not been completely turned on its head by the rate of social change seen in its smoggy factories, polluted rivers, teeming tenements, foreign-speaking immigrants, and vote-demanding women. Nature was a constant. The newspaper stories reassured a receptive audience that a simpler, quieter, more virtuous life could be had. It did not matter that few readers would ever attempt to do such a thing; it was sufficient to know that *someone* could do it. Part nostalgia, part agrarian myth, part transcendentalist, and a great deal Boy Scout, Nature Man was popular because people wanted to believe he was possible. To the readers, it did not really matter if the story was made up.

Coverage reflected the contention that modern man could successfully escape modernity. "He has made his main contention good—that modern man is not only the equal of primitive man in his adaptability to his environment, but, because he possesses the inherited knowledge of the race, he is far superior to his primitive ancestors," wrote the *Post*.[36] Physicians said the sudden change back to civilization for Knowles was apt to be a far more serious task than the relapse to savagery. "I do not believe that every man can do what I have done, but I felt confident that a man of good health, a knowledge of the woods and resourcefulness can accomplish the same thing," Knowles said.[37] The remnants of his primitive camp were not described as the scene of a physical presence, but as the "deeper, more impressive signs of a mental battle."[38]

The circulation fights among the ten daily newspapers in Boston in the early twentieth century often focused on William Randolph Hearst, the famous publisher who was building his national newspaper empire one city at a time. In Boston, his paper was the *American*. The *Post,* the *Globe,* and the *American* were the biggest rivals in town. All three were housed on Washington Street in Newspaper Row in downtown Boston. It was the densest geographical concentration of newspapers in an American city and helped fuel competition.[39] The other daily Boston papers were the *Herald,* the *Transcript,* the *Record,* the *Journal,* the *Advertiser,* the *Traveler,* and the *Christian Science Monitor.*

Knowles, who had worked for the *Post* as a graphic artist from 1907 to 1910, recalled events inconsistently, but at one time said both the *Post* and the *American* approached him with a proposal to head for the hills after another newspaper discussed his ideas about the possibility of a civilized man surviving in the wilderness. The *American* turned him down, for reasons that are unclear. The *Post* wasn't faring as well financially because Hearst was giving New England journalism his sensationalistic best, or worst, depending on one's perspective. Charles E. L. Wingate, who had just assumed editorship of the Sunday edition, welcomed Knowles at the *Post:* "To prove that atavism is not only easy and pleasant, but good for newspaper circulation as well . . . to learn whether the human race had become so sissified that it could no longer combat the rigors and dangers which beset Primitive Man."[40]

After sixty days of Nature Man stories, and a special syndication agreement with twenty other newspapers, the *Post* claimed its daily circulation went from 200,000 to 436,585, although in other reports its circulation gains were considerably more modest. In any event, Knowles was getting bigger headlines than baseball, the completion of the Panama Canal, and Massachusetts politics. Crowds lined the streets to hear Knowles speak upon his return to civilization.[41] Even the *Globe* covered his landing in Boston (on an inside page) after lampooning him in a cartoon. Amid the receptions, Hearst and the *American* (which refused to cover Knowles's return) grew envious. The paper hinted at skulduggery on the part of Knowles and the *Post* and promised shocking revelations to come.

The first mention of possible scandal from the *American* came on Friday, November 28. At the bottom of the front page, the Hearst paper previewed a story promised for Sunday's edition with the headline THE TRUTH ABOUT KNOWLES.[42] Saturday's paper followed with an even bigger promotion, complete with hints of what was next: the "alleged adventures" of Knowles, the "Dr. Cook of the Maine Woods."[43]

But Sunday came and went with mention of Knowles in only some editions of the *American*. Stories circulated that the front-page plate had been removed from the printing press and a replacement page substituted. Whatever happened, only a few copies of the Sunday *American* contained the exposé. Rumors flew of a lawsuit filed by the *Post* seeking a court injunction prohibiting the *American* from publishing.[44] If such a suit was threatened, the threat did not work for long. On Monday, December 1, the *American* said it would print the Knowles story in its entirety the following day, in all editions. Beginning on Tuesday and running for several days, the *American* exposed Joseph Knowles as a fraud.

The *American* claimed that Knowles had spent most of the two months lolling around a deserted but comfortable logging camp. The paper gathered evidence that he had guides, hunters, and a cook, and that a woman had visited him. The investigation by reporter Bert Ford for evidence on "Naked Tame Man" included a look at small holes in Knowles's bearskin robe, which looked suspiciously like bullet holes. William Hall, a trapper, claimed he shot the bear.[45] A leather expert was quoted as saying the bearskin looked like it had been tanned commercially.[46] Then the bearskin was reported to have mysteriously disappeared. The former chief of photography for the *Post,* Thomas A. Luke, said the stories may have been made up.[47] *Post* managing editor C. B. Carberry responded with a page-one letter to the public calling Luke a liar and disclosed that he was fired for drunkenness.[48]

Knowles responded to his critics with the affidavits of Maine guides, opinions of nationally known naturalists, and support from a former U.S. senator. He challenged his detractors to come forward, but outside of the Hearst paper they mostly remained silent. Knowles said he was willing to put up $20,000 that he could do it again—with observers—but he got no takers.[49] On the Keith Vaudeville Circuit, a few dozen steps from Newspaper Row, Knowles earned $400 per week for a twenty-week run. Nature Man threatened to sue the *American* for libel for $50,000 over the "slanderous story," but the dispute seems to have been resolved out of court.[50]

Perhaps the resolution involved the dismissal of some Hearst journalists. Knowles later claimed seven employees of the *American* were fired over the incident. He certainly buried the hatchet in a hurry with Hearst, who less than a year later sponsored Knowles's trip to the Siskiyous in Oregon.[51] More than any publisher, Hearst knew a circulation booster when he read it. To deter criticism of Knowles in the Siskiyous, Hearst paid two naturalists, Dr. Charles Lincoln Edwards, head of the nature study department of the Los Angeles school system, and Professor T. T. Waterman of the University of California, to pick up Nature Man's messages and wander at will in the area, acting as "guardians of the public interest."[52]

Unfortunately for the public interest and the circulation of Hearst's *San Francisco Examiner,* Knowles went into the woods on July 20, 1914, and Austria declared war on Serbia on July 28; Germany then quickly declared war on Russia. World war bumped Nature Man deep in the newspaper, next to the classified advertisements. Six weeks after the war broke out, Knowles left the woods. "What does the public care about a naked man in the wilderness when Belgian babies are having their hands cut off?" he asked, somewhat bitterly.[53]

After a few Boy Scout jamborees and some banquets, he was unemployed by 1916, when Hearst rehired him. Hearst sent

Knowles to New York, despite the continuing pressure of war news, to do for his *New York Evening Journal* and his morning *New York American* what his newspaper had missed in Boston. On a trip to Old Forge, in the Adirondacks, there was to be a Dawn Man and a Dawn Woman as well—both naked, but not together. Elaine Hammerstein, actress, society leader, and kin to Oscar Hammerstein, was to be the natural woman. DAWN GIRL SLIPS NAKED IN TO DARK FOREST read one headline, and young men everywhere took up woodcraft. But Dawn Woman, even after a week of (chaperoned) survival instruction from Dawn Man, lasted only a few days in the wilderness. (The mosquitoes were too much for her.) When Dawn Woman left him alone in the wilderness, Knowles returned to civilization and its discontents.

In 1938, when Knowles was in his seventies and living in a self-made driftwood shack on the Washington coast, a man named Michael McKeogh came forward to claim that Nature Man was a fraud and lend some credence to the charges brought by the *Boston American*. In a *New Yorker* article on the twenty-fifth anniversary of the trip, McKeogh, then fifty-five, said it was he, not Knowles, who had sold the idea to the newspapers.[54] Knowles never admitted to the fraud.

Human interest and dramatic events have been a part of newspapering since at least the penny press era, and it was only a short hop for reporters writing about novel events to begin writing about themselves in novel situations. (Nellie Bly, who attempted a circumnavigation of the globe in eighty days, was the most famous one.) And the argument could be made that novelty-as-news accelerated with the advent of more kinds of mass media, up to and including "reality television" in the twenty-first century. In 1929 Lippmann took note of radio and film: "Novelties crowd the consciousness of modern man; the press, the radio, the moving picture, have enormously multiplied the number of unseen events and strange people and queer doings with which he has to be concerned . . . He finds it increasingly difficult to believe that through it all there is order, permanence, and connecting principle."[55]

The brief, intense popularity of Knowles may be representative of a more subtle, underlying, long-term social change—what has been called modernity.[56] In 1913, when the media-friendly Knowles trotted into the Maine woods in his birthday suit, the forces of modernity—immigration, industrialization, and urbanization, to name three commonly mentioned ones—were wearing at the American psyche. The frontier, which defined so much of the national character, had been declared closed by the historian Frederick Jackson Turner in 1893; his writings accepted and reinforced Thomas Jefferson's dichotomy between rural good and urban evil.[57] For Turner, frontier agriculture and agrarian virtue were giving way to urban complexity. Pollution was one troubling form through which complexity revealed itself: water problems plagued big cities like New York, where millions of gallons of raw sewage poured into the city's rivers. Traffic jams, crowded subways, noise pollution, and piles of garbage added to the worries of the city dweller. In rural areas, a widespread but somewhat unorganized phenomenon called the country life movement arose to promote the attractions of rural living.[58] Of concern to others was the growing influence of early feminists on traditional American male culture. Moreover, slums, sweatshops, child labor, and trusts gnawed at the souls of reformers and others who sought answers to the growing social evils of the city. Historian David E. Shi has called the phenomenon, which appears in various forms throughout American history, as a search for the simple life.[59] Robert H. Wiebe noted that in the Progressive Era, change came at such a rapid rate that Americans searched for organizing principles to help them cope.[60]

The back-to-nature movement faded from prominence in the social system of the 1920s as people became accustomed to modernity. A system that had supported a presidential candidate (William Jennings Bryan) who espoused "rural fundamentalism"—and a president (Roosevelt) who appointed a Country Life Commission—slowly changed.[61] Nature loving continued, of course, but the urgency and rate at which the public devoured newspaper stories on Joseph Knowles, bought the books of John Burroughs, and supported the Boy Scouts seemed to lessen, especially after the onset of the Great Depression. Folks continued to move from the country into the city. Outdoor life was no longer considered a condition for the survival of the human species. "Yet withal [outdoor living] is a natural phenomenon, a form of social adjustment that has grown out of the exigencies of urban life," wrote sociologists Noel Gist and L. A. Halbert in their 1933 study of urban society.[62]

The critic Raymond Williams noted that the word *nature* is the most complex in the English language, and it is no simple task to divine its meanings.[63] In journalism history, one common assumption is that the content of the press tells us something about the audience, even if, in the end, the Nature Man stories were more like the moon hoax of 1835—which claimed the existence of intelligent life on the moon—than Nellie Bly's adventures in the 1880s.[64]

THE WORKPLACE ENVIRONMENT: WEST VIRGINIA

If Samuel Hays was correct about the economic foundation of environmentalism, it would follow that the economic calamity of the Great Depression would lessen interest in conservation and outdoor recreation as people grew more worried about basic human needs, like employment.[65] But even as back-to-nature stories fell from the pages of the press, urban and workplace environmental issues remained part of news routines in the 1930s.

In West Virginia, hundreds of men digging a diversion tunnel for a Union Carbide plant's hydroelectric project on the New River beginning in 1927 contracted the lung disease silicosis from the work and died. Most of the victims were poor African American southerners; they were issued no respirators or any other protection, although their white supervisors were equipped with safety devices. The respirators were critical because the work bore through a mountain that was up to 96 percent silica. A few workers soaked their handkerchiefs in water and wore them like a mask; most just breathed, coughed, and spat.

As men started to get sick, families of the victims sought assistance from the plant's owner as well as the government and the courts, but they got little relief—and little news coverage. In all of 1931, the largest construction project in the history of Fayette County received only three stories in local newspapers; the company had imposed a "gag rule" on employees, forbidding them to talk to the local press.

It is not surprising that the local press was not much help to the workers. The reaction of the newspapers was in line with a communication model proposed by researchers Philip Tichenor, George Donohue, and Clarice Olien, who suggested that small-town newspapers are more likely than large metro papers to be consensus-oriented rather than conflict-oriented.[66] Community newspapers are reluctant to shed light on environmental conflicts, for example, since they function in a "homogenous, interpersonal social structure."[67] The researchers further noted that when jobs are at stake, local news media will serve more of a "lapdog" function, protecting the interests of those in power, rather than the "watchdog" function so commonly ascribed to the press in popular thought.[68]

The main local newspaper, the *Fayette Tribune,* covered the silicosis issue—when it bothered to mention it at all—as a case of bureaucratic inspection of the conditions in the mines.[69] About the only reporting that could be considered critical came from the nearest metro daily, the *Charleston Gazette,* which dug up a clear conflict-of-interest case by the director of the state department of mines, who was also consulting for industry. However, the tenor of most of the coverage of the construction was not about problems, but about the triumph of man over nature. A sample headline: ARMY OF WORKMEN DRILLING THROUGH GAULEY MOUNTAIN.[70]

Company gag order or not, eventually the local papers could not completely ignore the sickness and deaths occurring in the work camps. On February 18, 1931, the *Charleston Journal* reported: "This is a great deal of comments [*sic*] about town regarding the unusually large number of deaths among the colored laborers at tunnel works of the New Kanawha Power Company. The deaths total about 37 in the past two weeks."[71] The first accounts attributed lung disease among the African Americans working in tunnels to "gambling out of doors before an open fire," poor habits of nutrition, unusual susceptibility among blacks to pneumonia, or their general inability to resist disease.[72]

In 1935 a reporter named Albert Maltz, working for the Communist publication *New Masses,* published a piece about the workers and their illnesses.[73] But Maltz's story was a fictionalized account of what happened and did not capture the attention of any other newspapers. Another *New Masses* reporter, writing under the byline of Bernard Allen, went to the scene and interviewed survivors and families of the dead.[74] Allen's stories did get noticed. A radical labor tabloid in Detroit, *People's Press,* sent a photographer to shoot what the editor called "the village of walking skeletons"; a reporter from a mainstream Pittsburgh daily saw the pictures and went to West Virginia to cover the story.[75] A New York congressman with labor sympathies read the articles and called for congressional hearings. Researcher Martin Cherniak, who wrote the definitive history of the incident, said the publicity generated by the congressional hearings was the tipping point: "The hearings indirectly achieved an objective of immense significance in awakening recognition of the need to protect workers exposed to silica."[76]

One of those testifying was "Bernard Allen," whose stories in *New Masses* had caught the attention of the Pittsburgh paper and the congressman. To the surprise of those at the hearing, "Bernard" was really Phillippa Allen, a New York social worker who had caught wind of the dangerous workplace conditions in the tunnel and had gone to the New River on her own to investigate.[77]

The hearings generated little help for the victims or any punishment for the company, but major news media, including the newsreels, took notice of the story. The secretary of labor called a national conference on silicosis and shortly thereafter the medical profession, for the first time, recognized acute silicosis as a disease. By the end of 1937, forty-six states included workers suffering from silicosis in their workers' compensation laws. Cherniak noted that the death toll will never be known for sure—at least several hundred and perhaps two thousand or more—in what he called America's worst industrial tragedy.[78]

THE WORKPLACE ENVIRONMENT: ST. LOUIS

Stories about the air we breathe and environmental hazards in the workplace earned Pulitzer Prizes in 1941 and 1948 for the *St. Louis Post-Dispatch*. An anti–air pollution editorial campaign won the first award; spot news coverage of a coal-mining disaster won the second.

St. Louis, like many other midwestern and eastern cities, suffered from the coal smoke of chimneys, smokestacks, and steam engines. The city attempted to curb the emissions as early as 1893, but that ordinance was weak and ineffectual.[79] One study conducted in 1907 found that St. Louis homeowners and small businesses were more likely to burn the dirtier bituminous coal than the less smoky anthracite.[80] At times smog was so bad that airplanes could not land at the St. Louis airport because they could not find it.[81]

Civic groups who worked on "smoke abatement campaigns" often had the support of city leaders, business groups, and other community elites who worried about the effects of pollution on the business climate. The *Post-Dispatch,* in both its editorial pages and news columns, had agitated for reform for several years. An editorial published on November 26, 1939, demanded an immediate campaign by the city government against smoke, "the evil that is ruining our city."[82] Only two days later, thick smog fell so heavily over the city that streetlights had to be lit in the daytime so people could see. The haze lasted for four days; no one was recorded as dying from it, but the dramatic event kicked the issue to the forefront in the city. In a story about the plight of those in the St. Louis slums called "Children of Darkness," reporter Virginia Irwin's first sentence said it all: "It was another daytime night."[83]

Dozens of stories about smoke abatement appeared in the

newspaper over the next two years, and the paper proposed a coal-buying cooperative for "smoke-free" fuels. Stronger ordinances were passed, and diesel engines replaced steam ones on the railroads. Industries complying with the ordinances were given free advertising in the newspaper on its "Anti-Smoke Roll of Honor."

The Pulitzer committee awarded the *St. Louis Post-Dispatch* its editorial prize in 1940. John Hohenburg, the longtime director of the prize committee, said the award was "the first instance in the Pulitzer files in which the pollution menace was recognized."[84] Raymond R. Tucker, an engineering professor at Washington University, was named the city's first smoke commissioner, and he parlayed the publicity from his work into a victorious mayoral campaign in 1953.

In the news columns of the *Post-Dispatch,* the lead reporter on the smoke abatement story was a man named Sam J. Shelton, who deserves consideration as one of the pioneers of environmental journalism. "A great city has washed its face, and its neck and ears, too," Shelton wrote as the cleanup progressed. "St. Louis is no longer the grimy old man of American municipalities. The plague of smoke and soot has been so well wiped off if not completely removed, that the shining countenance of the Missouri metropolis is now the envy of the other cities still subject to the winter's outpouring of dirt and fumes from thousands of chimneys."[85] According to the official history of the newspaper, representatives from other smoke-plagued cities traveled to St. Louis to talk with Shelton about the issue.[86]

Shelton, hired in 1913, was a general assignment reporter, a "well-tried talent" who also wrote about kidnappings, blackmailers, and graft.[87] He made himself an expert on the utilities industry; his stories on Union Electric's attempts to funnel campaign contributions to legislators and other illegal deeds sent two industry executives to jail.[88] Shelton was the only reporter invited to interview Kansas City political boss Tom Pendergast on his way to prison in 1939. In the mid-1940s Shelton covered the plans for a proposed Missouri Valley Authority (modeled after the TVA), as well as other conservation and outdoor issues.[89] In 1945 Shelton became publisher Joseph Pulitzer II's personal assistant; he wrote for the editorial pages of the paper until his retirement in 1957.[90]

Shelton was gone from the newsroom at the time of the next dramatic story, on the afternoon of March 25, 1947. An explosion in the Centralia Coal Company's Mine No. 5 near Centralia, Illinois, sixty-five miles east of St. Louis, trapped 142 miners, of whom 111 were killed. Coincidentally, the smoky, high-sulfur soft coal from the southern Illinois mines was precisely what Shelton and the *Post-Dispatch* were campaigning against. As early as two years before, four miners from the local union had written Illinois governor Dwight Green asking for help in improving the safety conditions at Centralia, and complaining about lax safety inspections: "Please save our lives," the men wrote.[91] Less than a week before the explosion, the *Post-Dispatch* broke a story about a possible shakedown of an Illinois coal mine operator by the Chicago Republican mayoral campaign, illustrating the corruption in the system.[92]

After the explosion, Pulitzer sent a team of reporters to the scene immediately. No one was rescued alive after the first day. A temporary morgue was established at the local Greyhound bus station. Many of the trapped miners had time to write notes before they perished. "If I don't make it, sell the house and go live with your folks," read one. "Please get the baby baptized," read another. "Oh Lord Help me," was a third.[93] After five days, the 111th and final body was recovered. The newspaper produced a twenty-four-page special section a month after the tragedy; Pulitzer decreed that the insert be distributed free throughout the southern Illinois coal country. The section contained articles, photographs, editorials, and cartoons.

The blast that killed the miners was caused by "coal dust raised into the air and ignited by explosives fired in a dangerous and non-permissible manner."[94] Other safety laws had been violated; federal inspectors' warnings had been ignored, and recommendations had not been followed. The reporters became convinced that part of the problem was with Governor Green's administration; seven journalists were dispatched to investigate the governor's role in the disaster. Stories began to appear about how Green had leaned on mine owners and operators for campaign contributions, and how he had ignored pleas for better safety inspections. The head of the state department of mines resigned.

The Illinois political machine retaliated and indicted one of the St. Louis reporters, Theodore C. Link, on trumped-up kidnapping charges.[95] Pulitzer became so convinced of the importance of the work of his journalists that he wrote an editorial opposing Green for reelection; he bought $12,000 in advertising space in eleven Illinois newspapers, representing three million in circulation, and ran an ad based on the editorial, titled "The Green Machine Fights Back." The final sentence of the editorial was "The *Post-Dispatch* will not be intimidated; it will not be gagged."[96] The story of the mine disaster reached a national audience when *Harper's* ran a cover story titled "The Blast in Centralia No. 5: A Mine Disaster No One Stopped."[97] One miner said "I used to cough up chunks of coal dust like walnuts after work."[98]

After the Centralia disaster and its news coverage, a lawyer from Chicago named Adlai Stevenson overwhelmingly defeated

Green in the 1948 gubernatorial election, the start of a political career that nearly ended up in the White House. Stevenson and others initiated changes in the Illinois mine inspection system, removing the inspectors from political pressure and making it a crime for any state mine officer to solicit campaign funds from mine operators, miners, or unions. The coal company was indicted, pleaded no defense, and paid a small fine.[99] The Illinois legislature voted down several attempts to appropriate money to the ninety-nine widows of the men killed in the explosion.[100]

JOURNALISM EVOLVES

In the 1950s, environmental concerns such as the controversy at Dinosaur National Monument and other land preservation issues became front-page news alongside smoke abatement campaigns and mine explosions. In the decade of the 1960s, social, political, and cultural trends combined to establish environmentalism in the public arena; journalists and their outlets reacted by institutionalizing environmental coverage in beats, a professional association, and other ways.

Some topics have remained relevant no matter the era. The Sago (W.Va.) mine disaster of January 2, 2006, that trapped thirteen miners and killed all but one received national attention from hundreds of media outlets; similarities between the stories of reporters such as Ken Ward Jr. and his colleagues at the *Charleston Gazette* on this disaster and the work of the *Post-Dispatch* in the 1940s were evident.[101] Miners attempting a rescue had to turn back; the doomed miners became resigned to their fate, wrote letters, and prayed. A company rescue attempt was disorganized and late. There was trouble with state workers' compensation benefits for the widows. One of Ward's stories noted that inspections from early October to late December the previous year had resulted in forty-six citations and three orders, eighteen of which were "serious and substantial." The "S&S" violations were those that the inspectors thought "likely to cause an accident that would seriously injure a miner." The *Gazette* organized its stories chronologically and created a free Web site with links to each story, a twenty-first-century way to print a special section and distribute it to interested audiences.

EIGHT

LATE MAINSTREAM JOURNALISM

By the 1960s and early 1970s, when environmental interests began to coalesce around books like *Silent Spring,* events such as Earth Day, and dramatic images such as the *Apollo 11* photograph of the Earth, environmental coverage had become part of standard news routines. In American society, ecological concerns were institutionalized in the Environmental Protection Agency and the Council for Environmental Quality, to name two; these government organizations were treated as authoritative sources by the news media. Environmental legislation and litigation, including the snail darter and other high-profile cases, marked the mid- to late 1970s. Antinuclear groups were strengthened after the accident at Three Mile Island (1979) and the disaster at Chernobyl (1986). In Niagara Falls (N.Y.) and Times Beach (Mo.), residents worried about toxic chemicals in their neighborhood. Oil spills, chemical accidents, species depletions, urban sprawl, and hundreds of other environmental issues became news. Membership in environmental groups grew substantially throughout the period, particularly during Ronald Reagan's presidency (1981–89). Green marketing became an established form of advertising for businesses looking to sell to an environmentally conscious public. "Green washing" critics called it.

Newspapers, magazines, and broadcast media created environmental beats and produced regular coverage. A professional organization, the Society of Environmental Journalists (SEJ), was formed in 1989–90 with an educational mission. It quickly grew to more than 1,400 members from thirty-three countries. Some newspapers and newsmagazines published environmental columns or separate sections. *National Geographic,* where editor Noel Grove was a key figure in SEJ, continued as a periodical leader. CNN produced an environmental television news program, *Earth Matters,* from 1993 to 2001. The radio show *Living on Earth* became a mainstay on National Public Radio in 1991, as did the Outdoor Life Network and the Discovery Channel on cable television. Newsletters such as those published by the Bureau of National Affairs and *Inside EPA* became important to policy makers and journalists. Specialty magazines such as *E/The Environmental Magazine* and the online *Grist* filled niches left by the mainstream media. And by the first decade of the twenty-first century, challenges to the growth of the genre were apparent: media budget cuts, shrinking news holes, a lack of advertiser support, other issues competing for attention, and a combative political culture.[1]

Environmental journalism became, after the late 1960s, a fair target for researchers as an important part of the news media. Scholarly journals and professional and academic organizations were dedicated to the topic, as was at least one educational service.[2] Several universities offered undergraduate or graduate degrees in the field; a few endowed chairs in environmental communication or science communication. Environmental journalism, as a routine component of the mainstream American press, emerged as a consequential factor in how citizens and their governments view, manage, debate, preserve, and exploit their natural surroundings.

It would be a fool's errand to try and identify the first newspaper or broadcast newsroom to appoint a reporter to the environmental beat. But by the late 1960s, mainstream newspapers such as the *Chicago Tribune, Los Angeles Times,* and *New York Times* had added an environmental reporter to the newsroom; network television news had not dedicated a full-time reporter to the beat, although some local stations did so, off and on. Environmental stories won public-service Pulitzers in 1967: one to the *Milwaukee Journal* for a campaign to stiffen water pollution laws, and the other to the *Louisville Courier-Journal* for coverage of strip mining in Kentucky. Robert Cahn of the *Christian Science Monitor* was awarded the Pulitzer for national reporting in 1969 for his series on the future of our parks.

At the *Chicago Tribune* in 1966, reporters Casey Bukro and Bill Jones were assigned to write about water pollution problems for a series called "Save Our Lakes." One of their first investigations was at the Indiana Harbor Ship Canal at its entry to Lake Michigan. The canal was full of an oily, filthy scum of an unknown origin; the two reporters pondered the problem of illustrating the dreck with a photograph. Jones stuck his arm into the ooze and grabbed a handful. Bukro picked up a camera and snapped a picture. "And that became our test for clean water," Bukro recalled thirty years later. "We traveled around the country doing that, to show what stuck to our hand."[3]

Their stories were as straightforward as the scene implied. "I didn't have to conduct any scientific experiments to prove that the air was black and the water was filthy," Bukro said. "Our pictures showed it, and your own senses proved it."[4]

Bukro, who was made environment editor at the *Tribune* in

1970, was at the forefront of a group of reporters who transformed stories about the environment from ones driven by dramatic events and government leaks to something more investigative, crusading, in-depth, and in many cases full-time. Some of the new environmental reporters had been covering science or agriculture, a few were writing about medicine and health, and one or two even came to it from outdoor adventure writing. One thing all of these reporters had in common was the influence of Rachel Carson's book *Silent Spring,* which appeared in 1962.

CARSON AND *SILENT SPRING*

While arguments in academic circles continue over when the modern environmental movement began or what started it, many observers note that Carson's book on the dangers of synthetic pesticides at least had something to do with 1960s environmental awareness. "There are still debates about *Silent Spring's* influence on the evolution of our thinking about earth's inhabitants and their resources," wrote Stewart Udall more than twenty-five years after the book's publication. "It would be difficult to understate Rachel Carson's contribution to science and culture. Her thinking had worldwide impact, and we have yet to assess the reach of her legacy."[5] Environmental historian John Opie noted that after the book's publication, "environmentalism, with ecology as its science, moved into the American mainstream and began to steer the national agenda in government, science, and industry."[6] The publication of the book and the ensuing controversy was "an epochal event in the history of environmentalism [that] can also be seen as helping launch a new decade of rebellion and protest in which the idea of Nature under stress also began to be seen as a question of the quality of life," wrote scholar Robert Gottlieb.[7]

Carson held a master's degree in marine biology from Johns Hopkins University, but she was also an accomplished journalist, showing an interest in writing from a young age. As a ten-year-old in 1918, she published the first of two stories in *St. Nicholas* magazine that paid her ten dollars. She entered what is now Chatham College as an English major, wrote for the school newspaper, and left with a biology degree in 1929. Carson began working at the U.S. Fish and Wildlife Service in 1935; her writing and editing skills were evident to her superiors, and she eventually wound up as editor in chief of the information division.

Carson's first stories on marine life and conservation appeared in the *Baltimore Sun* in 1936, and her breakthrough article for a national audience came the following year with a piece on oceans that appeared in the *Atlantic Monthly*.[8] A graceful writer who kept a copy of Thoreau's *Journal* by her bedside, Carson was also a dogged and careful researcher.[9] She became well known from a series of books, including *Under the Sea Wind* (1941), *The Sea Around Us* (1951), and *The Edge of the Sea* (1954), the latter of which nature writer Ann Zwinger called "the perfect book."[10] Her first attempt at tackling the dangers of DDT and other synthetic pesticides appeared in 1945; she wrote a short pitch letter to *Reader's Digest,* but there is no record of any response from its editors, and she dropped the subject.

Carson considered recruiting other writers, including E. B. White, to cover the issue but ultimately decided to take on the project alone.[11] By the time she started *Silent Spring* in 1958 she had retired from the fish and wildlife service. Several incidents spurred her to begin the work, including friends' property being soaked with DDT, reports of damage to birds and wildlife after the application of the highly toxic pesticides dieldrin and heptachlor, and

a court case on Long Island meant to enjoin the federal government from aerial pesticide spraying.[12] "Was it possible—even for
Rachel Carson—to write a best seller on such a dreary theme as
pesticides?" asked her editor at Houghton Mifflin, Paul Brooks.[13]
Rejections from editors at *Reader's Digest, Ladies' Home Journal,
Women's Home Companion,* and *Good Housekeeping* came in. The
Good Housekeeping editor forwarded Carson's pitch (made by Ma-
rie Rodell, her agent) to its chemical analysis laboratory, which
replied: "It is our feeling that the article proposed by Miss Rodell
is something which we should under no circumstances consider.
We doubt whether many of the things outlined in this letter could
be substantiated."[14] A major manufacturer of baby foods was also
quoted in the report as suggesting that the article would bring
"unwarranted fear" to mothers who used its products.[15]

Carson, who was diagnosed with breast cancer in 1960, had
reached an agreement with White and William Shawn to serialize
her work in the *New Yorker* (its circulation was a modest 430,000,
but its readers included opinion leaders such as President John F.
Kennedy) before publishing it in book form with Houghton Mifflin, which also published *Walden.* The stories began in June 1962.
They detailed the global impact of DDT, ranging from the death
of songbirds to the increased cancer threat to humans. Doing her
usual thorough research, Carson culled documents from scientific reports, case studies, court cases, interviews, and other sources.
"Overall, the effect and the rhythm of the pieces were—appro-
priately—that of an investigative, journalistic feature, beginning
with dramatic themes and anecdotes, supporting in the middle
mainly through the accuracy and lucidity of Carson's explanation
of scientific phenomena, and concluding with philosophic commentary," wrote Carson scholar Priscilla Coit Murphy.[16] Carson
knew the work would be controversial. The Swiss scientist who

discovered the use of DDT as a pesticide, Paul Mueller, had won a Nobel Prize for his work, and the powerful chemical industry and its generously funded academic researchers would protect their interests. "This was something I had not expected to do," Carson wrote a scientist friend, "but facts that came to my attention last winter disturbed me so deeply that I made the decision to postpone all other commitments and devote myself to what I consider a tremendously important problem."[17]

In the book, Carson did not reject all pest control efforts (something her critics often ignored), but rather she placed biological controls and an ecological whole as part of her solution. Her work was not original science; it was a more journalistic synthesis of the existing literature. She backed up her work with six hundred sources and more than fifty pages of footnotes, which were not in the magazine series.[18]

The chemical companies contested the book even before it hit the stores. "Perhaps not since the classic controversy over Charles Darwin's *The Origin of Species* just over a century earlier has a single book been more bitterly attacked by those who felt their interests threatened," Brooks wrote.[19] The agricultural chemical industry budgeted $250,000 for a public relations campaign to counter Carson's articles; an industry lawyer rattled the doors of both the *New Yorker* and Houghton Mifflin.[20] E. B. White wrote Carson that they were "the most valuable articles the magazine had ever published."[21] President Kennedy mentioned them in a press conference and instructed the President's Science Advisory Committee to look into their charges. The Book-of-the-Month Club announced that *Silent Spring* would be its October selection, and the Consumers' Union received permission to print a special edition for its members. In mid-October, two weeks after it was published, *Silent Spring* made the best-seller lists and was in first place by November, holding the top spot for about six weeks until John Steinbeck's *Travels with Charley* bumped it to No. 2. It was published in France, Norway, Spain, Denmark, Holland, Germany, Italy, Sweden, Finland, Brazil, Japan, Portugal, and Israel in 1963.[22]

The controversy surrounding the book raged on. One public official reached a low point when he wondered "why a spinster with no children was so concerned about genetics."[23] (Carson had an adopted son.) Chemical companies such as Monsanto and industry associations issued a series of press releases, brochures, pamphlets, speeches, and bulletins attacking the author, her scientific credentials, and her gender. Letters to the editor were written and media interviews conducted, and, as these things often go, much of the vitriol came from those who had not actually read her material. Houghton Mifflin responded with an advertising campaign quoting scientists and medical doctors praising the book; it mailed a pamphlet to newspaper editors around the country, but it could not equal the resources that the author's opponents brought to bear in attacking her.

The book was a top-ten best seller for six months, and CBS News broadcast a show on the book in April 1963 even after three of the show's five sponsors withdrew. (One might wonder as to why advertisers were scared off the TV show but did not withdraw from the *New Yorker* while the series ran.) Carson came off as dignified, calm, and reasonable on CBS, whereas her critics seemed uninformed and excitable. "Television allowed Carson and not her critics to define the issue," said her biographer, Linda Lear.[24] The Kennedy committee's report, issued on May 15, 1963, received more press attention and was widely seen as vindicating the book. Congressmen, spurred by the CBS show, held hearings in June, and Carson testified, although her breast cancer was in an advanced stage. Further vindication came in November 1963, when tiny amounts of the pesticide endrin—manufactured and dumped by the same company whose lawyers threatened the *New Yorker* and Houghton Mifflin—were responsible for a massive fish kill on the lower Mississippi River. "How does Rachel Carson look now?" a reporter asked Mississippi state public health officials. "She looks pretty good," said one scientist.[25]

Carson died in 1964 at age fifty-six. Eight years after her death, the federal government banned the use of DDT in the United States, but the book's toxic legacy was mixed: by 1977, pesticide use had increased two and a half times in America in the years since her work was published.[26]

Carson was not the first writer-scientist to point to the dangers of pesticide use. Murray Bookchin, writing as "Lewis Herber," published *Our Synthetic Environment* about six months before *Silent Spring*.[27] *Audubon* magazine was among the specialty publications writing about pesticides and their effect on avian life, while daily newspapers across the county, particularly in the Midwest, wrote about citizens' objections to roadside spraying programs and other heavy uses of pesticides.[28] Some scholars have argued that *Silent Spring* did not so much define the social problem of pesticide use (which had already been done) but rather accelerated public awareness of it; others have made the point that, as a result of earlier coverage, the book fit into an established news frame.[29] Certainly one of the reasons why *Silent Spring* received so much media attention—in addition to meeting the news criteria of conflict, impact, and prominence—was that controversial magazine articles, a book, congressional hearings, speeches, TV specials, a presidential report, and a large fish kill were all dramatic events, and journalists are better at covering what scholar G. Ray Funkhouser called "event summaries" than they are at covering complex issues.[30]

BURN ON, BIG RIVER

Why do some issues get media attention and others do not? As we have seen, throughout American history various groups have interacted on many levels to induce social change. Among these groups are the mass media, environmentalists, government, academia, business interests, civic organizations, churches, and others. Books, magazines, newspapers, and broadcast media have helped create regional and national communities of environmental awareness. The media perform this function in part by defining some issues as social problems and ignoring others.

How does this work? Take, for example, the highly publicized case of the heavily polluted Cuyahoga River in Cleveland, Ohio, which caught fire on June 22, 1969. The river had blazed up now and then since at least 1868, and few outside of northern Ohio had paid any attention. (An oil slick–fed inferno in 1952 caused almost $1.5 million in damage. A 1912 fire had killed five men.) And in those days it was not a problem just for northern Ohio. Rivers, canals, and harbors in Buffalo, Baltimore, Houston, and Detroit also regularly caught fire due to the high levels of industrial pollutants in them. When the Cleveland fires were covered in the newspapers of the 1930s, the news frame was not one of a dirty river, but inadequate fire protection services.[31]

Although there were some interesting aspects to the June 1969 blaze—it happened over the lunch hour, when people were out and about and could see the smoke, and witnesses reported flames five stories high—it was treated as routine by the authorities and local media. The Cleveland fire chief was not called, and the regular crew had it under control in less than thirty minutes. Photographers from the *Cleveland Plain Dealer* and the *Cleveland Press* arrived after the fire was out. The *Plain Dealer* ran a five-paragraph story and a photograph on the front page of the "C" section the next day.[32] The *Press* ran its photograph on page one with a caption only—there was no accompanying story.[33] No television crews arrived in time to film the blaze.[34] Damage to two train trestles was estimated between $50,000 and $85,000; one trestle was closed because its ties were warped in the fire, but the other remained open.[35] There was no loss of life or injuries.

That might have been the end of the news coverage but for the aggressive action of the political leader of the city. Cleveland mayor Carl Stokes, angry that the city's expensive cleanup efforts on the river were being stymied by the state of Ohio, held a press conference the next day in front of the charred railroad trestle ties. (The social critic Daniel Boorstin called press conferences and similar occurrences "pseudo-events"; journalists are well rehearsed as to how to cover them.)[36] "We have no jurisdiction over what is dumped in there . . . the state gives [industry] a license to pollute," Stokes told the press.[37]

The mayor was angry because the Ohio Water Pollution Control Board was allowed to issue permits to polluters, and the city had lost a court case trying to enforce its ordinances.[38] Congress had mandated Lake Erie remediation efforts, but did not appropriate the funds needed to do it. Attempts at cleaning the Cuyahoga River had been made since at least 1948, and it could be claimed that the stream was on its way to recovery.[39] In 1968 local voters approved a $100 million bond issue to finance a cleanup; fire codes were being enforced on neighboring industries, and boats were hired to skim the debris from the river. The city was spending $30 million on the construction of sewage treatment plants.[40] Stokes's angry comments were carried in the local news media (although not prominently), but he kept the focus on the Cuyahoga.[41] At his press conference, Stokes released copies of letters dated that day that he had sent to the governor and the state department of natural resources.

A month later, *Time* magazine ran a piece on the fire with a misleading but dramatic photo from the 1952 fire. "Some river! Chocolate-brown, oily, bubbling with subsurface gases, it oozes rather than flows," the story said.[42] "What a terrible reflection on our city," Stokes was quoted as saying.[43] Other national media, including *National Geographic* and at least one edition of the *New York Times,* matched the story from *Time;* it fit in a news frame with earlier reporting about pollution in Lake Erie, into which the Cuyahoga River fed, as well as other national environmental news of the day, especially the January oil spill near Santa Barbara, California.[44] National politicians were in the middle of a debate over what would become the Federal Water Pollution Control Act of 1972 (better known as the Clean Water Act); only weeks before the fire, Congress had debated the National Environmental Protection Act ("the most sweeping environmental law ever passed by a United States Congress"), which helped pave the way for the Environmental Protection Agency.[45]

More attention came Cleveland's way from Johnny Carson's jokes on *The Tonight Show,* a *New Yorker* cartoon, and, later, popular songwriter Randy Newman's tune "Burn On," which included the phrase "cause the Cuyahoga River goes smokin' through my dreams."[46] In August 1969 the federal government was shaken into action, and the Department of the Interior threatened six industrial firms with fines if they did not reduce their dumping into the river.[47] The symbolism of a river burning at a time when concern for the planet was nearing a peak was not lost on environmental advocates, who took advantage of it in their media relations, lobbying, and coalition-building efforts. In sum, a coalescence of interests created media attention where little had existed before. In this instance, the media played a critical role in setting the tempo at which policy formation took place.

A PROFESSIONAL ASSOCIATION

One way environmental journalists set themselves apart from their science-writing colleagues was by expanding the definition of what was news on their beats. "The environmental movement of the early 1970s focused journalists' attention on science's social, economic and political contexts," wrote scholar Sharon Friedman and her coauthors.[48] A content analysis of environmental stories in 1970 found a focus on environmental quality issues, which stood in contrast to earlier stories on environmental disasters.[49]

Only one journalist was identified as a "specialist" environmental reporter by an *Editor and Publisher* survey in 1968.[50] But by the 1970s and 1980s, the environment was an established beat at several mainstream newspapers and magazines in the United States. Another survey in 1972–73 found ninety-five reporters covering the environment at U.S. newspapers: the average reporter was a college-educated male and had been on the beat for more than three years and in the business for more than ten.[51] Only about one-third of them covered the environment full-time, and their coverage focused on pollution and government agencies.[52] A content analysis conducted at about the same time found that print journalists were often guilty of "environmental Afghanistanism"—covering problems outside their community, rather than local issues.[53] Both the survey and content analysis took note of the rapid pace of change in the field. More Pulitzers came in the period: one to the *Winston-Salem* [N.C.] *Journal and Sentinel* in 1971 for coverage of environmental problems in strip mining; one to James Risser of the *Des Moines Register* in 1979 for a series on the damage farming can do to the environment; and another to the staff of the *Philadelphia Inquirer* for its coverage of the Three Mile Island nuclear accident in 1979.

The late 1980s and early 1990s were salad days for the environmental beat in the United States. *Time* magazine, departing from its tradition of picking a human, selected the Earth as "Planet of the Year" for 1988. Publications that had previously ignored environmental coverage, such as *Business Week,* devoted staff to the topic; the *Rocky Mountain News* and other newspapers added a daily page for environment and science stories; local television stations created environmental teams; and PBS ran a ten-part series called *Race to Save the Planet* in fall 1990.[54] Organizers of the twentieth anniversary of Earth Day in 1990 took full advantage of the increased media attention to get their message out.

With that growth came challenges and problems, and some of them sounded familiar to reporters who had been in the field for decades. Many stories still suffered from poor sourcing (including the over-quoting of celebrity scientists such as Carl Sagan); some stories were superficial and underreported; and dramatic events still took precedence over harder-to-understand environmental problems. One survey in 1989 found that government officials accounted for nearly one-third of all sources in environmental stories, twice the percentage of any other category.[55] Sensationalism and gee-whiz reporting remained a concern, as did public relations efforts by industry to burnish its image with a technique known as green washing. Major foreign environmental disasters, like Chernobyl and Bhopal, were poorly understood, and some reporting on them lacked context, depth, and perspective. Journalists struggled with the idea of environmental risk and how to present it in everyday language. The 1989 coverage of the pesticide Alar on apples caused a significant decline in sales of the fruit, but one study showed that only 15 percent of the stories included some type of risk-assessment figure.[56]

As a response to these challenges on the beat in the 1980s, several environmental reporters began talking about a professional association partially based on the models already in place for science, agriculture, and outdoor adventure journalists. With a big push from Scripps-Howard executive David Stolberg, the Society of Environmental Journalists (SEJ) was officially founded in 1989–90. Stolberg had lobbied for the idea for a couple of years and finally found a receptive audience in the 1988 winners of a major journalism contest, the Edward J. Meeman Awards for environmental reporting. "I always believed in the value of networking," Stolberg recalled, "of the subliminal training that comes from an association with one's peers."[57]

Stolberg convinced nineteen journalists to meet in Washington, D.C., in December 1989 at the offices of the Environmental Health Center of the National Safety Council. In February 1990 a board of directors was elected, and Jim Detjen of the *Philadelphia Inquirer* was named the first president of the SEJ. There were 161 charter members. Stolberg persuaded his employer, Scripps-Howard, to provide $2,700 in start-up money, and the SEJ was incorporated as a nonprofit organization. Teya Ryan, a Turner Broadcasting producer; Bob Engelman, a journalist with Scripps-Howard; Rae Tyson of *USA Today;* and Noel Grove of *National Geographic* were elected officers. "Jim, Engelman and I were running the organization out of our newsrooms," Tyson said. "The workload grew, and we knew that as soon as we were able to afford it we would have to hire some staff."[58]

A newsletter, *SEJournal,* was created shortly thereafter, and the first national conference of environmental journalists was held in

Boulder, Colorado, in 1991. The environment got global attention in 1992, when the United Nations Conference on Environment and Development (known as the Earth Summit) in Rio de Janeiro received daily coverage for nearly two weeks. A total of 172 governments attended, along with around twenty-four hundred representatives of nongovernmental organizations and another seventeen thousand people at a parallel NGO conference. The conference led to an agreement on climate change that produced an international treaty and a controversial amendment called the Kyoto Protocol, which set mandatory targets for the reduction of greenhouse gases and generated voluminous amounts of news coverage well into the twenty-first century.

The awarding of a number of major honors, including three Pulitzer Prizes, to environmental stories in 1990 was a dramatic event in the history of environmental journalism and one that gave a boost to the fledgling SEJ. The Pulitzer winners included the *Seattle Times* for its coverage of the massive *Exxon Valdez* oil spill in Prince William Sound, Alaska, and a local newspaper's reporting on groundwater pollution in Washington, North Carolina (population nine thousand). The editorial writing award went to Tom Hylton of the *Pottstown* (Pa.) *Mercury* for a series on land preservation. (Two other Pulitzer finalists were environmental pieces.) Five of the Sigma Delta Chi Distinguished Service Awards in 1990 went to journalists for environmental coverage, as did two of the six awards given out by the Investigative Reporters and Editors group.

Environmental journalism stories had won awards in the past, as we have seen, but the attention given to the beat in 1990, helped in no small part by the coverage of the *Exxon Valdez* spill, highlighted its maturity and the receptiveness of the media to the subject matter.

A case in point came at the *Seattle Times*. The newspaper's coverage of the spill on March 24, 1989, that dumped an estimated eleven to thirty million gallons of crude oil into the Alaskan ecosystem could have begun and ended at the event itself, but the newspaper employed a team of experienced journalists that did more in-depth work, on deadline, and it illustrated how far environmental reporting had come. "The key to our coverage was the fact that we were able to step back, half a step, and write about the profound issues," said the assistant city editor, Dave Boardman, who was in charge of the story. "Not just cover what was happening day-to-day, but explain what it meant to people not living in Prince William Sound."[59] The stories included the event itself, reaction from the beaches of Alaska, the effect on the fisheries, the relationship between big oil and the state government, the regulation of the tanker industry, drinking among tanker men, and many other topics.

The visibility of environmental reporting rose with the prize-winning efforts of these journalists and others. With the increase came challenges. One of the most important issues facing the growing SEJ was its independence from organizations associated with environmental issues—businesses, government organizations, and environmental groups. The stresses and strains were not unlike those felt by the National Association of Science Writers (see chapter 3) and the Outdoor Writers Association of America (see chapter 4), but the leaders of the SEJ tried to be particularly vigilant in restricting full participation in the organization to "working journalists." Public relations professionals, who played such an important role in the OWAA, were not allowed to join the SEJ; academics were granted admission but in lesser roles.

Significantly, the SEJ's board of directors or staff did not attempt to evaluate the "objective quality" of any individual's journalism when it came to membership; it looked only at who signed the paycheck and whether it was a media employer or not. Scholar John Palen has examined the issue in depth and found that the ideal of objectivity as understood as "independence from vested interests" still held considerable sway in the environmental journalism field, although the SEJ recognized that it could not separate the individual beliefs and values of its members from the work the journalists were doing.[60]

The intensity of the debate was apparent from the SEJ's founding meeting in late 1989. For example, the meeting's location at the Environmental Health Center (EHC) offices of the National Safety Council, a nonprofit, nongovernmental, public-service organization, caused some concern among those wishing to maintain a position of independence. "There was—I hope there was—some trepidation about meeting at our place," said Bud Ward, executive director of the EHC. "Because of the need to be independent, there was some anxiety in the room."[61] Ward wound up as a key, if controversial, player in the development of the organization and its views of the proper role of persons not employed by a news organization (who came to be called associate members) in the group.[62]

Corporations offering financial support to the SEJ were turned down. Instead, Detjen and his board looked to media companies and foundations for money. Pete Myers, an ornithologist and executive director of the W. Alton Jones Foundation, was an early supporter, as was the Charles Stewart Mott Foundation. Myers and Detjen actually wrote one of the SEJ's first grant proposals in the newsroom of the *Inquirer,* "and in a remarkably short period of time we had a $50,000 grant," Detjen said.[63] The first full-time staff member, public radio producer Beth Parke, was hired in 1993 as executive director. By then the organization had more than six hundred members and $29,000 in the bank.

Funding and membership criteria remained critical issues for the SEJ leadership. Foundations associated with industry or environmental advocacy were off limits, but many media companies did not have the deep pockets or inclination to support the group. The Bacardi liquor company offered $1 million to fund an environmental journalism awards program, with the SEJ as a co-sponsor and the University of Missouri School of Journalism as its administrator, but Bacardi's offer was turned down after the board expressed its discomfort with a partnership with a multinational corporation and its public relations firm. (The SEJ eventually created and funded its own awards program.) Similarly, the Kellogg Foundation's offer of $1 million to promote sustainable agriculture was declined.

Time was spent at each board meeting examining membership roles and policies. Guidelines were written and rewritten, votes were taken, and points were debated. Detjen had to resign as an active member when he took an academic job at Michigan State University in 1994—holding one of the nation's first endowed chairs in environmental journalism—although the board appointed him as an ex officio member afterward.

LATER TRENDS

Sharon Friedman reviewed three decades of the environmental beat in 2004; she had written a not entirely optimistic essay in 1991 on the future of the field, but in 2004 she came to the conclusion that "what happened in environmental journalism during the decade [of the 1990s] was generally positive."[64] Friedman's analysis of the period credited the SEJ and the Internet with helping environmental coverage become more "sophisticated." Stories grew in complexity and intricacy to cover such topics as land use management, global warming, resource conservation, and bio-technology. Unfortunately for the field, as the stories grew more complicated and difficult to tell, newspapers, magazines, and broadcasters shrank the space allotted for them. Media owner-ship became more centralized, the demand for profits grew even greater as readership and revenues leveled off or declined, and new media forms based on the Internet provided more competition.

Economic trends, dramatic events, political and cultural leader-ship, and many other factors drive news coverage. The economist Anthony Downs described the yo-yo nature of public awareness as a five-stage "issue attention cycle."[65] He pointed to the fourth period in the cycle, where the social system realizes the high cost of solving a problem, as possibly leading to a period of discour-agement, suppression, or inattention.[66]

By the mid-1990s, environmental interest seemed to be on the downward side of the cycle.[67] Detjen blamed economic recession, which he said "shifted the public and media's attention to eco-nomic issues such as the loss of jobs and the inadequacy of health insurance."[68] The Harvard-produced magazine *Nieman Reports,* which covers news media issues, headlined its winter 1996 issue REVIVING ENVIRONMENTAL COVERAGE.[69] A survey by researchers at Michigan State University in 1996 found that 23 percent of news-paper environmental journalists and 44 percent of those work-ing for television stations were spending less time reporting about environmental issues than they had the year before.[70]

Mainstream news outlets could and did drive the social sys-tem's agenda in certain regions. The *News and Observer* in Raleigh, North Carolina, won a Pulitzer in 1996 for its coverage of the en-vironmental problems associated with corporate hog farming in its state. "Hogs were nobody's top agenda item in North Carolina, with the exception of a citizens' group concerned largely with odor from large hog farms. The *News and Observer* series changed that," recalled Melanie Sill, the series' editor.[71]

The election of George W. Bush in 2000 on a pro-energy, -oil, and -development platform increased the level of contention in Washington, D.C., and jump-started environmental coverage again, particularly over issues such as drilling for oil in the Arctic National Wildlife Refuge in Alaska. "The environment doesn't make news when green initiatives are going forward, it makes news when they are being rolled back," said one researcher. "That's because conflict makes news."[72] Almost as soon as the environment edged back toward center stage in American public life, the events of September 11, 2001, shoved it and other specialty beats to the wings again. Wars in Afghanistan and the Middle East assumed priority in news coverage. For example, Douglas Jehl was eighteen months into his new environmental beat at the *New York Times* on 9/11; within a few days, he was sent to the Middle East (he was the paper's former Cairo bureau chief). He spent six months reporting from the region before shifting stateside again. "But I think all beats in journalism became a casualty of the imperative of covering terrorism," he said.[73]

In Friedman's assessment of the news media field in 2004, she listed five important changes:

- Environmental journalists appeared to be using a larger number and wider variety of sources in their stories than in the early 1990s.
- Larger newspapers ran more investigative and enterprise stories on environmental subjects, but midsized and smaller papers ran few stories of that type.
- Local environmental issues were more prevalent in stories later in the period than earlier.
- Stories appeared with more graphics.

- Editorial support from newsroom managers for environmental journalism wavered under economic pressures.[74]

Nearly forty years had passed since the environment had become a legitimate beat at major American media outlets. "When I put my hand in the water now it comes out clean, and that's great," Bukro said in 1996. "But for that reason, people think we did our job and it's over. And of course, some people don't even remember those days and wonder what all the fuss is about. Maybe that's the price of success."[75] Jim Bruggers, an environmental reporter for several newspapers, wrote: "Sometimes I long for those days when I just wrote about buffalo in Montana."[76]

While the social system's attention to the environment ebbs and flows, it seems reasonable to conclude that the institutionalization of its coverage by the general-interest media is permanent, just as the environmental movement and the government bureaucracy built around it, industry, the courts, universities, and other societal structures are permanent. In this way, the environment has become what Everette E. Dennis called one of the "traditional news commitments."[77]

NINE

BROADCAST MEDIA

Sit in on a meeting of environmental journalists and it will not take long for the topic to turn to television news. What usually follows are comments about the poor to nonexistent job that TV does in covering the environment. There is a germ of truth in this assumption, but it is surrounded by a husk of exaggeration: in certain times and specific places, broadcast media have been responsible for important environmental journalism.

No doubt there are challenges. Jacques Rivard, a longtime Canadian Broadcasting Corporation environmental reporter, emphasized the difficulty in convincing editors to give him airtime for his work.[1] His most successful strategy, shared by many colleagues in the United States, was to package environmental issues as health or economic stories. "For example, the incidence of asthma in children living in the big cities is now endemic, and costs to the health care system are enormous," he wrote. "One contributing cause is atmospheric pollution."[2]

We have seen the print media struggle with the transition from environmental stories that were visible—coal-mining disasters, a river catching on fire, a hand stuck in a filthy lake—to the cov-

erage of issues that are often invisible, complex, and highly contentious, like global warming, endocrine disruptors, and ethanol.
Television, in particular among electronic media, often grapples
with that shift, in no small part because the "old" environmental problems—should we build a dam in this beautiful valley?—
are often extremely photogenic, while the "new" environmental
problems—how do you film a xenobiotic chemical?—are not. "In
newspapers across the country, environment reporters have been
covering these issues for years and have built-up expertise," wrote
Natalie Pawelski, a former CNN environmental correspondent.
"But, unlike newspapers, television networks don't recognize environment reporting as a real beat, one that deserves specialists."[3]
There is much less beat reporting of any kind in television newsrooms; often at the local level there are too few reporters and
producers and too many other priorities. "The bodies cost too
much and the commitment to in-depth coverage has never been
there," said David Ropeik, who worked in commercial television
news in Boston for many years.[4]

In the United States, radio news programs date from the 1920s;
regularly scheduled television news shows began shortly after
World War II. Weather-related environmental disasters were a
common story form—floods, hurricanes, and drought—as were
dramatic events like mining accidents, oil spills, and forest fires.
With the rise of environmental consciousness in the 1960s came
memorable visual images such as the *Apollo* photograph of the
Earth from the moon, the Santa Barbara oil spill, Earth Day
marchers, an ominous nuclear reactor, and others. Most of the
stories were treated as breaking news—something radio and television were particularly good at—and did not provide the depth
and context that the print media were also criticized for lacking.

In the late 1970s and early 1980s, broadcasters created programs dedicated to coverage of the environment, science, health, and the outdoors, in part as a response to those who said their reporting was superficial. Among the first regular environmental journalism shows on the radio, and the longest-lasting one, was the National Public Radio (NPR) show called *Living on Earth*.

LIVING ON EARTH

Living on Earth was the brainchild of Steve Curwood. Raised in Ohio and educated at Harvard, Curwood began his career as a print journalist in Boston, eventually winding up at the *Boston Globe* as an investigative reporter and columnist. Curwood was a man of many interests, including acting and opera, and his curiosity took him to radio news (he served as weekend host for *All Things Considered*) and longer-form narratives. In April 1991, a few months after the conclusion of the first Gulf War, *Living on Earth* debuted on National Public Radio.

The genesis of the show came from the interests of its founder. Curwood told the *Globe* that he had pondered writing a book on the environment. "But I wondered if it would be relevant two years later, so I thought of doing a radio series."[5] He traded some on-air hosting duties for production time in the studio at the Boston University public radio station, where the show began as a pilot in 1990.[6]

The first program on NPR featured stories related to the environment in the Middle East after the war: Kuwait, a conference on oil fires, desert ecology, the Saudi shoreline, Iraq, and military action and environmental planning. By the following week, the show's in-depth coverage shifted to a more typical environmental topic: water. A hydroelectric plant in Quebec, giant dams, and

Idaho salmon were the subjects. A typical show from the early days began with environmental news, and then was handed off to one of *Living on Earth*'s correspondents, who filed a nine- or ten-minute story, followed by a couple of shorter stories, perhaps an interview with a scientist or politician, and comments from listeners. Reporters from NPR member stations submitted stories as well.

Curwood, as creator and executive producer of the show, relied on the natural sound cuts that became familiar to public radio listeners. It was not uncommon for the audience to hear the wind rushing through the trees, the splash of a canoe paddle, crickets chirping, or the howling of a wolf. Peter Thomson, a founding editor at *Living on Earth,* wanted the natural sounds to carry listeners to the location of the story. "In environmental reporting, nothing is more elemental than the sense of place," he wrote. "The environment is, after all, that which surrounds us."[7]

NPR member stations were interested from the start: about one hundred stations signed on to carry the show in short order.[8] Part of the show's appeal lay in the broad nature of Curwood's concept of environmental journalism on the radio. "There's a whole field of environmental concerns that don't fit into any one category," he said. "It might be science, business, politics, economics—so it's not a field unto itself. It draws from so many different things, and they all need to be synthesized."[9] National Public Radio also had a long history of covering science, particularly at the hands of broadcast journalist Ira Flatow, who served as its science correspondent from 1971 to 1986 and became well known as the host of *Science Friday* on NPR and as a host and writer for *Newton's Apple,* a public television science program aimed at children.

Reviewers praised the content and pacing of *Living on Earth.* One commentator wrote of Curwood: "His radio shows are also organized around topics rather than individuals, and he moves rapidly but smoothly through brief, carefully edited conversations."[10]

The show became a staple in many public radio stations' schedules. By 2005, *Living on Earth* aired on nearly three hundred public stations across the United States and on Sirius satellite radio. *Living on Earth* had expanded to include a comprehensive Web page, podcasting, and reporting partnerships with the online magazine *Salon* and the University of California–Berkeley journalism school. Still, Curwood considered the show a tough sell, both to station managers and underwriters. "Environmental journalism is hard-hitting," he said. "We have to sometimes ask questions that make people uncomfortable."[11]

Curwood and the show's producers were also affected by the environmental journalism-as-advocacy charge; critics used it as a way to dismiss *Living on Earth*'s content, and some underwriters stayed away. "Industry often uses scientific doubt as a kind of tool to parry public inquiry into their practices. Which, if it weren't for the fact that the public isn't getting enough of this information, would be amusing," Curwood said.[12]

A *Living on Earth* collaboration with Michigan Public Radio and the Superior Radio Network produced the Great Lakes Radio Consortium (GLRC) in 1993, which provided environmental coverage of the Great Lakes region. A total of 140 stations signed on; the GLRC changed its name to Environmental Report in fall 2006.[13]

TURNER, CNN, AND THE ENVIRONMENT

Ted Turner secured himself a place in American journalism history when he created Cable News Network (CNN), the first twenty-four-hour news network. Given his personal interests, it was not surprising that he was instrumental in developing environmental journalism on television, pushing his stations to create the groundbreaking environmental news and documentary shows *Network Earth, Earth Matters,* and *Next@CNN* on TBS and CNN.

Science shows had been around on television since the days of Mr. Wizard (Don Herbert), who debuted on WNBQ-TV in Chicago in 1951. Another early popular science show was the MIT-produced *Science Reporter,* which ran on Boston station WGBH from 1955 to 1967 and featured a professor giving a lecture in front of a camera. No one made better science documentaries than the PBS show *Nova,* which started in the mid-1970s. (The word *news* is thought to come from the medieval Latin word *nova,* or "new things.") An occasional *National Geographic* TV documentary or Jacques Cousteau special contained some journalism, but Turner and CNN broadened the subject matter beyond science to the environment and all its political, social, cultural, and economic influences and attempted to treat it as a regular news subject.

For Turner, it was a labor of love. He came to his environmental interests the old-fashioned way—through hunting, fishing, sailing, and other outdoor activities. Turner collected and cared for animals as a child and, like Teddy Roosevelt decades before, learned taxidermy to preserve them.[14] As an adult, Turner was active in Ducks Unlimited in the 1970s, attending auctions and dinners and donating trips to his plantation in South Carolina to the highest bidder. The Ducks Unlimited mission of saving vanishing wetlands fit with Turner's somewhat gloomy outlook on the state of the world, particularly on the issue of overpopulation. In the late 1970s and early 1980s, Turner was deeply influenced by books on the subject, particularly *The Limits to Growth* from the Club of Rome and *The Global 2000 Report to the President,* a federal study commissioned by President Carter and issued in 1980. Both presented neo-Malthusian views of the state of the planet. "That [Carter] report was really, I think, the cornerstone for his philosophical views," said one of his friends. "Ted soaked it up. He just grabbed it."[15] Turner handed out gift-wrapped copies of the slim volume to his friends at the holidays.[16] Carter appointed Turner to the President's Council for Energy Efficiency.

Turner began CNN in 1980. *Time* magazine photographer Barbara Pyle, whom Turner had met at the America's Cup yacht races, was hired at the network as vice president for the environment; she was responsible for programming as well as company policy on environmental matters, "meaning everything from hour-long documentaries to compact fluorescent light bulbs and company car pools," recalled Peter Dykstra, a CNN colleague who produced many of the environmental journalism programs.[17]

Pyle had grown up in Oklahoma, where her parents founded the first Audubon Society chapter in the state, and she shared Turner's environmental interests. "If there was a person who educated Ted to the environment, it was Barbara and not the other way around," said Ira Miskin, a CNN executive, in 1995. "Despite what Barbara may say and despite what Ted believes, Barbara Pyle is the environmental conscience of Turner Broadcasting. Ted embraced those ideas, but Barbara has been talking about saving the environment since she could talk."[18]

Among CNN's first reporters on the air was John Holliman, who was billed as a "farm correspondent" and frequently did stories on nature and the environment. CNN also had a science unit. Pyle was asked to oversee environmental documentaries on subjects such as population, global warming, the health of the oceans, energy use, and nuclear disaster. Weekly half-hour shows, with titles such as *Future Watch* and *Science and Technology Week,* were aired in the 1980s.

Eventually Turner expanded his environmental coverage to include Cousteau; the CNN boss and his two sons had spent a week with the French captain on board his research vessel *Calypso* on the Amazon River in 1982 and loved it. He reached an agreement to fund Cousteau's documentaries. "I gave him $4 million for his work this year," Turner said. "We'll get four hours of programming out of it. Of course, I'm losing my shirt on it. That's double the budget of network programs. But at least I'm keeping Cousteau operating. He's on my team."[19]

In the 1980s there was little other environmental journalism on television. One of the nation's critics of environmental news coverage on television (or lack thereof), Sierra Club president Carl Pope, wrote: "Ted Turner's cable outlets cover the environment and population issues in much more depth than the competition because Turner has made it clear that he cares and is interested in these subjects."[20] Pope blamed television's obsession with celebrity news and tabloid gossip for pushing out news and current affairs programming from the airwaves.

In 1990 TBS began a half-hour newsmagazine show called *Earth Beat*. Renamed *Network Earth* the following year, the show aired first on TBS and later on CNN. Teya Ryan was senior producer and codeveloper of *Network Earth* and an early leader in the Society of Environmental Journalists. Ryan had begun her career as a print reporter in Canada, eventually moving to Los Angeles to work for public television at KCET-TV as a documentary producer. The show had a strong pro-environment viewpoint, which is why, according to Ryan, it was initially aired on TBS although it was created by a CNN production staff.[21] "Perhaps most important, *Network Earth* is a program that focuses on solutions,"

Ryan wrote in 1991. "We let our audience know there are an-swers, that there are ways they can influence the destiny of life on the Earth."[22] Shows included topics such as the effects of inter-national conflict on the Panamanian rain forest, global warming, nuclear waste, water pollution, pesticides, and hazardous chemi-cals. The environment news desk had about fifteen staffers at its peak. TBS eventually dropped the program after a few years, and on CNN it was renamed again, this time as *Earth Matters.*

Turner also funded other television shows that did some en-vironmental journalism. One of his holdings, WTBS, presented a quarterly series called *World of Audubon* by the National Audubon Society beginning in the mid-1980s. The show featured mostly personality profiles of scientists (such as biologist Margaret Ow-ings) and celebrities (such as retired anchorman Walter Cronkite); Turner provided $200,000 for the first episode, but the show be-gan to become self-sufficient through advertising sales.[23] The program tackled some tough issues, including a 1991 report on the conflicts between ranchers and wildlife in the American West from which the Ford Motor Company pulled its commercials.[24] Another Audubon show critical of the logging industry caused Ford, Citicorp, and Exxon to threaten to yank their advertising; Turner chose to lose the $250,000 in ad revenue rather than revise or not air the program.[25]

Entertainment programming with environmental themes popped up all over the schedule. On WTBS alone, in the 1990–91 season, 360 hours of environmental programming were shown.[26] Included in the schedule was an animated children's program that featured Captain Planet and the Planeteers, a superhero and his team who fought pollution, acid rain, and other problems.

CNN continued to air environmental documentaries through the 1990s, including an examination of the Rio de Janeiro climate meetings in 1992, but none of the shows earned great ratings. Meanwhile, ABC News was about the only other network to devote substantial resources to environmental coverage in the 1990s. A segment on the nightly news called "American Agenda" ran stories on the environment by correspondents Barry Serafin, Erin Hayes, and Ned Potter, under the eye of producer Bob Aglow. No one at CBS, NBC, or public television's news shows was assigned to cover the environment beat full-time. Local television news covered environmental stories with full or nearly full-time reporters in some markets, such as Seattle and Salt Lake City, but they mainly followed the lead of the networks. "Let's face it," said one reporter from a TV station in the Southwest in 1996. "Unless some chemical spill kills somebody, environmental stories are not lead material. They're still important and I think the audience still cares about them. But it won't lead the newscast because it doesn't bleed."[27]

Turner Broadcasting merged with Time Warner in 1996; AOL and Time Warner's ill-fated merger happened in 2001. With these actions, Ted Turner slowly began to lose control of the company; with his declining influence came the end for most of the environmental programming, including the journalism practiced on shows such as *Earth Matters.*

The work produced on *Earth Matters* included coverage of mountaintop removal in the coal country of West Virginia, the health of the oceans, PCB contaminations in Alabama, and snowmobiling in Yellowstone National Park. Some stories aired on *Earth Matters* were also edited for length and used on other CNN broadcasts.

Earth Matters was canceled in 2001, at about the same time as the science and technology shows got the ax. It ran for about eight years, by far the longest-running environmental news show on television. "Why did *Earth Matters* work?" asked Natalie Pawelski, one of its hosts. "I think it was because we stayed away from the thou-shalt-recycle, thou-shalt-hug-a-tree, activist-oriented school of environmental coverage. Instead, we used storytelling to illuminate environmental issues. In doing so, we tricked everyday viewers into paying attention to environmental news."[28]

After *Earth Matters* was canceled, the network continued with a combined science/technology/environment show called *Next@ CNN;* that show was put on hiatus after the events of 9/11 and much of the team was converted to covering the war in the Middle East and Afghanistan. *Next@CNN* was finally canceled in April 2005, about the time the last of the employees who devoted their full-time attention to the environment were laid off or quit. Camille Feanny was the last CNN producer assigned to the environment beat; she left the network rather than take another assignment. At the time, Feanny said she was the last television journalist at any major network covering the environment full-time.[29]

Turner never lost his interest in environmental causes. By 2002, he was America's largest private landowner.[30] His two million acres (an area larger than the state of Delaware) were spread over ten states, and he was the biggest bison rancher in the country with a herd of thirty thousand. Turner's environmental interests led him to fund fish and wildlife research on his properties, hire scientists, and establish the Turner Endangered Species Fund, a nonprofit organization to manage the lands. His foundation gave more to environmental causes than did any other single foundation in the year 2000. In June 2005 Turner addressed CNN employees at a twenty-fifth anniversary bash and asked for more international and environmental coverage, instead of "pervert of the day" stories.[31] The assembled staffers laughed and applauded. In May 2006, Turner left the board of Time Warner and the businesses he had spent more than thirty-five years building.

One of CNN's producers, Gary Streiker, found a new media niche in 2006 at the online site Yahoo.com. He began a video news show called *Assignment Earth;* stories ran from two to four minutes and were accessible through the Web site. His stories had a hard-news feel and tended to focus on global rather than local issues. "In the future it will all be 'news on demand,' and my theory is there is a demand for this news, and the number of clicks will show it," Streiker said. "All we have to do is make these stories compelling enough."[32]

OTHER ENVIRONMENTAL BROADCAST NEWS

While Turner was working on documentaries and news shows on the planet in the 1980s and 1990s, rival television channels were created and aimed at special market niches. Two of the most successful channels that frequently dealt with environmental issues were the Discovery Channel and the Outdoor Life Network.

The Discovery Channel began on June 17, 1985, with 156,000 subscribers and a program called "Iceberg Alley." Founder John Hendricks had created the idea for a station in 1982 and began buying up nature documentaries, many from the BBC. Hendricks started the channel with an investment from a large cable operator, Tele-Communications Inc., and expanded it to international television, multimedia and online ventures, and retail chains. Hendricks also bought or added channels such as Travel Channel, Learning Channel, and Animal Planet (with its highly popular "crocodile hunter," Steve Irwin).

Animal films were relatively inexpensive to produce or purchase, but documentaries on science and the environment could be much more costly. The first year, revenue was only $200,000, but after a little more than a decade Hendricks had used an aggressive growth strategy to create a $700 million business.[33] After ten years in business, the Discovery network had surpassed CNN to rank second (behind TBS) in the highest cable penetration in the United States.[34]

Hendricks relied heavily on nature, science, outdoors, and environmental documentaries and shows, but he considered himself in the business of nonfiction programming. "Non-fiction for a long time was regarded as programming for a minority audience," he said. "What we've proved and what cable TV has proved is that it's really for a majority audience."[35]

Discovery's early programming featured a plethora of dinosaurs and sharks; after more than twenty years on the air, documentaries seemed to get less time in favor of shows about motorcycles, war history, and auto repairs. "There's been a real collapse of the genres," said Clark Bunting, Discovery's executive vice president. "There are very few pure science or pure history programs around. Over a 19-year history, you've got to evolve to survive. It's a Darwinian environment out there."[36] The company described itself as featuring "culture, travel, history, wildlife, and lifestyle content" in a 2006 press release announcing its launch of a 100th and 101st network.[37] In 2005, Discovery Channel and ESPN became the first cable networks to cross the ninety-million subscriber mark.[38]

While the Discovery Channel grew out of nature shows and shark attacks, cable competitors looked to unmet markets; hunting, fishing, camping, and other topics related to the environment and explored by outdoor writers proved a successful formula. The Outdoors Channel, begun in California in 1990, and the Sportsman Channel, a Wisconsin-based company started in 2003, represented the format.[39] Perhaps the most successful was the Outdoor Life Network (OLN), founded in 1995 on the idea that what was needed in the cable landscape were stories about outdoor recreation, conservation, wilderness, and adventure/travel programming. OLN went through many ownership changes in its first few years (it was not created by the venerable hook-and-bullet magazine *Outdoor Life,* but rather paid a licensing fee for the use of the name). Eventually OLN was sold to the telecommunications giant Comcast, which shifted its focus away from outdoor programming to attract a broader, younger audience. "We started with hunting and fishing, which remained the base of our programming for years," said Roger Werner, OLN's first boss. "But we had a library of documentaries and some instructional programming on skiing and snowboarding and such sports. Because Times Mirror was one of the partners, we also had access to *Field and Stream* magazine and did some programs in conjunction with them."[40]

Some of the growth of OLN was attributed to nonoutdoor programming, particularly its exclusive daily coverage of the Tour de France bicycle race at a time when American audiences were becoming more and more interested in that event. By 2004, the channel's most popular show was on bull riding.[41] But the network also ran important original environmental programming, including a documentary series called *Earth Rescue.*

OLN changed its name to Versus in 2006 and saw itself as upstart competition for ESPN for a general sports audience, adding professional hockey to its programming in 2005.[42] It had begun with 4.8 million households in 1995 and had grown to nearly 65 million in a decade.[43]

THE ENVIRONMENTAL JOURNALISM CENTER

Traditional news values such as prominence, conflict, proximity, timeliness, and drama set priorities for broadcast journalists. Coverage of environmental stories on television is also affected by the availability of dramatic visual images, as well as by more practical considerations such as deadlines, cost, and convenience.[44] The challenges faced by broadcasters are often quite different from those confronted by their print brethren.

Audience surveys from the 1990s seemed to indicate that the public consistently ranked the environment in its top ten list of important issues. Yet the amount of local and network broadcast coverage did not reflect this high level of public interest. News directors worried about a lack of expertise among their producers and reporters on what could be a very complicated subject.

To help them, the trade association for broadcasters in the United States, the Radio and Television News Directors Association, through its educational arm, the Radio and Television News Directors Foundation (RTNDF), formed the Environmental Journalism Center in 1991. "The goal of the Center is to accurately inform reporters about environmental, science and health issues and to help you cover them in informed and compelling ways," according to an introductory statement.[45]

The center performed several functions for broadcasters, including serving as an information resource, a clearinghouse for contacting expert sources and documents, and as a host for roundtable discussions: "Its goal is to put the tools needed to understand environmental issues into the hands of as many radio and television news professionals as possible so that they may make their own informed journalistic decisions."[46] Story ideas included air and water quality, sprawl and other development issues, climate change, endangered species, wetlands, and others.

In 1991 the center published a handbook, produced by the Environmental Health Center, called *Covering Key Environmental Issues,* and by 1999 it was in its fourth edition. The handbook included story topics, key sources, story ideas, and trends. An appendix sorted out the alphabet soup of government acronyms, and a glossary defined technical terms. Three more resource guides, on the social, economic, and environmental impacts of sprawl, the science of hormone mimics and endocrine disruptors, and children's health, were produced. Further training tools, including a "best practices" videotape, were also made available. The RTNDF and the Society of Environmental Journalists combined to provide members with a weekly story tip sheet.

Surveys taken for the RTNDF showed that viewers wanted environmental news. Respondents to a 2006 survey ranked the environment at No. 6 in a list of "subjects people want to know about," and two other environment-related topics, weather (No. 1) and health care (No. 5), were also high on the list.[47]

Despite the best efforts of the RTNDF, one 2005 study reported that environmental coverage had dropped to nearly record low levels on the three national broadcast networks' nightly newscasts. Researcher Andrew Tyndall found that coverage of what he called "environment and man-made disasters" totaled only 168 minutes in all of 2005.[48] Data from 1988 through 2005 showed that the only years with less coverage were 1994 and 2003. Tyndall separated "natural disasters and weather" from his analysis; since 1988, the networks have devoted about 2 percent of their time to environmental stories and 4 percent of their time to natural disasters. Peak network TV coverage during his study was 1989, the year of the *Exxon Valdez* oil spill and the alleged cold fusion breakthrough.

Tyndall's study echoed other findings, including a 2004 survey that gave a generally discouraging assessment of environmental news on television, despite important stories told on public television by journalist Bill Moyers, the program *Front Line,* and occasional pieces on commercial television at the Weather Channel and from network reporters Bill Blakemore and Ned Potter of ABC,

Anne Thompson at NBC, and Miles O'Brien at CNN. One of the researchers said, "In a world of 'live, local and late-breaking' news, environmental stories of today lack the qualities that appeal to news managers, newsroom consultants, and advertisers."[49] That survey blamed the complexity of the environmental beat as being too difficult to translate into good television news: "It's hard to bring a sense of urgency to an issue with consequences that will not be felt for 10 or 20 years."[50]

PART III

ON THE HORIZON

TEN

CONCLUSION

Climate change, natural disasters, genetic discoveries, land use, workplace hazards—each day's headlines are full of environmental stories. Since the early days of the Republic, stories about the environment have played an important role in the fabric of the country. The precursors of modern environmental journalists were writers of ancient religious texts, outdoor adventurers, scientists and farmers, and dreamers and philosophers. Some of their key environmental questions are still relevant and urgent today. One consistent theme is that inherent tensions exist within a for-profit economic system that demands a certain level of resource use. Coupled with a basic desire not to foul one's own nest—minimal pollution, poisoning, and pillaging—this basic conflict will continue to provide journalists with material, in whatever media they operate. And no matter the economic system, people need to be housed, clothed, and fed, and natural resource management is a key ingredient in meeting those needs.

While resource use and a clean environment are hardy perennials in the environmental journalism garden, some issues wax and wane in their importance. After being ignored or dismissed for years, species depletion, for example, began to be mentioned by journalists in the late nineteenth century as the bison and passenger pigeon suffered catastrophic losses. But only a few decades earlier, the last pair of great auks had been killed off the coast of Iceland in June 1844, and their extinction did not generate extensive news coverage.[1] The environment itself as a news topic ebbs and flows; as discussed in chapter 8, there was a flood of interest in 1989–90, and again in early 2001; and then a drought after 9/11. The popularity of former vice president Al Gore's documentary on climate change, *An Inconvenient Truth,* and his Nobel Peace Prize seemed to kick-start coverage again in 2006–7.

While environmental journalism faces its own peculiar set of problems, one challenge faced by all modern journalists is the role of new media. Environmental journalists and their employers are responding and will continue to adapt to these in a variety of ways.

NEW MEDIA

While television, particularly local and network news shows, struggled with the complexities in coverage of the environment, several forms of so-called new media stepped in to provide information in different niches. Online and print/fax services such as Greenwire, Environmental News Service, and Environmental News Network began in the early 1990s to provide news on the environment and science; hard copies and faxes soon gave way to electronic distribution via the World Wide Web and e-mail.

Greenwire, under the care of former *New York Times* environment reporter Phil Shabecoff, began in 1991 as a print newsletter, was sold to *National Journal* (a Times Mirror company) in 1996, and was sold again to E&E Publishing in 2000. E&E linked Greenwire with *Environment and Energy Daily* in a Washington, D.C.–based service.[2] At the time of the sale, E&E employed twelve full-time reporters and editors to cover energy and the environment.[3]

Environmental News Service (ENS) was designed as a daily wire service for environmental journalism. ENS began in 1990 in the hands of Sunny Lewis, a former news broadcaster who was then working in Vancouver, British Columbia, and Jim Crabtree, who became managing editor. Independently owned, ENS used the work of freelance correspondents from around the world. The use of experts from the fields of business, law, biology, geography, and others as roving journalists set ENS apart. It gained credibility in its early years from a series of reports on the environmental consequences of the first Gulf War.

Another early innovator was Environmental News Network (ENN). Begun as a printed monthly report called *Environmental News Briefing* in 1993, ENN shifted to a Web-based format in 1995 at enn.com. Stephen Schowengerdt, a former reporter with the *Salt Lake City Deseret News,* was its founder and first editor.

ENN's first objective was to report and publish environmental news on the Web, but the expense of such an operation became too much to bear by 2001. "ENN saw itself as a gatherer of news," publisher Jerry Kay said in 2004. "They wanted to generate original content themselves, which was a noble cause, and they did it well."[4] Published by a for-profit company owned by shareholders but not publicly traded, ENN needed to make money. "How many writers can you employ to cover the world's environmental news?" Kay asked.[5]

ENN shifted its focus to become an environmental news aggregator, first posting news daily on its Web site, then moving to a Tuesday-through-Friday schedule. ENN was a member of the Associated Press wire service and used its material, as well as stories from the Reuters news service. Feature stories came from sources such as *E/The Environmental Magazine,* while regular columnists included high-profile environmentalists and scientists such as David Suzuki. Original content included the weekly *ENN Radio* show and ninety-second vignettes called "EarthNews Radio," which were syndicated nationally as well as broadcast on the Web. Interactive polls and quizzes also dotted the site. Podcasts, daily e-mails, desktop headlines, and other features were added.

Environmental Health Sciences, a not-for-profit organization working to increase public understanding of environmental exposures and human health, started an environmental news service and Web site in June 2003 called Environmental Health News (EHN). It grew out of Pete Myers's long career as a Ph.D. in animal ecology, a senior vice president of the Audubon Society, director of the W. Alton Jones Foundation (1990–2001), and as co-author, with scientist Theo Colborn and journalist Dianne Dumanowski, of the book *Our Stolen Future.* Environmental Health News was designed as a news aggregator Web site; the number of environmental news stories available to post on the site surprised Myers. "When I started EHN, I expected we'd be lucky to encounter 30 or 40 stories on any given day," he said in July 2006. "We average over 140 articles per day now and occasionally have exceeded 300. Admittedly not all of them are of the same importance, but what I've learned through this experience is that every day, 365 days per year, quality reporting is being published about environment and health, and lots of it—in local, regional and national outlets, on every continent except Antarctica."[6]

Myers, as the person in charge of a news aggregator, was in a position to evaluate the state of environmental journalism in the early years of the twenty-first century. He was not surprised by the event-driven coverage—Hurricane Katrina, mad cow disease, bird flu, SARS, chemical spills—but he identified four trends that went beyond the drama of the moment: climate coverage, energy use, the effects of environmental contaminants on human health, and local water quality. Myers estimated that more than one million people per month read EHN headlines and RSS feeds.[7]

By 2004, bloggers had also established themselves as part of the new media landscape. While debates continued over whether bloggers were journalists (or did journalism), there was less controversy about the number of readers attracted to their Web sites. By early 2006, one blog index listed more than seven hundred environmental blogs; some (Worldchanging, Gristmill) were a part of online magazines, while others were personal, introspective, or musing. Some blogs had specific focuses, such as green businesses or climate. Often highly opinionated, snarky, and culturally aware, blogs also had an immediacy and lightening-fast feedback loop that kept the writers on their toes. "In the interest of fairness," said Alex Steffen of Worldchanging, "journalists are obliged to give somebody who is doing something awful, or who holds a distinctly minority scientific opinion, a voice equal to that of those who are trying to alert people to a problem purely out of public interest."[8] Another popular green blogger, David Roberts of Gristmill, compared bloggers to the pamphleteers of early American journalism. "Having thousands of readers bird-dogging you keeps you pretty honest," he said.[9]

A few mainstream journalists added blogging to their daily chores. At the *Seattle Post-Intelligencer*, veteran environmental reporters Lisa Stiffler and Robert McClure began blogging in November 2005. The two journalists approached their online work at Dateline Earth differently from many environmental bloggers, using much of their space for localizing stories. "We wanted really to be able to write about the stuff that was falling through the cracks, whether it was something quirky and local or something national or international that was beyond the scope of what the *P-I*'s usual coverage includes," Stiffler said.[10]

AN EVOLVING FIELD

Blogging was made possible by technological change, which has been an influence on the craft of journalism since Gutenberg. In addition, professional practices, commercial pressures, and news routines all affect journalism, and all came under question during the first years of the twenty-first century. Commercial pressures were evident in falling newspaper readership, a continuing consolidation of ownership, and declining revenue, among other stresses. News routines, once as simple as a beat and one deadline per day, evolved into overlapping subject matter, video and audio components, and an Internet-driven deadline every minute.

Even storytelling was called into question. "Everything is in shades of gray," said one reporter from a Florida newspaper. "There aren't good guys and bad guys. The good guys are a little bad and the bad guys aren't all bad. So that's why it's so hard to report the way we used to—good versus bad."[11] A critical examination of professional practices, particularly the standard of all-sides storytelling and an Enlightenment-influenced detachment from the subject matter, provided some of the most controversy in the world of environmental journalism.

A common thread running through the new media landscape is a departure from the conventional objective role of the journalist. Bloggers, environmental magazines, online video producers, and others usually report and write for the new media with a point of view. The "traditional" standards of journalism—in place for most of the twentieth century, if not longer—were again in flux. Michael Kinsley, in the online magazine *Slate,* said that objectivity was yesterday's news standard. Writing about television news, Kinsley said that "objectivity is not a horse to bet the network on. Or the newspaper, either."[12] Most of the rest of the journalism world, including European newspapers and American newsmagazines, gave up on objectivity years ago, he asserted.

One practice related to objectivity—telling both sides of a story—was heavily criticized for failing to serve readers and listeners when it was performed at the expense of accuracy. "If the opinions of columnists count for too much in the American press, the intelligence of reporters is institutionally underused," wrote Ian Buruma in the *New York Times.* "The problem is that there are not always two sides to a story. Someone reporting on the persecution of Jews in Germany in 1938 would not have added 'balance' by quoting Joseph Goebbels."[13] Indeed, stories in the environmental journalism field that "balanced" lung cancer researchers with pro-tobacco industry scientists, or epidemiologists with those who denied a link between HIV and AIDS, seemed ridiculous a few years after they were published.

In 2006 the online magazine *Grist* asked the objectivity question of five of the nation's top mainstream environmental reporters.[14] Four of the five were not comfortable in an advocacy role, but all five had little use for the "he said, she said" stories of the beat. Felicity Barringer and Andrew Revkin of the *New York Times* said that the science should speak for itself; Revkin said his "activism" came from the subjects he chose to write about, such as climate change and biodiversity loss. "There is something of a false dichotomy in the notion that being an objective reporter is at odds with being a 'concerned citizen.' Of course I'm concerned about the quality of the environment," he said.[15] Ross Gelbspan, retired from the *Boston Globe,* said his work on climate change moved him from reporter to "advocate to semi-activist, although it's critically important to me not to say or write anything of substance that I have not documented or verified."[16]

As we have seen, serving niche audiences, which has a long history in American journalism, is alive and well in environmental journalism. Another example is the online magazine *Grist,* founded by Chip Giller in 1999. He had experience writing for the alternative mountain west weekly *High Country News,* worked at Greenwire, and served as a media person for Earth Day Network and its leader, Denis Hayes.

Grist began as a project at Earth Day Network. Based in Seattle, *Grist* attempted to link news of the environment to other important national issues. In 2003, Giller broke *Grist* from its Earth Day Network beginnings and formed an independent nonprofit organization to run the online magazine. Funding came from foundations and from e-mail and online solicitations aimed at regular readers.

Giller was less interested in the objective model of journalism than in environmental change; as such, the stories often were written with an edge or a touch of humor not often found in mainstream media. (Sample headline: RELAX, IT'S JUST POLLUTION.) "At *Grist,* we think that the best journalism inspires activism, and that the best activism is informed by outstanding journalism," Giller said. "Ecological crises are growing in urgency each day. During this important time, *Grist* is equipping average citizens, especially people in their 20s and 30s, with the information they need to help protect the environment."[17]

In 2006, *Grist* reported on the connections between poverty and the environment in a seven-week series that it said had 2.6

million readers.[18] The stories were influenced by the devastation in the wake of Hurricane Katrina in 2005. "We hope that when people think of environmental reporting, what comes to mind wouldn't simply be salmon protection or fights about national parks," Giller said. "We're asking that journalism begin to connect environmentalism back to communities in which people live."[19] *Grist* also attempted to put the news into historical perspective. The series included a historical essay tracing the elitist elements of the modern environmental movement to some of its early twentieth-century participants from the social upper crust such as Theodore Roosevelt.[20]

According to data from the *Grist* Web site, more than a half million people read the magazine each month in 2006. Forty percent of its readers were in their twenties and thirties.[21] That statistic on younger readers should have caught the attention of old media.

As commercial pressures, news routines, and professional practices work themselves out, what will environmental journalism look like in the years to come? Will environmental coverage, with its implied or stated values of ecosystem protection and other norms, represent a new form of values-based journalism? Or will it be an extension of the "moral journalism" sometimes practiced by investigative reporters? Or will a "social responsibility" role become a dominant standard, with environmental reporting leading by example? Environmental journalism has continued to ebb and flow, from its beginnings in ancient texts and Izaak Walton through nature writers and science writers to the beat system and online presentations. Continuity comes from the journalists who navigate the stream and tell the stories of the interaction of humans and the environment.

NOTES

FOREWORD

1. The member of the staff of CEQ with particular responsibility for drafting the land use legislation was William K. Reilly, later administrator of the Environmental Protection Agency in the George H. W. Bush administration. While the National Land Use Policy Act proposed by Nixon passed the Senate twice, it failed to pass in the House and eventually died.

2. These events are laid out in considerable detail in my book *Politics, Pollution, and Pandas* (Washington, D.C.: Island, 2003), which contains much material on environmental programs and the press.

PREFACE

1. Peter Hay, *Main Currents in Western Environmental Thought* (Bloomington: Indiana University Press, 2002), 10.

2. Ibid., 10.

3. That doesn't make me unusual. Research has shown that childhood experiences are key factors in adult careers, including the instance of environmental activists and the time they spent outdoors as kids. See Louise Chawla, "Childhood Place Attachments," in *Human Behavior and Environment: Advances in Theory and Research,* vol. 12, *Place Attachments,* ed. Irwin Altman and Setha M. Low (New York: Plenum, 1992), 63–84.

CHAPTER ONE

1. Douglas Quenqua, "Raelian Clone Claim Earns Serious Copy," *PR Week,* 6 January 2003, 24.

2. Chris Mooney, "Blinded by Science," *Columbia Journalism Review,* November/December 2004, 33.

3. "Journalist Rues Role in Rael Claim," Associated Press, 10 January 2003.

4. For an examination of the Raelian movement, see Susan J. Palmer, *Aliens Adored: Rael's UFO Religion* (New Brunswick, N.J.: Rutgers University Press, 2004).

5. Brenda Branswell, "Raelians Had Chortle over Cloning," *Montreal Gazette,* 9 October 2003, A8.

6. Nell Boyce and James M. Pethokoukis, "Clowns or Cloners?" *U.S. News and World Report,* 13 January 2003, 48.

7. Mooney, "Blinded by Science," 33.

8. Boyce and Pethokoukis, "Clowns or Cloners?" 48.

9. Len Ackland, *Making a Real Killing* (Albuquerque: University of New Mexico Press, 1999).

10. David Backes, *Canoe Country: An Embattled Wilderness* (Minocqua, Wis.: NorthWord, 1991).

11. Stuart Allan, Barbara Adam, and Cynthia Carter, *Environmental Risks and the Media* (New York: Routledge, 1999); Michael A. Kamrin, Dolores J. Katz, and Martha L. Walter, *Reporting on Risk: A Journalist's Handbook on Environmental Risk Assessment* (Ann Arbor: Michigan Sea Grant Program, 1995); Regina Lundgren and Andrea McMakin, *Risk Communication: A Handbook for Communicating Environmental, Safety, and Health Risks* (Columbus, Ohio: Battelle, 1998); and Peter Sandman and others, *Environmental Risk and the Press: An Exploratory Assessment* (New Brunswick, N.J.: Transaction, 1987).

12. See, for example, Anders Hansen, ed., *The Mass Media and Environmental Issues* (Leicester, Eng.: Leicester University Press, 1993); and Alison Anderson, *Media, Culture and the Environment* (New Brunswick, N.J.: Rutgers University Press, 1997).

13. See, for example, Julia Corbett, *Communicating Nature: How We Create and Understand Environmental Messages* (Washington, D.C.: Island, 2007); Robert Cox, *Environmental Communication in the Public Sphere* (Thousand

Oaks, Calif.: Sage, 2006); John S. Dryzek, *The Politics of the Earth: Environmental Discourses,* 2nd ed. (New York: Oxford University Press, 2005); Mark Meister and Phyllis M. Japp, *Enviropop: Studies in Environmental Rhetoric and Popular Culture* (Westport, Conn.: Praeger, 2002); Lea J. Parker, *Ecoculture: Environmental Messages in Music, Art, and Literature* (Dubuque, Iowa: Kendall Hunt, 2002); James Shanahan and Katherine McComas, *Nature Stories: Depictions of the Environment and Their Effects* (Cresskill, N.J.: Hampton, 1999); Rom Harré, Jens Brockmeier, and Peter Mühlhäusler, *Greenspeak: A Study of Environmental Discourse* (Thousand Oaks, Calif.: Sage, 1999); Lisa M. Benton and John R. Short, *Environmental Discourse and Practice* (Oxford: Blackwell, 1999); Craig Waddell, ed., *Landmark Essays on Rhetoric and the Environment* (Hillsdale, N.J.: Lawrence Erlbaum, 1997); George Myerson and Yvonne Rydin, *The Language of Environment: A New Rhetoric* (Vancouver: University of British Columbia Press, 1996); Carl G. Herndl and Stuart C. Brown, eds., *Green Culture: Environmental Rhetoric in Contemporary America* (Madison: University of Wisconsin Press, 1996); James G. Cantrill and Christine L. Oravec, eds., *The Symbolic Earth: Discourse and Our Creation of the Environment* (Lexington: University Press of Kentucky, 1996); and Bruce A. Williams and Albert R. Matheny, *Democracy, Dialogue, and Environmental Disputes: The Contested Languages of Social Regulation* (New Haven, Conn.: Yale University Press, 1995).

14. See, for example, Deborah Blum and Mary Knudson, eds., *A Field Guide for Science Writers* (New York: Oxford University Press, 1997); Lea J. Parker, *Environmental Communication: Messages, Media and Methods: A Handbook for Advocates and Organizations* (Dubuque, Iowa: Kendall Hunt, 1997); and Bernadette West, Peter M. Sandman, and Michael R. Greenberg, *The Reporter's Environmental Handbook* (New Brunswick, N.J.: Rutgers University Press, 1995).

15. Ted Kerasote, "A Short History of Hunting in America," in *State of the Wild 2006,* ed. Sharon Guynup (Washington, D.C.: Island, 2006), 100.

16. William Dietrich, *The Final Forest: The Battle for the Last Great Trees of the Pacific Northwest* (New York: Simon and Schuster, 1992).

17. Guy Berger, "Environmental Journalism Meets the 21st Century," *Intermedia* 30, no. 5 (December 2002): 10.

18. Neil Smelzer, *Theory of Collective Behavior* (Chicago: Free Press, 1963).

19. David E. Shi, *The Simple Life: Plain Living and High Thinking in American Culture* (New York: Oxford University Press, 1985).

20. Herbert Gans, *Deciding What's News* (New York: Vintage, 1979).

21. George A. Donohue, Philip J. Tichenor, and Clarice Olien, "A Guard Dog Perspective on the Role of the Media," *Journal of Communication* 45 (1995): 115–32.

22. See, for example, Julie J. Andsager and Leiott Smiley, "Evaluating the Public Information: Shaping News Coverage of the Silicone Implant Controversy," *Public Relations Review* 24 (1998): 183–201.

23. Frank Durham, "Exposed by Katrina: The Gulf Between the President and the Press," *Critical Studies in Mass Communication* 23, no. 1 (March 2006): 81–84.

24. Marc Fisher, "Essential Again," *American Journalism Review* 27, no. 5 (October/November 2005): 18–22.

25. Corinna Zarek, "Katrina Clampdown," *News Media and the Law* 29, no. 4 (Fall 2005): 4–7.

26. Peter Hay's book, *Main Currents in Western Environmental Thought,* also reflects this idea.

27. For example, A. Clay Schoenfeld posited that the roots of the specialized environmental magazine came from three sources: nature study/ outdoor recreation, professional natural resource management, and science/technology. See A. Clay Schoenfeld, "The Environmental Movement as Reflected in the *American Magazine,*" *Journalism Quarterly* 60, no. 3 (Autumn 1983): 470–75.

CHAPTER TWO

1. Edward Chauncey Baldwin, *The Prophet* (New York: Thomas Nelson and Son, 1927), 29–30.

2. Doug Underwood, *From Yahweh to Yahoo!: The Religious Roots of the Secular Press* (Champaign: University of Illinois Press, 2002), 21.

3. Ibid., 20.

4. Ezekiel 34:16 (New Revised Standard Version [NRSV]).

5. James L. Crouthamel, *Bennett's New York Herald and the Rise of the Popular Press* (Syracuse, N.Y.: Syracuse University Press, 1989), 95.

6. Barbara Lounsberry, *The Art of Fact: Contemporary Artists of Nonfiction* (Westport, Conn.: Greenwood, 1990), 37–64.

7. Art Kaul, "Hunter S. Thompson," in *Dictionary of Literary Biography*, vol. 185, *American Literary Journalists, 1945–1995* (Detroit: Gale, 1997), 311–23.

8. Theodore L. Glasser and James S. Ettema, "Investigative Journalism and the Moral Order," *Critical Studies in Mass Communication* 6, no. 1 (March 1989): 8.

9. Ibid., 9.

10. Richard Hofstadter, *The Age of Reform* (New York: Random House, 1955), 186.

11. David Paul Nord, *Faith in Printing* (New York: Oxford University Press, 2004).

12. Paul C. Gutjahr, *An American Bible: A History of the Good Book in the United States* (Stanford, Calif.: Stanford University Press, 1999).

13. Candy Gunther Brown, *The Word in the World: Evangelical Writing, Publishing, and Reading in America, 1789–1880* (Chapel Hill: University of North Carolina Press, 2004).

14. Erwin D. Canham, *Commitment to Freedom* (Boston: Houghton Mifflin, 1958), 39.

15. Mark 16:15 (NRSV).

16. *Webster's Collegiate Dictionary,* 3rd ed., s.v. "Gospel."

17. Ross Gelbspan, *The Heat Is On* (New York: Addison-Wesley, 1997), 162.

18. Ibid., 174, 173.

19. Gelbspan, *The Heat Is On,* 173.

20. Michael Oppenheimer, "The Heat Is On," http://www.environmentaldefense.org/article.cfm?contentid=505 (posted 1 June 1997).

21. Paul Driessen, "Prophets, False Prophets and Profiteers," www.intellectualconservative.com.

22. Prior to that, the works of prophets like Elijah were included in wider histories but were not separate narratives. Why the ideas of the later prophets were treated separately is a matter of conjecture.

23. Isaiah 24:4–5 (NRSV).

24. Baldwin, *The Prophet,* 32, 35–36.

25. Ibid.

26. Barry L. Bandstra, *Reading the Old Testament: An Introduction to the Hebrew Bible* (New York: Wadsworth, 1999).

27. Thomas Dunlap, *Faith in Nature: Environmentalism as Religious Quest* (Seattle: University of Washington Press, 2004), 148.

28. David Mazel, ed., *A Century of Early Ecocriticism* (Athens: University of Georgia Press, 2001), 228.

29. Ibid., 229.

30. Ibid., 235.

31. Ibid., 230.

32. Job 12:7–8 (NRSV).

33. Ezekiel 24:18 (NRSV).

34. Mazel, *Early Ecocriticism,* 232.

35. Ronald Bailey, *Eco-Scam: The False Prophets of Ecological Apocalypse* (New York: St. Martin's Press, 1993).

36. Ibid., 142.

37. Melvin J. Grayson, *The Disaster Lobby: Prophets of Ecological Doom and Other Absurdities* (River Grove, Ill.: Follett, 1973).

38. Bart Simon, *Undead Science: Science Studies and the Afterlife of Cold Fusion* (New Brunswick, N.J.: Rutgers University Press, 2002), 27.

39. "Taming H-Bombs," *Wall Street Journal,* 24 March 1989, 1ff.

40. Simon, *Undead Science,* 24.

41. Ibid., 30.

42. Jon Turney, "Lost in Limbo," *New Scientist,* 22 March 2003, 48.

43. Robert L. Park, "The Fizzle in Fusion," *Washington Post,* 15 May 1991, B4.

44. "Cold Fusion Farewell," *New Scientist,* 21 March 1998, 2323.

45. W. J. Weatherby, "Iben Browning: Under the Volcano," *Guardian,* 10 September 1991, 35.

46. "Scientist Expects New Madrid Tremors in '90," Associated Press, 29 November 1989; "Quake Predicted; Vacations Suspended," Associated Press, 19 March 1990.

47. William Allen, telephone interview, 7 March 2006.

48. Weatherby, "Iben Browning," 35.

49. Peter Hernon, "Pressing On . . . New Madrid Ready for Media to Leave," *St. Louis Post-Dispatch,* 4 December 1990, 1Aff.

50. I could not document the injury in the media coverage, so it may have been part of the folklore of the event.

51. Larry Fiquette, "How Quake Prediction Hysteria Grew," *St. Louis Post-Dispatch,* 9 December 1990, 1Dff.

52. Pamela Sands Showalter, "One Newspaper's Coverage of 1990 Earthquake Prediction," *Newspaper Research Journal* 16, no. 2 (Spring 1995): 7.

53. Ibid., 2–13.

54. Jon Payne, "Creating and Reporting the News," *Nuclear News,* February 1991, 27.

55. Fiquette, "Quake Prediction Hysteria," 1D.

56. Allen interview.

57. "AP Picks Top Stories," Associated Press, 21 December 1990; "Top Ten Missouri Stories," Associated Press, 30 December 1990.

58. Jack Lule, *Daily News, Eternal Stories: The Mythological Role in Journalism* (New York: Guilford, 2001), 25.

59. Ibid., 25.

60. Hayden White, *The Content of the Form: Narrative Discourse and Historical Representation* (Baltimore: Johns Hopkins University Press, 1987), 42–43.

61. The titles and subtitles of environmental biographies, books, and essays hint at this influence. For example, a biography of the nineteenth-century American scientist and writer George Perkins Marsh was subtitled *Prophet of Conservation.* In 1915 the horticulturalist and scholar of rural life Liberty Hyde Bailey titled his testament on the relationship of humans and the planet *The Holy Earth.* John Burroughs, one of America's most influential nature writers, called a 1912 essay "The Gospel of Nature." One biography of the preservationist and author John Muir (who believed wilderness was God's handiwork) was subtitled *The Apostle of Nature.*

62. R. R. Wilson, "Interpreting Israel's Religion: An Anthropological Perspective on the Problem of False Prophecy," in *The Place Is Too Small for Us: The Israelite Prophets in Recent Scholarship,* ed. Robert P. Gordon (Winona Lake, Ind.: Eisenbrauns, 1995), 334.

63. Genesis 9:12–13, 16 (NRSV).

64. Dunlap, *Faith in Nature,* 4.

65. Lule, *Daily News, Eternal Stories,* 173.

66. John McQuaid and Mark Schleifstein, "In Harm's Way," *New Orleans Times-Picayune,* 23 June 2002, 1ff.

67. Paloma Esquivel, "Reporters Discuss Hurricane Experiences," *Syracuse Post-Standard,* 7 February 2006, B3.

68. Glasser and Ettema, "Investigative Journalism," 1.

69. Bernard Brady, *The Moral Bond of Community* (Washington, D.C.: Georgetown University Press, 1998), 41–42.

70. Elizabeth Kolbert, "Watermark: Can Southern Louisiana Be Saved?" *New Yorker,* 27 February 2006, 46–57.

71. Brian Handwerk, "Louisiana Coast Threatened by Wetlands Loss," *National Geographic News,* http://news.nationalgeographic.com/news/2005/02/0209_050209_wetlands.html.

72. John McQuaid and Mark Schleifstein, "Left Behind," *New Orleans Times-Picayune,* 24 June 2002, 1ff.

73. MediaChannel, http://mediachannel.org/blog/node/2996.

74. Quicksilver, http://kaspit.typepad.com/weblog/2005/09/new_orleans_and.html.

75. Jonah 1–4 (NSRV).

76. Izaak Walton, *The Compleat Angler,* 6th ed. (London: Oxford University Press, 1921), 37–38.

77. Herman Melville, *Moby-Dick* (New York: Barnes and Noble Classics, 2003), 426–28.

78. George Orwell, *Such, Such Were the Joys* (New York: Harcourt, Brace, 1953), 154–99.

79. Aldous Huxley, *Jonah* (Oxford: Holywell, 1919), 2.

80. Frank Dumont, "De Gospel Raft," in *Minstrel Songs, Old and New* (Boston: Oliver Ditson, 1883), 176–77; New Lost City Ramblers, "The Old Fish Song," in *The Early Years 1958–1962,* Washington, D.C.: Folkways Recording, 1991; Grandpa Jones, "Jonah and the Whale," *16 Sacred Gospel Songs,* Cincinnati, Ohio: King Records, 1963.

81. In some versions of the myth, Cassandra is given the ability to communicate with animals instead of predicting the future.

82. Mark Schleifstein, Society of Environmental Journalists plenary session, Lyndon Baines Johnson Library and Museum, University of Texas–Austin, 30 September 2005.

83. Lule, *Daily News, Eternal Stories,* 184.

CHAPTER THREE

1. Mazel, *Early Ecocriticism,* 9.

2. Pliny the Elder, *The Natural History,* vol. 2., trans. Harris Rackham (Cambridge, Mass.: Harvard University Press, 1942), 509, 511.

3. A. G. Morton, "Pliny on Plants: His Place in the History of Botany," in *Science in the Early Roman Empire: Pliny the Elder, His Sources and His Influence,* ed. Roger French and Frank Greenaway (Totowa, N.J.: Barnes and Noble, 1986), 86.

4. French and Greenaway, *Science in the Early Roman Empire,* 252.

5. A. Locher, "The Structure of Pliny the Elder's Natural History," in French and Greenway, *Science in the Early Roman Empire,* 20.

6. Jerry Dennis, "Pliny's World: All the Facts and Then Some," *Smithsonian* 26, no. 8 (November 1995): 152–63.

7. Ibid.

8. Cato the Censor, *On Farming,* trans. Ernest Brehaut (New York: Octagon Books, 1966), 1.

9. Ibid., 19.

10. Daniel E. Vasey, *An Ecological History of Agriculture: 10,000 B.C.–A.D. 10,000* (Ames: Iowa State University Press, 1992), 138.

11. Cato, *On Farming,* 59.

12. Ibid., 59–60.

13. Ibid., 60.

14. Ibid., xviii.

15. Ibid., 1.

16. Lucius Junius Moderatus Columella, *On Agriculture,* trans. Harrison Boyd Ash (Cambridge, Mass.: Harvard University Press, 1941), xvii.

17. Ibid., 49.

18. Ibid., 61.

19. Ibid., xix.

20. Ibid., xx.

21. Charles Darwin, *The Variation of Animals and Plants Under Domestication* (London: John Murray, 1868), 262.

22. Tom Dickson, *Mass Media Education in Transition* (Mahwah, N.J.: Lawrence Erlbaum, 2000), 1.

23. Joseph Mirando, "Embracing Objectivity Early On: Journalism

Textbooks of the 1800s," *Journal of Mass Media Ethics* 16, no. 1 (2001): 23–32.

24. De Forest O'Dell, *A History of Journalism Education in the United States* (New York: Columbia University Press, 1935).

25. James Melvin Lee, "Schools of Journalism," *Review of Reviews* 49 (May 1914): 591.

26. Dickson, *Mass Media Education,* 4–5; Lee, "Schools of Journalism," 591.

27. Dickson, *Mass Media Education,* 5.

28. Ibid., 7.

29. Frank Luther Mott, *Time Enough: Essays in Autobiography* (Chapel Hill: University of North Carolina Press, 1962), 146.

30. Richard Terrill Baker, *A History of the Graduate School of Journalism* (New York: Columbia University Press, 1954), 15.

31. John A. Brubacher and Willis Rudy, *Higher Education in Transition: A History of American Colleges and Universities, 1636–1976* (New York: Harper and Row, 1976), 64.

32. David Host, *The Citizen and the News* (Milwaukee: Marquette University Press, 1962), 100.

33. Janice Ruth Wood, "The Foundation Years of American Journalism Education, 1908–1930," (M.A. thesis, University of South Carolina, 1981), 18.

34. Ibid., 81.

35. Ibid., 82.

36. Ibid., 29.

37. Ibid., 44.

38. Ibid., 46.

39. John Clay, "The Plough and the Book," address to Iowa State College, 30 May 1905, Agricultural Communications Documents Center, University of Illinois.

40. Stuart W. Shulman, "The Progressive Era Farm Press," *Journalism History* 25, no. 1 (Spring 1999): 27–36.

41. Edward L. Schapsmeier and Frederick H. Schapsmeier, "The Wallaces and Their Farm Paper: A Story of Agrarian Leadership," *Journalism Quarterly* 44 (Summer 1967): 289–96.

42. Shulman, "Progressive Era Farm Press."

43. Nora C. Quebral, "Wilmer Atkinson and the Early Farm Journal," *Journalism Quarterly* 47, no. 1 (Spring 1970): 69; Shulman, "Progressive Era Farm Press," 27–36.

44. Quebral, "Wilmer Atkinson," 65–70.

45. Charles E. Rogers, "Agricultural News and Comment," *Journalism Bulletin* 4 (March 1927): 8–10.

46. Schapsmeier and Schapsmeier, "Wallaces and Their Farm Paper," 292.

47. Wood, "Foundation Years," 90.

48. Stephen A. Banning, "The Cradle of Professional Journalistic Education in the Mid-Nineteenth Century," *Media History Monographs* 4, no. 1 (2000–2001), http://www.scripps.ohiou.edu/mediahistory/mhmjour4-1.htm.

49. Wood, "Foundation Years," 31.

50. Ibid., 43.

51. Laura Lane, "A Pioneer Who Didn't Feel Like One," in *Farm Magazines, Milestones and Memories: American Agricultural Editors' Association, 1921–1996,* ed. Wayne E. Swegle and John R. Harvey (New Prague, Minn.: American Agricultural Editors' Association, 1996), 14–15.

52. James W. Carey, "A Plea for the University Tradition," *Journalism Quarterly* 55, no. 4 (Winter 1978): 846–55.

53. Everette E. Dennis, "Whatever Happened to Marse Roberts' Dream?" *Gannett Center Journal* 2, no. 1 (Spring 1988): 12.

54. Dickson, *Mass Media Education,* 28.

55. Charles E. Rogers, "Survey of Agricultural Journalism," *Journalism Bulletin* 4 (January 1928): 45.

56. Murray Bookchin, "Radical Agriculture," in *Radical Agriculture,* ed. Richard Merrill (New York: New York University Press, 1976), 3–13.

57. Economic Research Service, U.S. Department of Agriculture, http://www.era.usda.gov.

58. ABC, "Publisher's Statement," 30 June 2005.

59. Michael Fritz, "Tribune Co. Near Deal to Bring Farm Magazines into Its Fold," *Crain's Chicago Business,* 25 April 1994/1 May 1994, 16.

60. Den Gardner, interview by author, 4 April 2006.

61. Thomas F. Pawlick, *The Invisible Farm: The Worldwide Decline in Farm News and Agricultural Journalism Training* (Chicago: Burnham, 2001), 3.

62. Ibid., 3.

63. Ann Reisner and Gerry Walter, "Agricultural Journalists' Assessment of Print Coverage of Agricultural News," *Rural Sociology* 59, no. 3 (1994): 525–37.

64. Ibid., 532.

65. Pawlick, *Invisible Farm,* 6.

66. Paul Raeburn, *The Last Harvest: The Genetic Gamble That Threatens to Destroy American Agriculture* (New York: Simon and Schuster, 1995).

67. Ibid., back cover.

68. Bernadette Longo, *Spurious Coin: A History of Science, Management, and Technical Writing* (Albany: State University of New York Press, 2000).

69. Aaron Sachs, *The Humboldt Current: Nineteenth-Century Exploration and the Roots of American Environmentalism* (New York: Viking, 2006), 89.

70. Ibid., 13.

71. Hillier Krieghbaum, *Science and the Mass Media* (New York: New York University Press, 1967), 19–20.

72. John C. Burnham, *How Superstition Won and Science Lost: Popularizing Science and Health in the United States* (New Brunswick, N.J.: Rutgers University Press, 1987), 22.

73. Frank Luther Mott, *A History of American Magazines,* vol. 1 (New York: Appleton, 1938), 152.

74. American Philosophical Society, http://www.amphilsoc.org/about/.

75. Mott, *American Magazines,* 1:149. See also David A. Kronick, *A History of Scientific and Technical Periodicals* (New York: Scarecrow, 1962), 73.

76. Mott, *American Magazines,* 1:305.

77. Frank Luther Mott, *A History of American Magazines,* vol. 2 (New York: Appleton, 1938), 324.

78. As quoted in Crosbie Smith and Ian Higginson, "'Improvised Europeans': Science and Reform in the *North American Review,* 1865–1880," in *Science Serialized: Representations of Science in Nineteenth-Century Periodicals,* ed. Geoffrey Cantor and Sally Shuttleworth (Cambridge, Mass.: MIT Press, 2004), 155.

79. Thomas Cooper, "The Connection Between Geology and the Pentateuch," *Knickerbocker Magazine* 8 (May 1836): 441–52.

80. Smith and Higginson, "'Improvised Europeans,'" 152.

81. Henry Adams, *The Education of Henry Adams* (New York: Modern Library, 1931), 226.

82. Jean Folkerts and Dwight L. Teeter Jr., *Voices of a Nation: A History of Mass Media in the United States,* 4th ed. (Boston: Allyn and Bacon, 2002), 208.

83. Frank Luther Mott, *A History of American Magazines,* vol. 3 (New York: Appleton, 1938), 496–97.

84. *Chicago Advance,* 30 January 1873, 11.

85. "Making Science Ridiculous," *Literary Digest,* 2 September 1922, 62.

86. As quoted in Krieghbaum, *Science and the Mass Media,* 26.

87. James C. Foust, "E. W. Scripps and the Science Service," *Journalism History* 21, no. 2 (Summer 1995): 58–65.

88. Israel Light, "Science Writing: Status and Needs," *Journalism Quarterly* 37, no. 4 (Winter 1960): 53.

89. Foust, "Scripps and the Science Service," 59.

90. Ibid.

91. Ibid.

92. Ibid.

93. "How the Chemist Moves the World," *Science News Letter,* 21 October 1922, 2; "Pupils Kept in Ignorance of Facts of Life Sciences," *Science News Letter,* 14 January 1939, 23.

94. Hillier Krieghbaum, "The Background and Training of Science Writers," *Journalism Quarterly* 17 (March 1940): 15–18.

95. Watson Davis, "Science, the Press, and Intellectual Advance," *Vital Speeches* 3 (1937): 207.

96. Benjamin Gruenberg, *Science and the Public Mind* (New York: McGraw-Hill, 1935), 93.

97. Foust, "Scripps and the Science Service."

98. Ibid., 65.

99. Krieghbaum, "Background and Training," 16.

100. Sharon M. Friedman, Sharon Dunwoody, and Carol L. Rogers, *Scientists and Journalists: Reporting Science as News* (New York: Free Press, 1986), xiii.

101. Pierre C. Fraley, "The Education and Training of Science Writers," *Journalism Quarterly* 40, no. 2 (Summer 1963): 325.

102. Krieghbaum, *Science and the Mass Media,* 9.

103. Light, "Science Writing," 53–60.

104. Hillier Krieghbaum, "Reporting Science Information Through the Mass Media," *Journalism Quarterly* 40, no. 2 (Summer 1963): 292.

105. Fraley, "Education and Training of Science Writers," 323–28. By 2006 the National Association of Science Writers numbered 2,400 members.

106. Victor K. McElheny, *Science in the Newspaper* (Washington, D.C.: American Association for the Advancement of Science, 1974), 8.

107. A 1973 survey of science writers found that environmental issues, as well as health and medicine, were "perceived as paramount" in their work. See ibid., 19.

CHAPTER FOUR

1. Paul G. Stanwood, *Izaak Walton* (New York: Twayne, 1998), 59.

2. Margaret Bottrall, *Izaak Walton* (London: Longmans, Green, 1955), 7.

3. Stanwood, *Izaak Walton,* 94.

4. Thomas A. Wikle, "A Comparison of Geographic Membership Patterns in Three National Environmental Organizations," *Journal of Environmental Education* 29, no. 3 (March 1998): 39–48. The Ikes, founded in 1922, had fifty-one thousand members in 1960, the most of any organization connected with the outdoors. In 2005 their membership was around forty thousand, according to the group's Web site.

5. John R. Cooper, *The Art of The Compleat Angler* (Durham, N.C.: Duke University Press, 1968), 4.

6. Ibid., 5.

7. As quoted in Bottrall, *Izaak Walton,* 13.

8. The quote is from John 21:3.

9. The New American Bible (2002) translates the verse as: "Simon Peter said to them, 'I am going fishing.' They said to him, 'We also will come with you.'"

10. Stanwood, *Izaak Walton,* 2.

11. Arthur F. Kinney, "Editor's Note," in Stanwood, *Izaak Walton,* xi.

12. Kinney (xi) and Stanwood (13), both writing in Stanwood, *Izaak Walton,* for example.

13. Bottrall, *Izaak Walton,* 13.

14. Izaak Walton, *The Compleat Angler,* 5th ed. (London: Oxford University Press, 1915), 120.

15. Stanwood, *Izaak Walton,* 62.

16. Ibid., 96.

17. Peter Oliver, *A New Chronicle of The Compleat Angler* (London: Paisley, 1936), xii.

18. Izaak Walton, *The Compleat Angler,* 1st ed., ed. Bryan Loughery (London: Penguin, 1985), 11.

19. Cooper, *Art of The Compleat Angler,* 153.

20. Walton, *Compleat Angler,* 1st ed., 62.

21. Ibid., 64.

22. Ibid., 65.

23. Ibid., 41 (italics in the original).

24. Charles Clover, "Licenses to Kill Cormorants Rise to 3,000," *London Daily Telegraph,* 31 August 2005, 4.

25. Lisa W. Foderaro, "Cormorants Take Over, Making Some Enemies," *New York Times,* 1 July 2005, B2.

26. Doug Smith, "About 2,000 Fish-Eating Birds Shot Near Leech Lake," Minneapolis *Star Tribune,* 22 May 2005, 13C.

27. D'Arcy Egan, "Crying Fowl over Copious Cormorant," *Cleveland Plain Dealer,* 10 June 2005, D8.

28. Foderaro, "Cormorants Take Over," B2.

29. Walton, *Compleat Angler,* 1st ed., 73 (italics in the original).

30. Frank Sargeant, "Study Shows Mortality Rates High Despite Catch-and-Release Plan," *Tampa Tribune,* 12 March 2006, 14.

31. Bryan Brasher, "Some Anglers Too Caught Up in Catch-and-Release," *Memphis Commercial Appeal,* 9 April 2006, C11.

32. Walton, *Compleat Angler,* 1st ed., 78 (italics and spelling in the original).

33. Ibid., 79 (italics in the original).

34. In this assumption Walton was incorrect. Mascall wrote and translated books on agriculture, gardening, and fishing in the late sixteenth century (he assisted in the introduction of another exotic, the pippin apple, to England). It is not probable, however, that he brought the carp to the island, since its existence there has been documented as early as 1496, but a Mascall ancestor may have facilitated its introduction. Dame

Juliana Berners's *Treatyse on Fysshynge with an Angle* from 1496 mentions carp in England on p. 16.

35. Paul Fisher, *The Angler's Souvenir* (London: Charles Tilt, 1835). "Fisher" was a pen name for W. A. Chatto.

36. John R. Betts, "Sporting Journalism in 19th Century America," *American Quarterly* 5 (1953): 41.

37. There was much crossover between farm writing and outdoor writing, as evidenced by the title of this publication.

38. Betts, "Sporting Journalism," 41.

39. *Mirror,* 6 January 1838. As quoted in Mott, *A History of American Magazines,* vol. 1, 481.

40. Mott, *History of American Magazines,* 1:481.

41. Frank Forester, *Fish and Fishing of the United States and British Provinces of North America,* rev. ed. (New York: W. A. Townsend, 1864), 294.

42. Ibid., 423, 426.

43. Betts, "Sporting Journalism," 42.

44. Stephen E. Meats, "Henry William Herbert," *The Literary Encyclopedia,* 24 June 2004, http://www.litencyc.com/php/speople.php?rec=true&UID=2099.

45. "Henry William Herbert, 'Frank Forester,'" *International Magazine of Literature, Art, and Science* 3, no. 2 (1 June 1851): 291.

46. Ibid., 291.

47. Porte Crayon, "The Mountains—VIII," *Harper's New Monthly Magazine* 47 (November 1873): 821.

48. "Americans at Play," *The Living Age* 214 (24 July 1897): 259.

49. Ibid., 259.

50. Paul Schullery, "Hope for the Hooks and Bullet Press," *New York Times,* 22 September 1985, sec. 7, pp. 1ff.

51. Thaddeus Norris, *American Angler's Book* (Philadelphia: Porter and Coates, 1864), 1.

52. Ibid., 33.

53. Ibid., 35.

54. Ibid., viii.

55. Thaddeus Norris, *American Fish Culture* (Philadelphia: Porter and Coates, 1868).

56. "Editor's Literary Record," *Harper's New Monthly Magazine* 46 (May 1873): 933.

57. Mark Neuzil and William Kovarik, *Mass Media and Environmental Conflict: America's Green Crusades* (Thousand Oaks, Calif.: Sage, 1996), 11.

58. Ibid., 13.

59. Ibid., 21.

60. Betts, "Sporting Journalism," 48.

61. "Announcement," *Forest and Stream,* 14 August 1873, 8–9.

62. Neuzil and Kovarik, *Mass Media and Environmental Conflict,* 22.

63. "Pigeon Matches," *Forest and Stream,* 17 February 1879, 145, 171.

64. Kerasote, "Short History of Hunting," 105.

65. Ed Dentry, "Is Hunting a Sport? That's Your Call," *Rocky Mountain News,* 9 April 1997, 14C.

66. As quoted in Peter Steinhart, "The Longer View," *Audubon,* March 1987, 10.

67. "Dr. G. B. Grinnell, Naturalist, Dead," *New York Times,* 12 April 1938, 23.

68. Schullery, "Hooks and Bullet Press," 1.

69. Frank Luther Mott, *A History of American Magazines,* vol. 4 (Cambridge, Mass.: Harvard University Press, 1958), 635.

70. Theodore Roosevelt, *The Wilderness Hunter* (New York: Putnam's, 1893), 275–76.

71. Schullery, "Hooks and Bullet Press."

72. Roosevelt, *Wilderness Hunter,* 274.

73. Ibid., 270.

74. *Spectator,* 16 January 1886, 82.

75. Edmund Morris, *The Rise of Theodore Roosevelt* (New York: Putnam, 1979), 792n8.

76. "Comment on New Books," *Atlantic Monthly,* December 1893, 850.

77. As quoted in Daniel J. Philippon, *Conserving Words: How American Nature Writers Shaped the Environmental Movement* (Athens: University of Georgia Press, 2004), 64.

78. Philippon, *Conserving Words,* 53.

79. Ibid., 66.

80. Boone and Crockett Club, www.boone-crockett.org.

81. Philippon, *Conserving Words,* 71.

82. Garvey Winegar, "Izaak Walton League Doesn't Conserve Noise This Time," *Washington Post,* 1 August 1999, D12.

83. Gene Mueller, "Izaak Walton League Helps Hunters and Landowners Cooperate on Access," *Washington Times,* 17 June 1998, B8.

84. William Voigt Jr., *Born with Fists Doubled: Defending Outdoor America* (Spirit Lake, Iowa: Izaak Walton League of America, 1992), 15.

85. Ibid., 16.

86. Ibid., 17.

87. Ibid., 18.

88. John Opie, *Nature's Nation: An Environmental History of the United States* (New York: Harcourt Brace, 1998), 419.

89. Don G. Cullimore and Edwin W. Hanson, *Sixty-Five Years of OWAA, 1927–1992* (State College, Pa.: Outdoor Writers Association of America, 1993), 1.

90. Ibid., 3.

91. Ibid., 4.

92. Ibid., 5.

93. The National Wildlife Federation's "Conservation Hall of Fame" contains many people famous for their media careers: John Burroughs, Rachel Carson, Jacques Cousteau, Marjory Stoneman Douglas, Ding Darling, George Grinnell, Aldo Leopold, John Muir, Sigurd Olson, Roger Tory Peterson, Ernest Thompson Seton, Wallace Stegner, and Henry David Thoreau.

94. Cullimore and Hanson, *Sixty-Five Years of OWAA,* 11.

95. Ibid., 12.

96. Ibid., 22.

97. Ibid., 44.

98. Ibid., 66.

99. Outdoor Writers Association of America, http://www.owaa.org/about_owaa.php#PositionOnHunting.

100. Blaine Harden, "NRA and Outdoor Writers Have Falling Out," *Washington Post,* 9 July 2004, A3.

101. Schullery, "Hooks and Bullet Press," 1.

102. Ibid.

103. Ibid.

104. Mark Freeman, "Keeping the Bean-Counters Happy," *Outdoors Unlimited,* January 2006, http://www.owaa.org/Tech-E_archives/JanFeb06 .htm#feature3.

105. Ibid.

106. Walton, *Compleat Angler,* 1st ed., 123.

CHAPTER FIVE

1. Hamilton Wright Mabie, *Short Studies in Literature* (New York: Dodd, Mead, 1891).

2. Hamilton Wright Mabie, *Essays on Nature and Culture* (New York: Dodd, Mead, 1896), 38.

3. Hamilton Wright Mabie, *Books and Culture* (New York: Dodd, Mead, 1896), 64.

4. Diane Ackerman, "King Penguins," in *By the Light of the Glow-Worm Lamp: Three Centuries of Reflections on Nature,* ed. Alberto Manguel (New York: Plenum, 1998), 241.

5. Thomas J. Lyon, *This Incomperable Lande: A Book of American Nature Writing* (Boston: Houghton Mifflin, 1989), 3.

6. Peter A. Fritzell, *Nature Writing and America* (Ames: Iowa State University Press, 1990), 4.

7. Hamilton Wright Mabie, "John Burroughs," *Century Magazine,* August 1897, 560–68.

8. John Burroughs, *Time and Change* (Boston: Houghton Mifflin, 1912), 245.

9. Bill McKibben, "The Call of the Not So Wild," in *Sharp Eyes: John Burroughs and American Nature Writing,* ed. Charlotte Zoe Walker (Syracuse, N.Y.: Syracuse University Press, 2000), 12–18.

10. Peter Matthiessen, *The Snow Leopard* (New York: Viking, 1978), 129.

11. Fritzell, *Nature Writing and America,* 6.

12. Francis Halsey, "The Rise of Nature Writers," *American Monthly Review of Reviews,* November 1902, 567–71.

13. See, for example, the following articles by John Burroughs: "The True Test of Good Nature Literature," *Country Life,* May 1904, 51–53; "The Literary Treatment of Nature," *Atlantic Monthly,* July 1904, 38–43;

"Gilbert White's Book," *Lippincott's,* August 1886, 133–40; "Henry D. Thoreau," *Century Magazine,* May 1882, 368–79; and "Nature in Literature," *Critic,* July 1881, 185.

14. Burroughs, "Henry D. Thoreau," 378.

15. Joseph Wood Krutch, *Great American Nature Writing* (New York: William Sloane, 1950), 3–86.

16. Ibid., 6.

17. Ibid., 5.

18. Michael P. Branch, ed., *Reading the Roots: American Nature Writing Before Walden* (Athens: University of Georgia Press, 2004).

19. Krutch, *Great American Nature Writers,* 6.

20. Ibid., 87 (emphasis in the original).

21. Ibid.

22. Ralph Waldo Emerson, "Nature," in *The Selected Writings of Ralph Waldo Emerson,* ed. Brooks Atkinson (New York: Random House, 1940), 6.

23. Donald Worster, *Nature's Economy: The Roots of Ecology* (Garden City, N.Y.: Anchor/Doubleday, 1979).

24. Roderick Nash, *Wilderness and the American Mind,* 3rd ed. (New Haven, Conn.: Yale University Press, 1982), 95.

25. Joel Myerson, *The New England Transcendentalists and "The Dial": A History of the Magazine and Its Contributors.* (Rutherford, N.J.: Fairleigh Dickinson University Press, 1980).

26. Margaret Fuller, "Preliminary Note," in Henry David Thoreau, *Thoreau: Collected Essays and Poems,* ed. Elizabeth Hall Witherell (New York: Library of America, 2001), 20.

27. Thoreau, *Thoreau: Collected Essays and Poems,* 22.

28. Henry David Thoreau, "Walking," *Atlantic Monthly,* June 1862, 657.

29. Ibid., 665.

30. Thoreau, *Thoreau: Collected Essays and Poems,* 653. See also Walter Harding, *A Thoreau Handbook* (New York: New York University Press, 1959), 176.

31. Frank Stewart, *A Natural History of Nature Writing* (Washington, D.C.: Island, 1995), xx.

32. Henry David Thoreau, *Walden* (New Haven, Conn.: Yale University Press, 2004), 195.

33. Ibid., 97.

34. Krutch, *Great American Nature Writing,* 92.

35. Opie, *Nature's Nation,* 196.

36. Lawrence Buell, *The Environmental Imagination: Thoreau, Nature Writing, and the Formation of American Culture* (Cambridge, Mass.: Belknap Press of Harvard University Press, 1995), 2.

37. Harding, *Thoreau Handbook,* 175–76.

38. Ibid., 178.

39. Ibid., 176–77.

40. Ibid., 179.

41. Ibid., 182.

42. Peter J. Schmitt, *Back to Nature: The Arcadian Myth in Urban America* (New York: Oxford University Press, 1969).

43. Fannie Eckstrom, "Fannie Eckstrom on Thoreau's *The Maine Woods,*" in Mazel, *Early Ecocriticism,* 163–72.

44. Harding, *Thoreau Handbook,* 184.

45. Ibid., 185.

46. Buell, *Environmental Imagination,* 9.

47. John Burroughs, *Wake-Robin* (Boston: Houghton Mifflin, 1902), x–xi.

48. Walker, *Sharp Eyes,* xxv.

49. Burroughs, *Wake-Robin,* 39.

50. Mazel, *Early Ecocriticism,* 12.

51. Clara Barrus, *The Life and Letters of John Burroughs* (Boston: Houghton Mifflin, 1925), 2:336.

52. John Burroughs, *Field and Study* (Boston: Houghton Mifflin, 1919), 3–4.

53. Ibid., 4.

54. William Kaufmann, "Rediscovering John Burroughs," in Walker, *Sharp Eyes,* 282.

55. John Burroughs, "Real and Sham Natural History," *Atlantic Monthly,* March 1903, 298. See also Ralph Lutts, *The Nature Fakers: Wildlife, Science and Sentiment* (Golden, Colo.: Fulcrum, 1990), 102.

56. Edward J. Renehan Jr., *John Burroughs: An American Naturalist* (Post Mills, Vt.: Chelsea Green, 1992), 231.

57. Lutts, *Nature Fakers.*

58. Frank Bergon, "'Sensitive to the Verge of the Horizon': The Envi-

ronmentalism of John Burroughs," in Walker, *Sharp Eyes,* 19–25.

59. William H. Goetzmann and Kay Sloan, *Looking Far North: The Harriman Expedition to Alaska, 1899* (Princeton, N.J.: Princeton University Press, 1982).

60. Perry Westbrook, *John Burroughs* (New York: Twayne, 1974), 96.

61. McKibben, "Call of the Not So Wild," 12–18.

62. Ibid., 17.

63. William D. Perkins, *Index to the Collected Works of John Burroughs* (New York: John Burroughs Association, 1995).

64. Renehan, *John Burroughs,* 205.

65. Stephen Fox, *John Muir and His Legacy: The American Conservation Movement* (Boston: Little, Brown, 1981), 43.

66. Stewart, *Natural History of Nature Writing,* 112.

67. Ibid., 120.

68. Fox, *John Muir,* 56.

69. John Muir, "Snow-Storm on Mount Shasta," *Harper's New Monthly Magazine,* September 1877, 527.

70. Fox, *John Muir,* 98.

71. Stewart, *Natural History of Nature Writing,* 110.

72. John Muir, *A Thousand-Mile Walk to the Gulf* (New York: Houghton Mifflin, 1916), 136.

73. Aldo Leopold, *A Sand County Almanac* (New York: Oxford University Press, 1949), xix.

74. J. Baird Callicott, "The Scientific Substance of the Land Ethic," in *Aldo Leopold: The Man and His Legacy,* ed. Thomas Tanner (Ankeny, Iowa: Soil Conservation Society of America, 1987), 90.

75. Susan Flader, *Thinking Like a Mountain* (Madison: University of Wisconsin Press, 1994), 9–10.

76. Ibid., 29.

77. Leopold, *A Sand County Almanac,* xviii.

78. Ibid., 262.

79. Curt Meine, "Moving Mountains: Aldo Leopold and *A Sand County Almanac,*" in *Aldo Leopold and the Ecological Conscience,* ed. Richard L. Knight and Suzanne Riedel (New York: Oxford University Press, 2002), 23.

80. Aldo Leopold Foundation, http://www.aldoleopold.org.

81. Flader, *Thinking Like a Mountain,* 5.

82. Roderick Nash, "Aldo Leopold and the Limits to Liberalism," in Tanner, *Aldo Leopold,* 55.

83. Scott Russell Sanders, "Introduction," in *Aldo Leopold: For the Health of the Land,* ed. J. Baird Callicott and Eric T. Freyfogle (Washington, D.C.: Island, 1999), xiii.

84. Wallace Stegner, "The Legacy of Aldo Leopold," in *Companion to A Sand County Almanac,* ed. J. Baird Callicott (Madison: University of Wisconsin Press, 1987), 233.

85. Curt Meine, *Aldo Leopold: His Life and Works* (Madison: University of Wisconsin Press, 1988), 526.

86. Flader, *Thinking Like a Mountain,* 130.

87. David Backes, *A Wilderness Within: The Life of Sigurd F. Olson* (Minneapolis: University of Minnesota Press, 1997), 187.

88. Ibid., 254–55.

89. Sigurd Olson, *The Singing Wilderness* (New York: Knopf, 1956), 6.

90. Ibid., 29.

91. Backes, *Wilderness Within,* 248.

92. Ibid., 248.

93. Ibid., 330.

94. Ibid., 339.

95. Ibid., 327–28.

96. Don Scheese, "Annie Dillard," in *American Nature Writers,* 2 vols., ed. John Elder (New York: Scribner's, 1996), 1:215.

97. "Nature's Finest," *Sierra,* November/December 2000, 48–55.

98. "Best-Loved Books," *Sierra,* March/April 2001, 9.

99. Elder, *American Nature Writers.*

100. Stewart, *Natural History of Nature Writing,* 220.

101. For example, see Stephanie L. Sarver, *Uneven Land: Nature and Agriculture in American Writing* (Lincoln: University of Nebraska Press, 1999); and Lorraine Anderson, *Sisters of the Earth* (New York: Vintage, 1991).

102. Paul Brooks, *Speaking for Nature: How Literary Naturalists from Henry Thoreau to Rachel Carson Have Shaped America* (Boston: Houghton Mifflin, 1980), 237.

103. Michael Pearson, "John McPhee," in Elder, *American Nature Writers,* 1:583.

104. Stephen Trimble, ed., *Words from the Land: Encounters with Natural History Writing* (Salt Lake City: Gibbs Smith, 1989), 5.

105. Ibid., 23–24.

106. Yvonne Baskin, *A Plague of Rats and Rubbervines: The Growing Threat of Species Invasions* (Washington, D.C.: Island, 2002), 225, 285.

107. William Allen, *Green Phoenix: Restoring the Tropical Rain Forests of Guanacaste, Costa Rica* (New York: Oxford University Press, 2001), xx.

108. Karen Schaefer, interview by author, 20 June 2006.

109. Daniel Glick, *Powder Burn: Arson, Money and Mystery on Vail Mountain* (New York: Public Affairs, 2001), 237.

110. Robert Cahn, "Books (Not Thneeds) Are What Everyone Needs," in *Media and the Environment,* ed. Craig L. LaMay and Everette E. Dennis (Washington, D.C.: Island, 1991), 227.

111. Trimble, *Words from the Land,* 21. In her book *Kindred Nature,* Barbara T. Gates attempts to remedy the omission of women from the nature-writing canon in England. She looks at the contributions of Victorian and Edwardian women to the study, protection, and description of nature. Gates's edited anthology, *In Nature's Name,* includes more female British authors who wrote about nature.

112. Esther Lanigan Stineman, *Mary Austin: Song of a Maverick* (New Haven, Conn.: Yale University Press, 1989).

113. Stewart, *Natural History of Nature Writing,* 135.

114. Mabel Osgood Wright, *The Friendship of Nature: A New England Chronicle of Birds and Flowers* (Baltimore: Johns Hopkins University Press, 1999).

115. Philippon, *Conserving Words,* 73.

CHAPTER SIX

1. Philip J. Tichenor and Mark Neuzil, "Advocacy, the Uncomfortable Issue," *Nieman Reports,* Winter 1996, 41–44.

2. William J. Coughlin, "Think Globally, Act Locally," in LaMay and Dennis, *Media and the Environment,* 121.

3. Teya Ryan, "Network Earth: Advocacy, Journalism and the Environment," in LaMay and Dennis, *Media and the Environment,* 85.

4. Tom Knudson, "Environment, Inc." *Sacramento Bee,* 22–26 April 2001, 1ff.

5. Debra A. Schwartz, "In the Lion's Mouth: Advocacy and Investigative Reporting About the Environment in the Early 21st Century" (Ph.D. diss., University of Maryland, 2004), 201–2.

6. Michael Frome, *Green Ink: An Introduction to Environmental Journalism* (Salt Lake City: University of Utah Press, 1998), 29.

7. Ibid., 31.

8. David Sachsman, JoAnn Valenti, and James Simon, "Regional Issues, National Norms: A Four-Region Analysis of U.S. Environment Reporters" (paper presented at the annual meeting of the International Communications Association, May 2005).

9. Ibid., 19.

10. LaMay and Dennis, *Media and the Environment,* 8.

11. Craig L. LaMay, "Heat and Light: The Advocacy-Objectivity Debate," in LaMay and Dennis, *Media and the Environment,* 109.

12. Frome, *Green Ink,* 23.

13. Ibid., 26.

14. Michael Frome, *Greenspeak: Fifty Years of Environmental Muckraking and Advocacy* (Knoxville: University of Tennessee Press, 2002), 189.

15. Ryan, "Network Earth," 84.

16. David Mindich, *Just the Facts: How "Objectivity" Came to Define American Journalism* (New York: New York University Press, 1998).

17. *Pennsylvania Gazette,* 23–30 August 1739, 1.

18. A. M. McMahon, "'Small Matters': Benjamin Franklin, Philadelphia, and the Progress of Cities," *Pennsylvania Magazine of History and Biography* 66, no. 2 (April 1992): 157–82.

19. Michael McMahon, "Dock Creek and the Origins of Urban Technology," in *Early American Technology: Making and Doing Things from the Colonial Era to 1850,* ed. Judith C. McGaw (Chapel Hill: University of North Carolina Press, 1994), 130.

20. Ibid., 127.

21. McMahon, "'Small Matters,'" 167.

22. Ibid., 170.

23. McMahon, "Dock Creek," 114–47.

24. Oliver H. Orr Jr., *Saving America's Birds: T. Gilbert Pearson and the Founding of the Audubon Movement* (Gainesville: University Press of Florida, 1992), 27.

25. Frank Graham Jr., *The Audubon Ark: A History of the National Audubon Society* (New York: Knopf, 1990), 12.

26. Orr, *Saving America's Birds,* 25.

27. "The Audubon Society," *Forest and Stream,* 11 February 1886, 41.

28. Ibid.

29. Orr, *Saving America's Birds,* 27.

30. Ibid., 7.

31. Ibid., 29.

32. Ibid.

33. Harriet Kofalk, *No Woman Tenderfoot: Florence Merriam Bailey, Pioneer Naturalist* (College Station: Texas A&M University Press, 1989), 34.

34. Graham, *Audubon Ark,* 3.

35. Robin W. Doughty, *Feather Fashions and Bird Preservation: A Study in Nature Protection* (Berkeley: University of California Press, 1975), 101–2.

36. Graham, *Audubon Ark,* 13.

37. Orr, *Saving America's Birds,* 48. The other *a* in *Harper's Bazaar* was added in 1929.

38. Theodore Peterson, *Magazines in the Twentieth Century* (Champaign: University of Illinois Press, 1956), 218–20.

39. Doughty, *Feather Fashions,* 52.

40. Graham, *Audubon Ark,* 13.

41. William A. Gamson, *The Strategy of Social Protest,* 2nd ed. (Belmont, Calif.: Wadsworth, 1990).

42. Jennifer Price, "Hats Off to Audubon," *Audubon,* November/December 2004, 46.

43. Witmer Stone, "Report of the A.O.U. Committee on Protection of North American Birds," *The Auk,* January 1900, 51–52.

44. Doughty, *Feather Fashions,* 54n.

45. Philippon, *Conserving Words,* 95–103.

46. Felton Gibbons and Deborah Strom, *Neighbors to the Birds: A History of Birdwatching in America* (New York: Norton, 1988), 110–11.

47. Graham, *Audubon Ark,* 16.

48. One of Franklin's popular stories concerned the blackbird and the farmer's corn. In an attempt to create an analogy between the mechanical and natural worlds, he told of the farmer who netted or shot blackbirds that he thought were raiding his fields, not knowing that the birds were also eating insects harmful to the corn.

49. Graham, *Audubon Ark,* 13.

50. Jennifer Price, *Flight Maps: Adventures with Nature in Modern America* (New York: Basic Books, 1999).

51. Kofalk, *No Woman Tenderfoot,* 90.

52. Price, *Flight Maps,* 79–80.

53. Ibid., 99.

54. National Audubon Society, http://www.audubon.org/bird/cbc/history.html.

55. Doughty, *Feather Fashions,* 15, 80–81.

56. Ibid., 22–23.

57. Price, *Flight Maps,* 86.

58. Philippon, *Conserving Words,* 92.

59. Price, "Hats Off," 48.

60. Florence Merriam Bailey, "Olive Thorne Miller," *The Auk,* April 1919, 168.

61. George F. Hoar, "The Birds' Petition to the Massachusetts General Court," *New England Magazine,* July 1897, 614.

62. Graham, *Audubon Ark,* 62, 66.

63. Price, *Flight Maps,* 87.

64. Price, "Hats Off," 50.

65. Graham, *Audubon Ark,* 56.

66. Ibid., 58.

67. "Notes and News," *The Auk,* April 1905, 232.

68. Graham, *Audubon Ark,* 35.

69. Price, *Flight Maps,* 65–69.

70. See, for example, Robert W. Righter, *The Battle over Hetch Hetchy: America's Most Controversial Dam and the Birth of Modern Environmentalism* (New York: Oxford University Press, 2005); and John Warfield Simpson, *Dam! Water Power, Politics, and Preservation in Hetch Hetchy and Yosemite National Park* (New York: Pantheon, 2005).

71. Historian Mark Harvey has noted the importance of a series of stories by A. G. Birch in the *Denver Post* in 1928 that helped raise awareness of the area.

72. As quoted in Philip Fradkin, *A River No More: The Colorado River and the West,* rev. ed. (Berkeley: University of California Press, 1996), 191.

73. As quoted in Russell Martin, *A Story That Stands Like a Dam: Glen Canyon and the Struggle for the Soul of the West* (New York: Holt, 1989), 52.

74. Mark W. T. Harvey, *A Symbol of Wilderness: Echo Park and the American Conservation Movement* (Albuquerque: University of New Mexico Press, 1994), 77.

75. Bernard DeVoto, "Shall We Let Them Ruin Our National Parks?" in *DeVoto's West,* ed. Edward K. Muller (Athens: Ohio University Press, 2005), 192.

76. Ibid., 193.

77. Fradkin, *A River No More,* 191.

78. Martin, *Stands Like a Dam,* 55.

79. Roderick Nash, *Wilderness and the American Mind,* 3rd ed. (New Haven, Conn.: Yale University Press, 1982), 212.

80. Harvey, *Symbol of Wilderness,* 270.

81. Ibid., 87.

82. Ibid., 168.

83. Fradkin, *A River No More,* 192; Nash, *Wilderness and the American Mind,* 212.

84. Martin, *Stands Like a Dam,* 59.

85. Righter, *Battle over Hetch Hetchy,* 213.

86. Harvey, *Symbol of Wilderness,* 169.

87. Sierra Club, http://www.sierraclub.org/history/origins/chapter7.asp.

88. Wallace Stegner, ed., *This Is Dinosaur: Echo Park Country and Its Magic Rivers* (New York: Knopf, 1955). *This Is Dinosaur* was the spark for a successful run of publications from 1960 to 1968 called the Sierra Club Exhibit Format Series.

89. Ibid., 17.

90. Marc Reisner, *Cadillac Desert: The American West and Its Disappearing Water* (New York: Viking, 1986), 294.

91. Martin, *Stands Like a Dam,* 59.

92. Harvey, *Symbol of Wilderness,* 92.

93. Nash, *Wilderness and the American Mind,* 218.

94. Harvey, *Symbol of Wilderness,* 276.

95. Fradkin, *A River No More,* 193.

96. Harvey, *Symbol of Wilderness,* 166–67.

97. Ibid., 265.

98. Nash, *Wilderness and the American Mind,* 213.

99. Fradkin, *A River No More,* 193.

100. Martin, *Stands Like a Dam,* 67.

101. Ibid., 69.

102. Ibid., 71.

103. Nash, *Wilderness and the American Mind,* 219.

104. Donald Worster, *Rivers of Empire: Water, Aridity, and the Growth of the American West* (New York: Pantheon, 1985).

105. Byron E. Pearson, *Still the Wild River Runs: Congress, the Sierra Club, and the Fight to Save Grand Canyon* (Tucson: University of Arizona Press, 2002). Pearson's view on the Grand Canyon struggle was that Stewart Udall's political pragmatism, not the conservationists' campaigns, stopped the dams.

106. Michael Cohen, *History of the Sierra Club* (San Francisco: Sierra Club Books, 1988).

107. Samuel P. Hays, *Beauty, Health, and Permanence: Environmental Politics in the United States, 1955–1985* (New York: Cambridge University Press, 1987).

108. John McPhee, *Encounters with the Archdruid* (New York: Farrar, Straus and Giroux, 1971), 164.

109. Paul Rogers, "Should They Drain Hetch Hetchy?" *San Jose Mercury News,* 20 July 2006, 1ff.

CHAPTER SEVEN

1. Mitchell Stephens, *A History of News* (New York: Viking, 1988), 228.

2. Ted Curtis Smythe, "The Reporter, 1880–1900: Working Conditions and Their Influence on the News," *Journalism History* 7, no. 1 (Spring 1980): 1.

3. Hazel Dicken-Garcia, *Journalistic Standards in Nineteenth-Century America* (Madison: University of Wisconsin Press: 1989), 63.

4. Stephen Ponder, "'Nonpublicity' and the Unmaking of a President: William Howard Taft and the Ballenger-Pinchot Controversy of 1909–1910," *Journalism History* 19, no. 4 (Winter 1994): 111–21.

5. Donald A. Ritchie, *Press Gallery: Congress and the Washington Correspondents* (Cambridge, Mass.: Harvard University Press, 1991). See also George Juergens, *News from the White House: The Presidential-Press Rela-*

tionship in the Progressive Era (Chicago: University of Chicago Press, 1981).

6. Stephen Ponder, *Managing the Press: Origins of the Media Presidency, 1897–1933* (New York: St. Martin's Press, 1999).

7. Edward G. Lowry, "The White House Now," *Harper's Weekly,* 15 May 1909, 7.

8. Ponder, "'Nonpublicity,'" 1.

9. James Penick Jr., *Progressive Politics and Conservation: The Ballinger-Pinchot Affair of 1909–1910* (Chicago: University of Chicago Press, 1968).

10. Walter Lippmann, *Drift and Mastery* (Madison: University of Wisconsin Press, 1985), 25.

11. Robert K. Otterbourg, "Gifford Pinchot: Conservationist and Publicist," *Public Relations Quarterly,* Summer 1974, 19–23.

12. Harold T. Pinkett, *Gifford Pinchot* (Urbana: University of Illinois Press, 1970), 53.

13. Edward Bernays, *Public Relations* (Norman: University of Oklahoma Press, 1952), 51.

14. Fox, *John Muir,* 134.

15. Char Miller, *Gifford Pinchot and the Making of Modern Environmentalism* (Washington, D.C.: Island, 2001), 211.

16. Ponder, "'Nonpublicity,'" 3.

17. Ibid., 3.

18. Neuzil and Kovarik, *Mass Media and Environmental Conflict,* 86.

19. Samuel P. Hays, *Conservation and the Gospel of Efficiency* (Cambridge, Mass.: Harvard University Press, 1958).

20. Neuzil and Kovarik, *Mass Media and Environmental Conflict,* 94.

21. Arthur Weinberg and Lila Weinberg, eds., *The Muckrakers* (Urbana: University of Illinois Press, 2001), 147.

22. Ibid.

23. Gifford Pinchot, *Breaking New Ground* (Washington, D.C.: Island, 1998), 446.

24. John L. Mathews, "The Ballinger-Pinchot Controversy," *Hampton's,* November 1909, 674.

25. "Can This Be Whitewashed Also?" *Collier's,* 18 December 1909, 8–9.

26. Penick, *Progressive Politics and Conservation,* 130.

27. Neuzil and Kovarik, *Mass Media and Environmental Conflict,* 99.

28. Miller, *Gifford Pinchot,* 218.

29. A. T. Mason, *Bureaucracy Convicts Itself* (New York: Viking, 1941), 107.

30. Penick, *Progressive Politics and Conservation,* 150.

31. Otterbourg, "Gifford Pinchot," 23.

32. Ponder, "'Nonpublicity.'"

33. George E. Mowry, *The Era of Theodore Roosevelt, 1900–1912* (New York: Harper, 1958), 258.

34. "Naked He Plunges into the Maine Woods to Live Alone Two Months," *Boston Post,* 4 August 1913, 1ff.

35. An important difference is that Nellie Bly participated and wrote the stories herself, while Knowles wrote and supplied the details, but he was not a journalist. Reporters back at the *Post* composed the stories from Knowles's writings. See Brooke Kroeger, *Nelly Bly: Daredevil, Reporter, Feminist* (New York: Times Books, 1994).

36. "Knowles Last Day in the Woods," *Boston Post,* 3 October 1913, 9.

37. Paul Waitt, "Knowles, Clad in Skins, Comes Out of the Forest," *Boston Post,* 5 October 1913, 1ff.

38. Ibid., 10.

39. Herbert A. Kenny, *Newspaper Row: Journalism in the Pre-Television Era* (Chester, Conn.: Globe-Pequot, 1987).

40. Stewart Holbrook, "The Original Nature Man," *American Mercury* 39 (1936): 419–22.

41. "Knowles, the Modern Forest Man, Welcomed by Cheering Thousands," *Boston Post,* 10 October 1913, 1ff.

42. "The Truth About Knowles," *Boston American,* 28 November 1913, 1ff.

43. Ibid. The reference to Dr. Cook was to Frederick Albert Cook, an American explorer-surgeon who claimed to have reached the North Pole on April 21, 1908, almost a year before Admiral Richard Perry reached the pole. Cook's claims were widely credited and he received honorary degrees, filled lecture halls, and authored a best-selling book. His North Pole claims were discovered to be fraudulent, however, though he maintained that his experiences as an explorer were authentic.

44. If this injunction was indeed issued, it would be a rare example of prior restraint in American media law history, but I have not been able to find a record of the court action.

45. "Bullet Holes in Knowles' Bearskin," *Boston American,* 9 December 1913, 4.

46. "Indisputable Evidence Modern Tools Were Used," *Boston American,* 7 December 1913, 1ff.

47. "Knowles Official Photographer Says Ford Story Is Right," *Boston American,* 14 December 1913, 1ff.

48. "Another Unjust Attack on Knowles Refuted," *Boston Post,* 15 December 1913, 1ff.

49. "Artist Knowles on Homeward Journey," *Boston Post,* 6 October 1913, 3.

50. Holbrook, "Original Nature Man."

51. "Nature Man," *Hearst's Magazine,* 13 December 1913, 954ff.

52. Holbrook, "Original Nature Man."

53. Richard O. Boyer, "Where Are They Now? The Nature Man," *New Yorker,* 18 June 1938, 21–25.

54. Ibid.

55. Catherine L. Covert and John D. Stevens, *Mass Media Between the Wars: Perceptions of Cultural Tension, 1918–1941* (Syracuse, N.Y.: Syracuse University Press, 1984), xiii.

56. T. J. Jackson Lears, *No Place of Grace* (New York: Pantheon and Tripps, 1981); C. Dean, "Modernization Theory and the Comparative Study of Societies," *Comparative Studies in Society and History* 15 (1973): 199–226.

57. Frederick Jackson Turner, *The Frontier in American History* (New York: Holt, 1920).

58. William L. Bowers, *The Country Life Movement in America* (Port Washington, N.Y.: Kennikat, 1974).

59. Shi, *The Simple Life.*

60. Robert H. Wiebe, *The Search for Order, 1877–1920* (New York: Hill and Wang, 1967).

61. Samuel P. Hays, *The Response to Industrialism, 1885–1914,* 2nd ed. (Chicago: University of Chicago Press, 1995).

62. Noel Gist and L. A. Halbert, *Urban Society* (New York: Thomas Crowell, 1933), 285.

63. Thomas Slaughter, *The Natures of John and William Bartram* (New York: Knopf, 1996).

64. Mark Neuzil, "The Great Moon Hoax of 1835," *History Channel*

Magazine, September/October 2005, 34–37. The moon hoax was perpetuated in 1835 by the *New York Sun* and a reporter named Richard Adams Locke. His made-up reports, framed around a real-life astronomer, spoke of winged men and women on the moon, surrounded by lush forests full of blue unicorns and bipedal beavers. The stories fooled some and entertained many in the public and the scientific community.

65. Hays, *Beauty, Health, and Permanence.*

66. Philip J. Tichenor, George A. Donohue, and Clarice Olien, *Community Conflict and the Press* (Beverly Hills, Calif.: Sage, 1980).

67. Joseph C. Harry, "Covering Conflict: A Structural-Pluralist Analysis of How a Small-Town and Big-City Newspaper Reported an Environmental Controversy," *Journalism and Mass Communication Quarterly* 78, no. 3 (Summer 2001): 419–36.

68. Clarice Olien, George A. Donohue, and Philip J. Tichenor, "Conflict, Consensus, and Public Opinion," in *Public Opinion and the Communication of Consent,* ed. Theodore L. Glasser and Charles T. Salmon (New York: Guilford, 1995), 301–22.

69. Martin Cherniak, *The Hawk's Nest Incident* (New Haven, Conn.: Yale University Press, 1986), 50–51.

70. Ibid., 53.

71. Ibid., 52.

72. Ibid., 53.

73. Albert Maltz, "Man on the Road," *New Masses,* 8 January 1935, 19–21.

74. Bernard Allen, "Two Thousand Men Dying on a Job," *New Masses,* 15 January 1935, 18–19, and 22 January 1935, 19–21.

75. Judith Serrin and William Serrin, *Muckraking! The Journalism That Changed America* (New York: New Press, 2002), 37.

76. Cherniak, *Hawk's Nest Incident,* 80.

77. Serrin and Serrin, *Muckraking!* 37.

78. Cherniak, *Hawk's Nest Incident,* 89–105.

79. W. S. Cooper, "Solving Interstate Air Pollution Problems," in *Proceedings of the National Conference on Air Pollution, November 18–20, 1958* (Washington, D.C.: Government Printing Office, 1958), 416.

80. E. C. Halliday, "An Historical Review of Air Pollution," in *Air Pollution* (New York: World Health Organization, Columbia University Press, 1961), 9–37.

81. Neuzil and Kovarik, *Mass Media and Environmental Conflict,* 182.

82. *The Story of the St. Louis Post-Dispatch* (St. Louis: Pulitzer, 1954), 18.

83. Virginia Irwin, "Children of Darkness," *Everyday Magazine,* 18 January 1940, 3D.

84. John Hohenburg, *The Pulitzer Prizes* (New York: Columbia University Press, 1974), 128.

85. As quoted in Mary Delach Leonard, "Post-Dispatch Crusade Led to Cleaner Air in St. Louis," *St. Louis Post-Dispatch,* 14 January 2003, 18.

86. *Story of the St. Louis Post-Dispatch,* 18.

87. James W. Markham, *Brovard of the Post-Dispatch* (Baton Rouge: Louisiana State University Press, 1954), 111.

88. Ibid., 121–25.

89. *Story of the St. Louis Post-Dispatch,* 38.

90. Daniel W. Pfaff, *Joseph Pulitzer II and the Post-Dispatch* (College Station: Pennsylvania State University Press, 1991), 314, 320.

91. Serrin and Serrin, *Muckraking!* 37.

92. *Story of the St. Louis Post-Dispatch,* 41.

93. John Bartlow Martin, "The Blast in Centralia No. 5: A Mine Disaster No One Stopped," *Harper's,* March 1948, 24.

94. Serrin and Serrin, *Muckraking!* 39.

95. John Hohenberg, ed., *The Pulitzer Prize Story* (New York: Columbia University Press, 1959), 58.

96. *Story of the St. Louis Post-Dispatch,* 43.

97. Martin, "The Blast in Centralia No. 5," 1–28.

98. Ibid., 5.

99. Hohenberg, *Pulitzer Prize Story,* 59.

100. Martin, "The Blast in Centralia No. 5," 28.

101. *Charleston Gazette,* http://www.wvgazette.com/section/Series/The+Sago+Mine+Disaster.

CHAPTER EIGHT

1. Stephen R. Miller, "Disappearing Green Ink," *Sierra,* November/December 2003, 50.

2. The scholarly journals include *Environmental Communication, Public Understanding of Science, Science Communication,* and *ISLE: Interdisciplinary*

Studies in Literature and Environment. Professional societies include the Society of Environmental Journalists, the National Association of Science Writers, and the Outdoor Writers Association of America. Academic organizations include the Science Communication Interest Group of the Association for Education in Journalism and Mass Communication, the American Society on Literature and the Environment, and the Conference on Communication and Environment. The education service is the Environmental Communication Network.

3. Chris Bowman, "Needed: A Recommitment," *Nieman Reports,* Winter 1996, 5.

4. Ibid., 7.

5. Stewart Udall, *The Quiet Crisis and the Next Generation* (Salt Lake City: Gibbs Smith, 1988), 201–2.

6. Opie, *Nature's Nation,* 414.

7. Robert Gottlieb, *Forcing the Spring: The Transformation of the American Environmental Movement* (Washington, D.C.: Island, 1993), 81.

8. Mary A. McCay, *Rachel Carson* (New York: Twayne, 1993), xv–xvi.

9. Paul Brooks, *Speaking for Nature: How Literary Naturalists from Henry Thoreau to Rachel Carson Have Shaped America* (Boston: Houghton Mifflin, 1980), 278.

10. Trimble, *Words from the Land,* 22.

11. Udall, *Quiet Crisis,* 197.

12. See ibid., 197; Opie, *Nature's Nation,* 413.

13. Paul Brooks, *House of Life: Rachel Carson at Work* (Boston: Houghton Mifflin, 1972), 227.

14. Ibid., 235.

15. Ibid.

16. Priscilla Coit Murphy, *What a Book Can Do: The Publication and Reception of Silent Spring* (Amherst: University of Massachusetts Press, 2005), 10.

17. Brooks, *House of Life,* 248.

18. Rachel Carson, *Silent Spring* (Boston: Houghton Mifflin, 1962).

19. Brooks, *House of Life,* 293.

20. Murphy, *What a Book Can Do,* 4.

21. Linda Lear, *Rachel Carson: Witness for Nature* (New York: Holt, 1997), 420.

22. H. Patricia Hynes, *The Recurring Silent Spring* (New York: Pergamon, 1989), 40.

23. Ibid., 19.

24. Lear, *Rachel Carson,* 450.

25. Ibid., 470–71.

26. Hynes, *Recurring Silent Spring,* 156.

27. Ibid., 3–4.

28. Murphy, *What a Book Can Do,* 15.

29. Ibid., 16.

30. G. Ray Funkhouser, "The Issues of the Sixties: An Exploratory Study in the Dynamics of Public Opinion," *Public Opinion Quarterly* 37 (1973): 62–75; also in G. Ray Funkhouser, "Trends in Media Coverage of the Issues of the '60s," *Journalism Quarterly* 50, no. 3 (Autumn 1973): 533–38.

31. Robert H. Clifford, "City's Lakes and River Fronts in Constant Peril Without the Protection of Fire Tugs," *Cleveland Press,* 25 April 1936, 1.

32. "Oil Slick Fire Damages 2 River Spans," *Cleveland Plain Dealer,* 23 June 1969, 1C.

33. "The Cuyahoga River Caught Fire," *Cleveland Press,* 23 June 1969, 1.

34. Jonathan H. Adler, "Fables of the Cuyahoga: Reconstructing a History of Environmental Protection," *Fordham Environmental Law Journal* 14, no. 1 (Fall 2002): 98.

35. Ibid., 96.

36. Daniel Boorstin, *The Image: A Guide to Pseudo-Events in America* (New York: Atheneum, 1961), 11–12, 205–10.

37. Stacie Thomas, "The Cuyahoga Revisited," *The Freeman: Ideas on Liberty,* May 2000, 38.

38. Ibid.

39. Adler, "Fables of the Cuyahoga," 102.

40. Ibid., 110.

41. Betty Klaric, "Stokes Promises to Lead Pollution Fight," *Cleveland Press,* 24 June 1969, D3.

42. "The Cities: The Price of Optimism," *Time,* 1 August 1969, 41.

43. Ibid.

44. "Sad, Soiled Waters: The Cuyahoga River and Lake Erie," *National Geographic,* December 1970, 743–44.

45. Richard Liroff, *A National Policy for the Environment* (Bloomington: Indiana University Press, 1976). Nearly every major U.S. newspaper failed to cover the passage of the National Environmental Protection Act. See A. Clay Schoenfeld, "The Press and NEPA: The Case of the Missing Agenda," *Journalism Quarterly* 56, no. 2 (August 1979): 577–85, 587.

46. Randy Newman, "Burn On," *Sail Away* (Los Angeles: Rhino Records #78244, 1972).

47. Adler, "Fables of the Cuyahoga," 136.

48. Friedman, Dunwoody, and Rogers, *Scientists and Journalists,* xiv.

49. Erick Howenstine, "Environmental Reporting: Shift from 1970 to 1982," *Journalism Quarterly* 64, no. 3 (Autumn 1987): 842–46.

50. John DeMott and Emmanuel Tom, "The Press Corps of Spaceship Earth: A Trend Analysis, 1968–1988," *Newspaper Research Journal* 11, no. 4 (Fall 1990): 12–23.

51. William Witt, "The Environmental Reporter on U.S. Daily Newspapers," *Journalism Quarterly* 51, no. 4 (Winter 1974): 697–704.

52. Ibid.

53. Steven E. Hungerford, "Covering the Environment: A New 'Afghanistanism'?" *Journalism Quarterly* 50, no. 3 (Autumn 1973): 475–81.

54. Sharon Friedman, "Two Decades of the Environmental Beat," in LaMay and Dennis, *Media and the Environment,* 18.

55. Ibid., 21.

56. Ibid., 24.

57. John Palen, "Objectivity as Independence," *Science Communication* 21, no. 2 (December 1999): 159.

58. Ibid., 160.

59. Eric Nalder, "Covering Valdez: No Place for Those Bean Counters," *SEJournal* 1, no. 1 (Fall 1990): 1, 5–6.

60. Palen, "Objectivity as Independence," 159.

61. Ibid., 160.

62. The highly respected Ward lost his associate member status in the mid-1990s after he worked on a project for the U.S. Department of Energy that the SEJ board considered to be public relations. He was later named an honorary member.

63. Palen, "Objectivity as Independence," 161.

64. Sharon Friedman, "And the Beat Goes On: The Third Decade of Environmental Reporting," in *The Environmental Communication Yearbook,* vol. 1, ed. Susan Senecah (Mahwah, N.J.: Lawrence Erlbaum, 2004), 175.

65. Anthony Downs, "Up and Down with Ecology: The 'Issue-Attention' Cycle," *Public Interest* 28 (Summer 1972): 38–50.

66. Ibid., 40.

67. Allan Mazur, "Global Environmental Change in the News," *International Sociology* 13, no. 4 (December 1998): 457–72.

68. Jim Detjen, "Erosion of Serious Reporting," *Quill* 83, no. 8 (October 1995): 8.

69. *Nieman Reports,* Winter 1996.

70. Friedman, "And the Beat Goes On," 177.

71. Melanie Sill, "Needed: Long-Haul Commitment," *Nieman Reports,* Winter 1996, 17.

72. Paul Rogers, "Complexity in Environment Reporting Is Critical to Public Decision-Making," *Nieman Reports,* Winter 2002, 32.

73. Ibid., 32.

74. Friedman, "And the Beat Goes On," 182–83.

75. Bowman, "Needed: A Recommitment," 7.

76. James Bruggers, "The Beat Is a Tougher One Today," *Nieman Reports,* Winter 2002, 38.

77. Everette E. Dennis, "In Context: Environmentalism in the System of News," in LaMay and Dennis, *Media and the Environment,* 57.

CHAPTER NINE

1. Jacques Rivard, "Fighting to Get Environmental Stories on Television," *Nieman Reports,* Winter 2002, 74–75.

2. Ibid., 75.

3. Natalie Pawelski, "Networks Aren't Tuned into the Environment," *Nieman Reports,* Winter 2002, 70.

4. David Ropeik, "The Challenge to TV," *Nieman Reports,* Winter 1996, 21.

5. Susan Bickelhaupt, "NPR Launches 'Living on Earth,'" *Boston Globe,* 20 April 1991, 28.

6. Clea Simon, "It's a Tough Sell for Stations, But 'Living on Earth'

Returns," *Boston Globe,* 13 August 2005, D7.

7. Peter Thomson, "Radio Uses Sound and Script to Transport Listeners to a Place," *Nieman Reports,* Winter 2002, 70.

8. Bickelhaupt, "NPR Launches 'Living on Earth,'" 28.

9. Ibid., 28.

10. "Amid the Static and the Screeching, Science Talk Radio Stands Out," *Buffalo News,* 7 May 2001, B2.

11. Simon, "Tough Sell for Stations," D7.

12. Ibid.

13. Great Lakes Radio Consortium, http://www.environmentreport.org/.

14. Robert Goldberg and Gerald Jay Goldberg, *Citizen Turner: The Wild Rise of an American Tycoon* (New York: Harcourt, Brace, 1995), 323.

15. Ibid., 325.

16. Ibid.

17. Peter Dykstra, interview by author, 13 September 2006.

18. Goldberg and Goldberg, *Citizen Turner,* 329.

19. Ibid., 327.

20. Carl Pope, "Television Misses the Picture," *Sierra,* March/April 1996, 12.

21. Ryan, "Network Earth," 83.

22. Ibid.

23. Ruth Norris, "More Than a Nature Show," *Audubon,* March 1985, 22ff.

24. Stuart Elliott, "Ford Pulls Commercials from Audubon Show," *New York Times,* 12 June 1991, D18.

25. Goldberg and Goldberg, *Citizen Turner,* 424.

26. Ibid., 423.

27. Ropeik, "The Challenge to TV," 23.

28. Pawelski, "Networks Aren't Tuned," 69.

29. Bill Dawson, "CNN's Environment Unit: End of the Road for What Remained," *Environment Writer,* August 2005, http://www.environmentwriter.org/.

30. Krista West, "The Billionaire Conservationist," *Scientific American* 287, no. 2 (August 2002): 34–35.

31. Dawson, "CNN's Environment Unit."

32. Christian Kallen, "'Assignment Earth' Fills a Gap in the News," Yahoo.com, 29 August 2006, www.yahoo.com.

33. Peter Kaplan, "Cable Pioneer Discovers Value of Putting Substance over Style," *Washington Times,* 23 December 1996, D11.

34. Ed Kirchdoerffer, "Tribute: Exploring John Hendricks' World," *RealScreen,* 1 September 1997, 53.

35. Ibid.

36. Jacque Jones, "Discovery Channel Pioneered Format," *Television Week,* 24 May 2004, 22.

37. "Discovery Communications Announces 100th Network Milestone," Discovery Communications Inc. press release, 3 October 2006.

38. "Discovery, ESPN Reach 90 Million Viewers," *Television Week,* 30 May 2005, 4.

39. Joel Brown, "Outdoor Cable Networks Find Their Own Space," *Broadcasting and Cable,* 10 October 2005, 16.

40. Lee Alan Hill, "Bikes, Bulls Raise Ratings," *Television Week,* 25 July 2005, 49.

41. Shannon Peavey, "Outdoor Focus: Cable Networks Zero in on Niche Events, Athletics," *Television Week,* 12 July 2004, 18.

42. Larry Stewart, "OLN Switches to 'Versus,'" *Los Angeles Times,* 25 September 2006, 7.

43. Hill, "Bikes, Bulls Raise Ratings," 49.

44. Michael Greenberg and others, "Risk, Drama, and Geography in Coverage of Environmental Risk by Network TV," *Journalism Quarterly* 66: no. 2 (Summer 1989), 267–76.

45. *Covering Key Environmental Issues: A Handbook for Journalists,* 4th ed. (Washington, D.C.: Radio and Television News Directors Foundation, 1994), 3.

46. Ibid., 3.

47. "Executive Summary of RTNDF's News Study," Poynter Online, 3 October 2006, www.poynter.org.

48. Bill Dawson, "Network TV News E-Coverage Plummeted in 2005, Survey Finds," *Environment Writer,* July 2006, http://www.environmentwriter.org/.

49. "'State of Beat' Report Paints Grim Picture of Broadcast, Cable TV Coverage," *Environment Writer,* October 2004, http://www.environmentwriter.org/.

50. Ibid.

CHAPTER TEN

1. Kerasote, "Short History of Hunting," 100.

2. Jerry Walker, "Ex-N.Y. Times Reporter to Edit Newsletter," *Jack O'Dwyer's Newsletter,* 15 May 1991, 4.

3. "National Journal Group Announces Sale of Greenwire to E&E Publishing," *PR Newswire,* 5 October 2000.

4. Bill Dawson, "ENN—Environmental News Network—A Decade Old and Moving Forward," *Environment Writer,* June 2004, http://www.environmentwriter.org/.

5. Ibid.

6. "EW-Q&A: Pete Myers of Environmental Health News," *Environment Writer,* August 2006, http://www.environmentwriter.org/.

7. Ibid.

8. Gregory Dicum, "Green Blogs: The Revolution Moves Online," SFGate.com (online site of the *San Francisco Chronicle*), www.SFGate.com.

9. Ibid.

10. "EW-Q&A: Lisa Stiffler and Robert McClure," *Environment Writer,* April 2006, http://www.environmentwriter.org/.

11. Erika Archibald, "Problems with Environmental Reporting: Perspectives of Daily Newspaper Reporters," *Journal of Environmental Education* 30, no. 4 (Summer 1999): 28.

12. Michael Kinsley, "The Twilight of Objectivity," *Slate,* 31 March 2006, http://www. slate.com/id/2139042.

13. Ian Buruma, "Theater of War," *New York Times,* 17 September 2006, sec. 7, pp. 1ff.

14. "They Walk the Line," *Grist,* www.grist.org.

15. Ibid.

16. Ibid.

17. "Tides Foundation Honors Chip Giller, Founder and President of *Grist Magazine,* with the Prestigious Jane Bagley Lehman Award for Excellence in Public Advocacy," *Grist,* www.grist.org.

18. "Audience for *Grist*'s Coverage of 'Poverty and the Environment' Surpasses 2.6 Million," *Grist,* www.grist.org.

19. Kevin Friedl, "The Poorest for the Trees," *Columbia Journalism Re-*

view, May/June 2006, 17.

20. Matthew Klingle and Joseph E. Taylor III, "Caste from the Past: Environmentalism's Elitist Tinge Has Roots in the Movement's History," *Grist,* www.grist.org.

21. *Grist,* www.grist.org.

BIBLIOGRAPHY

BOOKS

Ackland, Len. *Making a Real Killing.* Albuquerque: University of New Mexico Press, 1999.

Adams, Henry. *The Education of Henry Adams.* New York: Modern Library, 1931.

Allan, Stuart, Barbara Adam, and Cynthia Carter. *Environmental Risks and the Media.* New York: Routledge, 1999.

Allen, William. *Green Phoenix: Restoring the Tropical Rain Forests of Guanacaste, Costa Rica.* New York: Oxford University Press, 2001.

Anderson, Alison. *Media, Culture and the Environment.* New Brunswick, N.J.: Rutgers University Press, 1997.

Anderson, Lorraine. *Sisters of the Earth.* New York: Vintage, 1991.

Atkinson, Brooks, ed. *The Selected Writings of Ralph Waldo Emerson.* New York: Random House, 1940.

Backes, David. *Canoe Country: An Embattled Wilderness.* Minocqua, Wis.: NorthWord, 1991.

———. *A Wilderness Within: The Life of Sigurd F. Olson.* Minneapolis: University of Minnesota Press, 1997.

Bailey, Ronald. *Eco-Scam: The False Prophets of Ecological Apocalypse.* New York: St. Martin's Press, 1993.

Baker, Richard Terrill. *A History of the Graduate School of Journalism.* New York: Columbia University Press, 1954.

Baldwin, Edward Chauncey. *The Prophet.* New York: Thomas Nelson and Son, 1927.

Bandstra, Barry L. *Reading the Old Testament: An Introduction to the Hebrew Bible.* New York: Wadsworth, 1999.

Barrus, Clara. *The Life and Letters of John Burroughs.* 2 vols. Boston: Houghton Mifflin, 1925.

278   BIBLIOGRAPHY

Baskin, Yvonne. *A Plague of Rats and Rubbervines: The Growing Threat of Species Invasions.* Washington, D.C.: Island, 2002.

Benton, Lisa M., and John R. Short. *Environmental Discourse and Practice.* Oxford: Blackwell, 1999.

Bernays, Edward. *Public Relations.* Norman: University of Oklahoma Press, 1952.

Blum, Deborah, and Mary Knudson, eds. *A Field Guide for Science Writers.* New York: Oxford University Press, 1997.

Boorstin, Daniel. *The Image: A Guide to Pseudo-Events in America.* New York: Atheneum, 1961.

Bottrall, Margaret. *Izaak Walton.* London: Longmans, Green, 1955.

Bowers, William L. *The Country Life Movement in America.* Port Washington, N.Y.: Kennikat, 1974.

Brady, Bernard. *The Moral Bond of Community.* Washington, D.C.: Georgetown University Press, 1998.

Branch, Michael P., ed. *Reading the Roots: American Nature Writing Before Walden.* Athens: University of Georgia Press, 2004.

Brooks, Paul. *House of Life: Rachel Carson at Work.* Boston: Houghton Mifflin, 1972.

———. *Speaking for Nature: How Literary Naturalists from Henry Thoreau to Rachel Carson Have Shaped America.* Boston: Houghton Mifflin, 1980.

Brown, Candy Gunther. *The Word in the World: Evangelical Writing, Publishing and Reading in America, 1789–1880.* Chapel Hill: University of North Carolina Press, 2004.

Brubacher, John A., and Willis Rudy. *Higher Education in Transition: A History of American Colleges and Universities, 1636–1976.* New York: Harper and Row, 1976.

Buell, Lawrence. *The Environmental Imagination: Thoreau, Nature Writing, and the Formation of American Culture.* Cambridge, Mass.: Belknap Press of Harvard University Press, 1995.

Burnham, John C. *How Superstition Won and Science Lost: Popularizing Science and Health in the United States.* New Brunswick, N.J.: Rutgers University Press, 1987.

Burroughs, John. *Field and Study.* Boston: Houghton Mifflin, 1919.

———. *Time and Change.* Boston: Houghton Mifflin, 1912.

————. *Wake-Robin.* Boston: Houghton Mifflin, 1902.

Canham, Erwin D. *Commitment to Freedom.* Boston: Houghton Mifflin, 1958.

Cantrill, James G., and Christine L. Oravec, eds. *The Symbolic Earth: Discourse and Our Creation of the Environment.* Lexington: University Press of Kentucky, 1996.

Carson, Rachel. *Silent Spring.* Boston: Houghton Mifflin, 1962.

Cato the Censor. *On Farming.* Translated by Ernest Brehaut. New York: Octagon Books, 1966.

Cherniak, Martin. *The Hawk's Nest Incident.* New Haven, Conn.: Yale University Press, 1986.

Cohen, Michael. *History of the Sierra Club.* San Francisco: Sierra Club Books, 1988.

Columella, Lucius Junius Moderatus. *On Agriculture.* Translated by Harrison Boyd Ash. Cambridge, Mass.: Harvard University Press, 1941.

Cooper, John R. *The Art of The Compleat Angler.* Durham, N.C.: Duke University Press, 1968.

Corbett, Julia. *Communicating Nature: How We Create and Understand Environmental Messages.* Washington, D.C.: Island, 2007.

Covering Key Environmental Issues: A Handbook for Journalists, 4th ed. Washington, D.C.: Radio and Television News Directors Foundation, 1994.

Covert, Catherine L., and John D. Stevens. *Mass Media Between the Wars: Perceptions of Cultural Tension, 1918–1941.* Syracuse, N.Y.: Syracuse University Press, 1984.

Cox, Robert. *Environmental Communication in the Public Sphere.* Thousand Oaks, Calif.: Sage, 2006.

Crouthamel, James L. *Bennett's New York Herald and the Rise of the Popular Press.* Syracuse, N.Y.: Syracuse University Press, 1989.

Cullimore, Don G., and Edwin W. Hanson. *Sixty-Five Years of OWAA, 1927–1992.* State College, Pa.: Outdoor Writers Association of America, 1993.

Darwin, Charles. *The Variation of Animals and Plants Under Domestication.* London: John Murray, 1868.

Dicken-Garcia, Hazel. *Journalistic Standards in Nineteenth-Century America.* Madison: University of Wisconsin Press, 1989.

Dickson, Tom. *Mass Media Education in Transition.* Mahwah, N.J.: Lawrence Erlbaum, 2000.

Dietrich, William. *The Final Forest: The Battle for the Last Great Trees of the Pacific Northwest.* New York: Simon and Schuster, 1992.

Doughty, Robin W. *Feather Fashions and Bird Preservation: A Study in Nature Protection.* Berkeley: University of California Press, 1975.

Dryzek, John S. *The Politics of the Earth: Environmental Discourses,* 2nd ed. New York: Oxford University Press, 2005.

Dunlap, Thomas. *Faith in Nature: Environmentalism as Religious Quest.* Seattle: University of Washington Press, 2004.

Elder, John, ed. *American Nature Writers.* New York: Scribner's, 1996.

Fisher, Paul. *The Angler's Souvenir.* London: Charles Tilt, 1835.

Flader, Susan. *Thinking Like a Mountain.* Madison: University of Wisconsin Press, 1994.

Folkerts, Jean, and Dwight L. Teeter Jr. *Voices of a Nation: A History of Mass Media in the United States,* 4th ed. Boston: Allyn and Bacon, 2002.

Forester, Frank. *Fish and Fishing of the United States and British Provinces of North America.* Rev. ed. New York: W. A. Townsend, 1864.

Fox, Stephen. *John Muir and His Legacy: The American Conservation Movement.* Boston: Little, Brown, 1981.

Fradkin, Philip. *A River No More: The Colorado River and the West,* rev. ed. Berkeley: University of California Press, 1996.

French, Roger, and Frank Greenaway, eds. *Science in the Early Roman Empire: Pliny the Elder, His Sources and His Influence.* Totowa, N.J.: Barnes and Noble, 1986.

Friedman, Sharon M., Sharon Dunwoody, and Carol L. Rogers. *Scientists and Journalists: Reporting Science as News.* New York: Free Press, 1986.

Fritzell, Peter A. *Nature Writing and America.* Ames: Iowa State University Press, 1990.

Frome, Michael. *Green Ink: An Introduction to Environmental Journalism.* Salt Lake City: University of Utah Press, 1998.

———. *Greenspeak: Fifty Years of Environmental Muckraking and Advocacy.* Knoxville: University of Tennessee Press, 2002.

Gamson, William A. *The Strategy of Social Protest,* 2nd ed. Belmont, Calif.: Wadsworth, 1990.

Gans, Herbert. *Deciding What's News.* New York: Vintage, 1979.

Gates, Barbara T., ed. *In Nature's Name: An Anthology of Women's Writing and Illustration, 1780–1930.* Chicago: University of Chicago Press, 2002.

———. *Kindred Nature: Victorian and Edwardian Women Embrace the Loving World.* Chicago: University of Chicago Press, 1999.

Gelbspan, Ross. *The Heat Is On.* New York: Addison-Wesley, 1997.

Gibbons, Felton, and Deborah Strom. *Neighbors to the Birds: A History of Birdwatching in America.* New York: Norton, 1988.

Gist, Noel, and L. A. Halbert. *Urban Society.* New York: Thomas Crowell, 1933.

Glick, Daniel. *Powder Burn: Arson, Money and Mystery on Vail Mountain.* New York: Public Affairs, 2001.

Goetzmann, William H., and Kay Sloan. *Looking Far North: The Harriman Expedition to Alaska, 1899.* Princeton, N.J.: Princeton University Press, 1982.

Goldberg, Robert, and Gerald Jay Goldberg. *Citizen Turner: The Wild Rise of an American Tycoon.* New York: Harcourt, Brace, 1995.

Gordon, Robert P., ed. *The Place Is Too Small for Us: The Israelite Prophets in Recent Scholarship.* Winona Lake, Ind.: Eisenbrauns, 1995.

Gottlieb, Robert. *Forcing the Spring: The Transformation of the American Environmental Movement.* Washington, D.C.: Island, 1993.

Graham, Frank, Jr. *The Audubon Ark: A History of the National Audubon Society.* New York: Knopf, 1990.

Grayson, Melvin J. *The Disaster Lobby: Prophets of Ecological Doom and Other Absurdities.* River Grove, Ill.: Follett, 1973.

Gruenberg, Benjamin. *Science and the Public Mind.* New York: McGraw-Hill, 1935.

Gutjahr, Paul C. *An American Bible: A History of the Good Book in the United States.* Stanford, Calif.: Stanford University Press, 1999.

Guynup, Sharon, ed. *State of the Wild 2006.* Washington, D.C.: Island, 2006.

Hansen, Anders, ed. *The Mass Media and Environmental Issues.* Leicester, Eng.: Leicester University Press, 1993.

Harding, Walter. *A Thoreau Handbook.* New York: New York University Press, 1959.

Harré, Rom, Jens Brockmeier, and Peter Mühlhäusler. *Greenspeak: A Study of Environmental Discourse.* Thousand Oaks, Calif.: Sage, 1999.

Harvey, Mark W. T. *A Symbol of Wilderness: Echo Park and the American Conservation Movement.* Albuquerque: University of New Mexico Press, 1994.

Hay, Peter. *Main Currents in Western Environmental Thought.* Bloomington: Indiana University Press, 2002.

Hays, Samuel P. *Beauty, Health, and Permanence: Environmental Politics in the United States, 1955–1985.* New York: Cambridge University Press, 1987.

———. *Conservation and the Gospel of Efficiency.* Cambridge, Mass.: Harvard University Press, 1958.

———. *The Response to Industrialism, 1885–1914,* 2nd ed. Chicago: University of Chicago Press, 1995.

Herndl, Carl G., and Stuart C. Brown, eds. *Green Culture: Environmental Rhetoric in Contemporary America.* Madison: University of Wisconsin Press, 1996.

Hofstadter, Richard. *The Age of Reform.* New York: Random House, 1955.

Hohenberg, John, ed. *The Pulitzer Prize Story.* New York: Columbia University Press, 1959.

———. *The Pulitzer Prizes.* New York: Columbia University Press, 1974.

The Holy Bible: New Revised Standard Version. Grand Rapids, Mich.: Zondervan, 1990.

Host, David. *The Citizen and the News.* Milwaukee: Marquette University Press, 1962.

Huxley, Aldous. *Jonah.* Oxford: Holywell, 1919.

Hynes, H. Patricia. *The Recurring Silent Spring.* New York: Pergamon, 1989.

Irwin, Kevin W., and Edmund D. Pellegrino, eds. *Preserving the Creation: Environmental Theology and Ethics.* Washington, D.C.: Georgetown University Press, 1994.

Juergens, George. *News from the White House: The Presidential-Press Relationship in the Progressive Era.* Chicago: University of Chicago Press, 1981.

Kamrin, Michael A., Dolores J. Katz, and Martha L. Walter. *Reporting on Risk: A Journalist's Handbook on Environmental Risk Assessment*. Ann Arbor: Michigan Sea Grant Program, 1995.

Kenny, Herbert A. *Newspaper Row: Journalism in the Pre-Television Era*. Chester, Conn.: Globe-Pequot, 1987.

Kofalk, Harriet. *No Woman Tenderfoot: Florence Merriam Bailey, Pioneer Naturalist*. College Station: Texas A&M University Press, 1989.

Krieghbaum, Hillier. *Science and the Mass Media*. New York: New York University Press, 1967.

Kroeger, Brooke. *Nelly Bly: Daredevil, Reporter, Feminist*. New York: Times Books, 1994.

Kronick, David A. *A History of Scientific and Technical Periodicals*. New York: Scarecrow, 1962.

Krutch, Joseph Wood. *Great American Nature Writing*. New York: William Sloane, 1950.

LaMay, Craig L., and Everette E. Dennis, eds. *Media and the Environment*. Washington, D.C.: Island, 1991.

Lear, Linda. *Rachel Carson: Witness for Nature*. New York: Holt, 1997.

Lears, T. J. Jackson. *No Place of Grace*. New York: Pantheon and Tripps, 1981.

Leopold, Aldo. *A Sand County Almanac*. New York: Oxford University Press, 1949.

Lippmann, Walter. *Drift and Mastery*. Madison: University of Wisconsin Press, 1985.

Liroff, Richard. *A National Policy for the Environment*. Bloomington: Indiana University Press, 1976.

Longo, Bernadette. *Spurious Coin: A History of Science, Management, and Technical Writing*. Albany: State University of New York Press, 2000.

Lounsberry, Barbara. *The Art of Fact: Contemporary Artists of Nonfiction*. Westport, Conn.: Greenwood, 1990.

Lule, Jack. *Daily News, Eternal Stories: The Mythological Role in Journalism*. New York: Guilford, 2001.

Lundgren, Regina, and Andrea McMakin. *Risk Communication: A Handbook for Communicating Environmental, Safety, and Health Risks*. Columbus, Ohio: Battelle, 1998.

Lutts, Ralph. *The Nature Fakers: Wildlife, Science and Sentiment.* Golden, Colo.: Fulcrum, 1990.

Lyon, Thomas J. *This Incomperable Lande: A Book of American Nature Writing.* Boston: Houghton Mifflin, 1989.

Mabie, Hamilton Wright. *Books and Culture.* New York: Dodd, Mead, 1896.

———. *Essays on Nature and Culture.* New York: Dodd, Mead, 1896.

———. *Short Studies in Literature.* New York: Dodd, Mead, 1891.

Markham, James W. *Brovard of the Post-Dispatch.* Baton Rouge: Louisiana State University Press, 1954.

Martin, Russell. *A Story That Stands Like a Dam: Glen Canyon and the Struggle for the Soul of the West.* New York: Holt, 1989.

Mason, A. T. *Bureaucracy Convicts Itself.* New York: Viking, 1941.

Matthiessen, Peter. *The Snow Leopard.* New York: Viking, 1978.

Mazel, David, ed. *A Century of Early Ecocriticism.* Athens: University of Georgia Press, 2001.

McCay, Mary A. *Rachel Carson.* New York: Twayne, 1993.

McElheny, Victor K. *Science in the Newspaper.* Washington, D.C.: American Association for the Advancement of Science, 1974.

McPhee, John. *Encounters with the Archdruid.* New York: Farrar, Straus and Giroux, 1971.

Meine, Curt. *Aldo Leopold: His Life and Works.* Madison: University of Wisconsin Press, 1988.

Meister, Mark, and Phyllis M. Japp. *Enviropop: Studies in Environmental Rhetoric and Popular Culture.* Westport, Conn.: Praeger, 2002.

Melville, Herman. *Moby-Dick.* New York: Barnes and Noble Classics, 2003.

Miller, Char. *Gifford Pinchot and the Making of Modern Environmentalism.* Washington, D.C.: Island, 2001.

Mindich, David. *Just the Facts: How "Objectivity" Came to Define American Journalism.* New York: New York University Press, 1998.

Morris, Edmund. *The Rise of Theodore Roosevelt.* New York: Putnam, 1979.

Motavalli, Jim. *Naked in the Woods: Joseph Knowles and the Legacy of Frontier Fakery.* New York: Da Capo Press, 2008.

Mott, Frank Luther. *A History of American Magazines,* vol. 1. New York: Appleton, 1938.

————. *A History of American Magazines,* vol. 2. New York: Appleton, 1938.

————. *A History of American Magazines,* vol. 3. New York: Appleton, 1938.

————. *A History of American Magazines,* vol. 4. Cambridge, Mass.: Harvard University Press, 1958.

————. *Time Enough: Essays in Autobiography.* Chapel Hill: University of North Carolina Press, 1962.

Mowry, George E. *The Era of Theodore Roosevelt, 1900–1912.* New York: Harper, 1958.

Muir, John. *A Thousand-Mile Walk to the Gulf.* New York: Houghton Mifflin, 1916.

Murphy, Priscilla Coit. *What a Book Can Do: The Publication and Reception of Silent Spring.* Amherst: University of Massachusetts Press, 2005.

Myerson, George, and Yvonne Rydin. *The Language of Environment: A New Rhetoric.* Vancouver: University of British Columbia Press, 1996.

Myerson, Joel. *The New England Transcendentalists and "The Dial": A History of the Magazine and Its Contributors.* Rutherford, N.J.: Fairleigh Dickinson University Press, 1980.

Nash, Roderick. *Wilderness and the American Mind,* 3rd ed. New Haven, Conn.: Yale University Press, 1982.

Neuzil, Mark, and William Kovarik. *Mass Media and Environmental Conflict: America's Green Crusades.* Thousand Oaks, Calif.: Sage, 1996.

Nord, David Paul. *Faith in Printing.* New York: Oxford, 2004.

Norris, Thaddeus. *American Angler's Book.* Philadelphia: Porter and Coates, 1864.

————. *American Fish Culture.* Philadelphia: Porter and Coates, 1868.

O'Dell, De Forest. *A History of Journalism Education in the United States.* New York: Columbia University Press, 1935.

Oliver, Peter. *A New Chronicle of The Compleat Angler.* London: Paisley, 1936.

Olson, Sigurd. *The Singing Wilderness.* New York: Knopf, 1956.

Opie, John. *Nature's Nation: An Environmental History of the United States.* New York: Harcourt Brace, 1998.

Orr, Oliver H., Jr. *Saving America's Birds: T. Gilbert Pearson and the Founding of the Audubon Movement.* Gainesville: University Press of Florida, 1992.

Orwell, George. *Such, Such Were the Joys*. New York: Harcourt, Brace, 1953.

Palmer, Susan J. *Aliens Adored: Rael's UFO Religion*. New Brunswick, N.J.: Rutgers University Press, 2004.

Parker, Lea J. *Ecoculture: Environmental Messages in Music, Art, and Literature*. Dubuque, Iowa: Kendall Hunt, 2002.

―――. *Environmental Communication: Messages, Media and Methods: A Handbook for Advocates and Organizations*. Dubuque, Iowa: Kendall Hunt, 1997.

Pawlick, Thomas F. *The Invisible Farm: The Worldwide Decline in Farm News and Agricultural Journalism Training*. Chicago: Burnham, 2001.

Pearson, Byron E. *Still the Wild River Runs: Congress, the Sierra Club, and the Fight to Save Grand Canyon*. Tucson: University of Arizona Press, 2002.

Penick, James, Jr. *Progressive Politics and Conservation: The Ballinger-Pinchot Affair of 1909–1910*. Chicago: University of Chicago Press, 1968.

Perkins, William D. *Index to the Collected Works of John Burroughs*. New York: John Burroughs Association, 1995.

Peterson, Theodore. *Magazines in the Twentieth Century*. Champaign: University of Illinois Press, 1956.

Pfaff, Daniel W. *Joseph Pulitzer II and the Post-Dispatch*. State College: Pennsylvania State University Press, 1991.

Philippon, Daniel J. *Conserving Words: How American Nature Writers Shaped the Environmental Movement*. Athens: University of Georgia Press, 2004.

Pinchot, Gifford. *Breaking New Ground*. Washington, D.C.: Island, 1998.

Pinkett, Harold T. *Gifford Pinchot*. Urbana: University of Illinois Press, 1970.

Pliny the Elder. *The Natural History*, vol. 2. Translated by Harris Rackham. Cambridge, Mass.: Harvard University Press, 1942.

Ponder, Stephen. *Managing the Press: Origins of the Media Presidency, 1897–1933*. New York: St. Martin's Press, 1999.

Price, Jennifer. *Flight Maps: Adventures with Nature in Modern America*. New York: Basic Books, 1999.

Raeburn, Paul. *The Last Harvest: The Genetic Gamble That Threatens to Destroy American Agriculture*. New York: Simon and Schuster, 1995.

Reisner, Marc. *Cadillac Desert: The American West and Its Disappearing Water.* New York: Viking, 1986.

Renehan, Edward J., Jr. *John Burroughs: An American Naturalist.* Post Mills, Vt.: Chelsea Green, 1992.

Righter, Robert W. *The Battle over Hetch Hetchy: America's Most Controversial Dam and the Birth of Modern Environmentalism.* New York: Oxford University Press, 2005.

Ritchie, Donald A. *Press Gallery: Congress and the Washington Correspondents.* Cambridge, Mass.: Harvard University Press, 1991.

Roosevelt, Theodore. *The Wilderness Hunter.* New York: Putnam's, 1893.

Sachs, Aaron. *The Humboldt Current: Nineteenth-Century Exploration and the Roots of American Environmentalism.* New York: Viking, 2006.

Sandman, Peter, David Sachsman, Michael Greenberg, and Michael Gochfeld. *Environmental Risk and the Press: An Exploratory Assessment.* New Brunswick, N.J.: Transaction, 1987.

Sarver, Stephanie L. *Uneven Land: Nature and Agriculture in American Writing.* Lincoln: University of Nebraska Press, 1999.

Schmitt, Peter J. *Back to Nature: The Arcadian Myth in Urban America.* New York: Oxford University Press, 1969.

Serrin, Judith, and William Serrin. *Muckraking! The Journalism That Changed America.* New York: New Press, 2002.

Shanahan, James, and Katherine McComas. *Nature Stories: Depictions of the Environment and Their Effects.* Cresskill, N.J.: Hampton, 1999.

Shi, David E. *The Simple Life: Plain Living and High Thinking in American Culture.* New York: Oxford University Press, 1985.

Simon, Bart. *Undead Science: Science Studies and the Afterlife of Cold Fusion.* New Brunswick, N.J.: Rutgers University Press, 2002.

Simpson, John Warfield. *Dam! Water Power, Politics, and Preservation in Hetch Hetchy and Yosemite National Park.* New York: Pantheon, 2005.

Slaughter, Thomas. *The Natures of John and William Bartram.* New York: Knopf, 1996.

Smelzer, Neil. *Theory of Collective Behavior.* Chicago: Free Press, 1963.

Stanwood, Paul G. *Izaak Walton.* New York: Twayne, 1998.

Stegner, Wallace, ed. *This Is Dinosaur: Echo Park Country and Its Magic Rivers.* New York: Knopf, 1955.

Stephens, Mitchell. *A History of News.* New York: Viking, 1988.

Stewart, Frank. *A Natural History of Nature Writing*. Washington, D.C.: Island, 1995.

Stineman, Esther Lanigan. *Mary Austin: Song of a Maverick*. New Haven, Conn.: Yale University Press, 1989.

The Story of the St. Louis Post-Dispatch. St. Louis: Pulitzer, 1954.

Tanner, Thomas, ed. *Aldo Leopold: The Man and His Legacy*. Ankeny, Iowa: Soil Conservation Society of America, 1987.

Thoreau, Henry David. *Thoreau: Collected Essays and Poems*. Edited by Elizabeth Hall Witherell. New York: Library of America, 2001.

———. *Walden*. New Haven, Conn.: Yale University Press, 2004.

Tichenor, Philip J., George A. Donohue, and Clarice Olien. *Community Conflict and the Press*. Beverly Hills, Calif.: Sage, 1980.

Trimble, Stephen, ed. *Words from the Land: Encounters with Natural History Writing*. Salt Lake City: Gibbs Smith, 1989.

Turner, Frederick Jackson. *The Frontier in American History*. New York: Holt, 1920.

Udall, Stewart. *The Quiet Crisis and the Next Generation*. Salt Lake City: Gibbs Smith, 1988.

Underwood, Doug. *From Yahweh to Yahoo!: The Religious Roots of the Secular Press*. Champaign: University of Illinois Press, 2002.

United Nations Food and Agriculture Organization. *The State of Food and Agriculture, 1994*. Rome: Food and Agriculture Organization, 1994.

Vasey, Daniel E. *An Ecological History of Agriculture: 10,000 B.C.–A.D. 10,000*. Ames: Iowa State University Press, 1992.

Voigt, William, Jr. *Born with Fists Doubled: Defending Outdoor America*. Spirit Lake, Iowa: Izaak Walton League of America, 1992.

Waddell, Craig, ed. *Landmark Essays on Rhetoric and the Environment*. Hillsdale, N.J.: Lawrence Erlbaum, 1997.

Walker, Charlotte Zoe, ed. *Sharp Eyes: John Burroughs and American Nature Writing*. Syracuse, N.Y.: Syracuse University Press, 2000.

Walton, Izaak. *The Compleat Angler*, 1st ed. Edited by Bryan Loughery. London: Penguin, 1985.

———. *The Compleat Angler*, 5th ed. London: Oxford University Press, 1915.

Weinberg, Arthur, and Lila Weinberg, eds. *The Muckrakers*. Urbana: University of Illinois Press, 2001.

West, Bernadette, Peter M. Sandman, and Michael R. Greenberg. *The Reporter's Environmental Handbook*. New Brunswick, N.J.: Rutgers University Press, 1995.

Westbrook, Perry. *John Burroughs.* New York: Twayne, 1974.

White, Hayden. *The Content of the Form: Narrative Discourse and Historical Representation*. Baltimore: Johns Hopkins University Press, 1987.

Wiebe, Robert H. *The Search for Order, 1877–1920.* New York: Hill and Wang, 1967.

Williams, Bruce A., and Albert R. Matheny. *Democracy, Dialogue, and Environmental Disputes: The Contested Languages of Social Regulation*. New Haven, Conn.: Yale University Press, 1995.

Worster, Donald. *Nature's Economy: The Roots of Ecology.* Garden City, N.Y.: Anchor/Doubleday, 1979.

———. *Rivers of Empire: Water, Aridity, and the Growth of the American West*. New York: Pantheon, 1985.

Wright, Mabel Osgood. *The Friendship of Nature: A New England Chronicle of Birds and Flowers*. Baltimore: Johns Hopkins University Press, 1999.

ARTICLES AND CHAPTERS

ABC, "Publisher's Statement," 30 June 2005.

Ackerman, Diane. "King Penguins." In *By the Light of the Glow-Worm Lamp: Three Centuries of Reflections on Nature,* ed. Alberto Manguel, 241–46. New York: Plenum, 1998.

Adler, Jonathan H. "Fables of the Cuyahoga: Reconstructing a History of Environmental Protection." *Fordham Environmental Law Journal* 14, no. 1 (Fall 2002): 89–146.

Allen, Bernard. "Two Thousand Men Dying on a Job." *New Masses,* 15 January 1935, 18–19, and 22 January 1935, 19–21.

"Americans at Play." *The Living Age* 214, 24 July 1897, 217–80.

"Amid the Static and the Screeching, Science Talk Radio Stands Out." *Buffalo News,* 7 May 2001, B2.

Andsager, Julie J., and Leiott Smiley. "Evaluating the Public Information: Shaping News Coverage of the Silicone Implant Controversy." *Public Relations Review* 24 (1998): 183–201.

"Announcement." *Forest and Stream,* 14 August 1873, 8–9.

"Another Unjust Attack on Knowles Refuted." *Boston Post,* 15 December 1913, 1ff.

"AP Picks Top Stories." Associated Press, 21 December 1990.

Archibald, Erika. "Problems with Environmental Reporting: Perspectives of Daily Newspaper Reporters." *Journal of Environmental Education* 30, no. 4 (Summer 1999): 27–32.

"Artist Knowles on Homeward Journey." *Boston Post,* 6 October 1913, 3.

"Audience for *Grist's* Coverage of 'Poverty and the Environment' Surpasses 2.6 Million." *Grist.* www.grist.org.

"The Audubon Society." *Forest and Stream,* 11 February 1886, 41.

Bailey, Florence Merriam. "Olive Thorne Miller." *Auk,* April 1919, 168.

Banning, Stephen A. "The Cradle of Professional Journalistic Education in the Mid-Nineteenth Century." *Media History Monographs* 4, no. 1 (2000–2001). http://www.scripps.ohiou.edu/mediahistory/mhmjour4-1.htm.

Berger, Guy. "Environmental Journalism Meets the 21st Century." *Intermedia* 30, no. 5 (December 2002): 8–11.

Bergon, Frank. "'Sensitive to the Verge of the Horizon': The Environmentalism of John Burroughs." In *Sharp Eyes: John Burroughs and American Nature Writing,* ed. Charlotte Zoe Walker, 19–25. Syracuse, N.Y.: Syracuse University Press, 2000.

"Best-Loved Books." *Sierra,* March/April 2001, 9–11.

Betts, John R. "Sporting Journalism in 19th Century America." *American Quarterly* 5 (1953): 39–56.

Bickelhaupt, Susan. "NPR Launches 'Living on Earth.'" *Boston Globe,* 20 April 1991, 28.

Bookchin, Murray. "Radical Agriculture." In *Radical Agriculture,* ed. Richard Merrill, 3–13. New York: New York University Press, 1976.

Bowman, Chris. "Needed: A Recommitment." *Nieman Reports,* Winter 1996, 5–8.

Boyce, Nell, and James M. Pethokoukis. "Clowns or Cloners?" *U.S. News and World Report,* 13 January 2003, 48.

Boyer, Richard O. "Where Are They Now? The Nature Man." *New Yorker,* 18 June 1938, 21–25.

Branswell, Brenda. "Raelians Had Chortle over Cloning." *Montreal Gazette,* 9 October 2003, A8.

Brasher, Bryan. "Some Anglers Too Caught Up in Catch-and-Release." *Memphis Commercial Appeal,* 9 April 2006, C11.

Brown, Joel. "Outdoor Cable Networks Find Their Own Space." *Broadcasting and Cable,* 10 October 2005, 16.

Bruggers, James. "The Beat Is a Tougher One Today." *Nieman Reports,* Winter 2002, 36–38.

"Bullet Holes in Knowles' Bearskin." *Boston American,* 9 December 1913, 4.

Burroughs, John. "Gilbert White's Book." *Lippincott's,* August 1886, 133–40.

———. "Henry D. Thoreau." *Century Magazine,* May 1882, 368–79.

———. "The Literary Treatment of Nature." *Atlantic Monthly,* July 1904, 38–43.

———. "Nature in Literature." *Critic,* July 1881, 185.

———. "Real and Sham Natural History." *Atlantic Monthly,* March 1903, 298–310.

———. "The True Test of Good Nature Literature." *Country Life,* May 1904, 51–53.

Buruma, Ian. "Theater of War." *New York Times,* 17 September 2006, sec. 7, pp. 1ff.

Cahn, Robert. "Books (Not Thneeds) Are What Everyone Needs." In *Media and the Environment,* ed. Craig L. LaMay and Everette E. Dennis, 225–44. Washington, D.C.: Island, 1991.

Callicott, J. Baird. "The Scientific Substance of the Land Ethic." In *Aldo Leopold: The Man and His Legacy,* ed. Thomas Tanner, 87–104. Ankeny, Iowa: Soil Conservation Society of America, 1987.

"Can This Be Whitewashed Also?" *Collier's,* 18 December 1909, 8–9.

Carey, James W. "A Plea for the University Tradition." *Journalism Quarterly* 55, no. 4 (Winter 1978): 846–55.

Chawla, Louise. "Childhood Place Attachments." In *Human Behavior and Environments: Advances in Theory and Research.* Vol. 12, *Place Attachments,* ed. Irwin Altman and Setha M. Low, 63–84. New York: Plenum, 1992.

Chicago Advance, 30 January 1873, 11.

"The Cities: The Price of Optimism." *Time,* 1 August 1969, 41.

Clifford, Richard. "The Bible and the Environment." In *Preserving the Creation: Environmental Theology and Ethics,* ed. Kevin W. Irwin and

Edmund D. Pellegrino, 1–26. Washington, D.C.: Georgetown University Press, 1994.

Clifford, Robert H. "City's Lakes and River Fronts in Constant Peril Without the Protection of Fire Tugs." *Cleveland Press,* 25 April 1936, 1.

Clover, Charles. "Licenses to Kill Cormorants Rise to 3,000." *London Daily Telegraph,* 31 August 2005, 4.

"Cold Fusion Farewell." *New Scientist,* 21 March 1998, 2323.

"Comment on New Books." *Atlantic Monthly,* December 1893, 850.

Cooper, Thomas. "The Connection Between Geology and the Pentateuch." *Knickerbocker Magazine* 8, May 1836, 441–52.

Cooper, W. S. "Solving Interstate Air Pollution Problems." In *Proceedings of the National Conference on Air Pollution, November 18–20, 1958,* 416–26. Washington, D.C.: Government Printing Office, 1958.

Coughlin, William J. "Think Globally, Act Locally." In *Media and the Environment,* ed. Craig L. LaMay and Everette E. Dennis, 115–24. Washington, D.C.: Island, 1991.

Crayon, Porte. "The Mountains—VIII." *Harper's New Monthly Magazine* 47, November 1873, 821–32.

"The Cuyahoga River Caught Fire." *Cleveland Press,* 23 June 1969, 1.

Davis, Watson. "Science, the Press and Intellectual Advance." *Vital Speeches* 3 (1937): 207–15.

Dawson, Bill. "CNN's Environment Unit: End of the Road for What Remained." *Environment Writer,* August 2005. http://www.environmentwriter.org/.

———. "ENN—Environmental News Network—A Decade Old and Moving Forward." *Environment Writer,* June 2004. http://www.environmentwriter.org/.

———. "Network TV News E-Coverage Plummeted in 2005, Survey Finds." *Environment Writer,* July 2006. http://www.environmentwriter.org/.

Dean, C. "Modernization Theory and the Comparative Study of Societies." *Comparative Studies in Society and History* 15 (1973): 199–226.

DeMott, John, and Emmanuel Tom. "The Press Corps of Spaceship Earth: A Trend Analysis, 1968–1988." *Newspaper Research Journal* 11, no. 4 (Fall 1990): 12–23.

Dennis, Everette E. "In Context: Environmentalism in the System of News." In *Media and the Environment,* ed. Craig L. LaMay and Everette E. Dennis, 55–66. Washington, D.C.: Island, 1991.

———. "Whatever Happened to Marse Roberts' Dream?" *Gannett Center Journal* 2, no. 1 (Spring 1988): 1–22.

Dennis, Jerry. "Pliny's World: All the Facts and Then Some." *Smithsonian* 26, no. 8, November 1995, 152–63.

Dentry, Ed. "Is Hunting a Sport? That's Your Call." *Rocky Mountain News,* 9 April 1997, 14C.

Detjen, Jim. "Erosion of Serious Reporting." *Quill* 83, no. 8 (October 1995): 8.

DeVoto, Bernard. "Shall We Let Them Ruin Our National Parks?" In *DeVoto's West,* ed. Edward K. Muller, 189–202. Athens: Ohio University Press, 2005.

Dicum, Gregory, "Green Blogs: The Revolution Moves Online." SFGate.com (online site of the *San Francisco Chronicle*). www.SFGate.com.

"Discovery, ESPN Reach 90 Million Viewers." *Television Week,* 30 May 2005, 4.

"Discovery Communications Announces 100th Network Milestone." Discovery Communications Inc. press release, 3 October 2006.

Donohue, George A., Philip J. Tichenor, and Clarice Olien. "A Guard Dog Perspective on the Role of the Media." *Journal of Communication* 45 (1995): 115–32.

Downs, Anthony. "Up and Down with Ecology: The 'Issue-Attention' Cycle." *Public Interest* 28 (Summer 1972): 38–50.

"Dr. G. B. Grinnell, Naturalist, Dead." *New York Times,* 12 April 1938, 23.

Driessen, Paul. "Prophets, False Prophets and Profiteers." www.intellectualconservative.com.

Dumont, Frank. "De Gospel Raft." In *Minstrel Songs, Old and New,* 176–77. Boston: Oliver Ditson, 1883.

Durham, Frank. "Exposed by Katrina: The Gulf Between the President and the Press." *Critical Studies in Mass Communication* 23, no. 1 (March 2006): 81–84.

Eckstrom, Fannie. "Fannie Eckstrom on Thoreau's *The Maine Woods.*" In *A Century of Early Ecocriticism,* ed. David Mazel, 163–72. Athens: University of Georgia Press, 2001.

"Editor's Literary Record." *Harper's New Monthly Magazine* 46, May 1873, 933.

Egan, D'Arcy. "Crying Fowl over Copious Cormorant." *Cleveland Plain Dealer,* 10 June 2005, D8.

Elliott, Stuart. "Ford Pulls Commercials from Audubon Show." *New York Times,* 12 June 1991, D18.

Emerson, Ralph Waldo. "Nature." In *The Selected Writings of Ralph Waldo Emerson,* ed. Brooks Atkinson, 3–42. New York: Random House, 1940.

Esquivel, Paloma. "Reporters Discuss Hurricane Experiences." *Syracuse Post-Standard,* 7 February 2006, B3.

"EW-Q&A: Lisa Stiffler and Robert McClure." *Environment Writer,* April 2006. http://www.environmentwriter.org/.

"Executive Summary of RTNDF's News Study." Poynter Online, 3 October 2006. www.poynter.org.

Fiquette, Larry. "How Quake Prediction Hysteria Grew." *St. Louis Post-Dispatch,* 9 December 1990, 1Dff.

Fisher, Marc. "Essential Again." *American Journalism Review* 27, no. 5, October/November 2005, 18–22.

Foderaro, Lisa W. "Cormorants Take Over, Making Some Enemies." *New York Times,* 1 July 2005, B2.

Foust, James C. "E. W. Scripps and the Science Service." *Journalism History* 21, no. 2 (Summer 1995): 58–65.

Fraley, Pierre C. "The Education and Training of Science Writers." *Journalism Quarterly* 40, no. 2 (Summer 1963): 323–28.

Freeman, Mark. "Keeping the Bean-Counters Happy." *Outdoors Unlimited,* January 2006. http://www.owaa.org/Tech-E_archives/Jan-Feb06.htm#feature3.

Friedl, Kevin. "The Poorest for the Trees." *Columbia Journalism Review,* May/June 2006, 17.

Friedman, Sharon. "And the Beat Goes On: The Third Decade of Environmental Reporting." In *The Environmental Communication Yearbook,* vol. 1., ed. Susan Senecah, 175–88. Mahwah, N.J.: Lawrence Erlbaum, 2004.

———. "Two Decades of the Environmental Beat." In *Media and the Environment,* ed. Craig L. LaMay and Everette E. Dennis, 17–28. Washington, D.C.: Island, 1991.

Fritz, Michael. "Tribune Co. Near Deal to Bring Farm Magazines into Its Fold." *Crain's Chicago Business,* 25 April 1994/1 May 1994, 16.

Fuller, Margaret. "Preliminary Note." In Henry David Thoreau, *Thoreau: Collected Essays and Poems,* ed. Elizabeth Hall Witherell, 20. New York: Library of America, 2001.

Funkhouser, G. Ray. "The Issues of the Sixties: An Exploratory Study in the Dynamics of Public Opinion." *Public Opinion Quarterly* 37 (1973): 62–75.

———. "Trends in Media Coverage of the Issues of the '60s." *Journalism Quarterly* 50, no. 3 (Autumn 1973): 533–38.

Glasser, Theodore L., and James S. Ettema. "Investigative Journalism and the Moral Order." *Critical Studies in Mass Communication* 6, no. 1 (March 1989): 1–20.

Greenberg, Michael, David Sachsman, Peter Sandman, and Kandice Salomone. "Risk, Drama, and Geography in Coverage of Environmental Risk by Network TV." *Journalism Quarterly* 66: no. 2 (Summer 1989): 267–76.

Halliday, E. C. "An Historical Review of Air Pollution." In *Air Pollution,* 9–37. New York: World Health Organization, Columbia University Press, 1961.

Halsey, Francis. "The Rise of Nature Writers." *American Monthly Review of Reviews,* November 1902, 567–71.

Handwerk, Brian. "Louisiana Coast Threatened by Wetlands Loss." *National Geographic News.* http://news.nationalgeographic.com/news/2005/02/0209_050209_wetlands.html.

Harden, Blaine. "NRA and Outdoor Writers Have Falling Out." *Washington Post,* 9 July 2004, A3.

Harry, Joseph C. "Covering Conflict: A Structural-Pluralist Analysis of How a Small-Town and Big-City Newspaper Reported an Environmental Controversy." *Journalism and Mass Communication Quarterly* 78, no. 3 (Summer 2001): 419–36.

"Henry William Herbert, 'Frank Forester.'" *International Magazine of Literature, Art, and Science* 3, no. 2, 1 June 1851, 289–92.

Hernon, Peter. "Pressing On . . . New Madrid Ready for Media to Leave." *St. Louis Post-Dispatch,* 4 December 1990, 1Aff.

Hill, Lee Alan. "Bikes, Bulls Raise Ratings." *Television Week,* 25 July 2005, 49.

Hoar, George F. "The Birds' Petition to the Massachusetts General Court." *New England Magazine,* July 1897, 614–16.

Holbrook, Stewart. "The Original Nature Man." *American Mercury* 39, 1936, 419–22.

"How the Chemist Moves the World," *Science News Letter,* 21 October 1922, 2.

Howenstine, Erick. "Environmental Reporting: Shift from 1970 to 1982." *Journalism Quarterly* 64, no. 3 (Autumn 1987): 842–46.

Hungerford, Steven E. "Covering the Environment: A New 'Afghanistanism'?" *Journalism Quarterly* 50, no. 3 (Autumn 1973): 475–81.

"Indisputable Evidence Modern Tools Were Used." *Boston American,* 7 December 1913, 1ff.

Irwin, Virginia. "Children of Darkness." *Everyday Magazine,* 18 January 1940, 3D.

Jones, Jacque. "Discovery Channel Pioneered Format." *Television Week,* 24 May 2004, 22.

"Journalist Rues Role in Rael Claim." Associated Press, 10 January 2003.

Kallen, Christian. "'Assignment Earth' Fills a Gap in the News." Yahoo .com, 29 August 2006. www.yahoo.com.

Kaplan, Peter. "Cable Pioneer Discovers Value of Putting Substance over Style." *Washington Times,* 23 December 1996, D11.

Kaufmann, William. "Rediscovering John Burroughs." In *Sharp Eyes: John Burroughs and American Nature Writing,* ed. Charlotte Zoe Walker, 279–86. Syracuse, N.Y.: Syracuse University Press, 2000.

Kaul, Art. "Hunter S. Thompson." In *Dictionary of Literary Biography.* Vol. 185, *American Literary Journalists, 1945–1995,* 311–23. Detroit: Gale, 1997.

Kerasote, Ted. "A Short History of Hunting in America." In *State of the Wild 2006,* ed. Sharon Guynup, 99–105. Washington, D.C.: Island, 2006.

Kinney, Arthur F. "Editor's Note." In Paul G. Stanwood, *Izaak Walton.* New York: Twayne, 1998, xi.

Kinsley, Michael. "The Twilight of Objectivity." *Slate,* 31 March 2006. http://www.slate.com/id/2139042.

Kirchdoerffer, Ed. "Tribute: Exploring John Hendricks' World." *RealScreen,* 1 September 1997, 53.

Klaric, Betty. "Stokes Promises to Lead Pollution Fight." *Cleveland Press,* 24 June 1969, D3.

Klingle, Matthew, and Joseph E. Taylor III. "Caste from the Past: Environmentalism's Elitist Tinge Has Roots in the Movement's History." *Grist.* www.grist.org.

"Knowles, the Modern Forest Man, Welcomed by Cheering Thousands." *Boston Post,* 10 October 1913, 1ff.

"Knowles Last Day in the Woods." *Boston Post,* 3 October 1913, 9.

"Knowles Official Photographer Says Ford Story Is Right." *Boston American,* 14 December 1913, 1ff.

Knudson, Tom. "Environment, Inc." *Sacramento Bee,* 22–26 April 2001, 1ff.

Kolbert, Elizabeth. "Watermark: Can Southern Louisiana Be Saved?" *New Yorker,* 27 February 2006, 46–57.

Krieghbaum, Hillier. "The Background and Training of Science Writers." *Journalism Quarterly* 17 (March 1940): 15–18.

———. "Reporting Science Information Through the Mass Media." *Journalism Quarterly* 40, no. 2 (Summer 1963): 291–92.

LaMay, Craig L. "Heat and Light: The Advocacy-Objectivity Debate." In *Media and the Environment,* ed. Craig L. LaMay and Everette E. Dennis, 103–13. Washington, D.C.: Island, 1991.

Lane, Laura. "A Pioneer Who Didn't Feel Like One." In *Farm Magazines, Milestones and Memories: American Agricultural Editors' Association, 1921–1996,* ed. Wayne E. Swegle and John R. Harvey, 14–15. New Prague, Minn.: American Agricultural Editors' Association, 1996.

Lee, James Melvin. "Schools of Journalism." *Review of Reviews* 49 (May 1914): 591–93.

Leonard, Mary Delach. "Post-Dispatch Crusade Led to Cleaner Air in St. Louis." *St. Louis Post-Dispatch,* 14 January 2003, 18.

Light, Israel "Science Writing: Status and Needs." *Journalism Quarterly* 37, no. 4 (Winter 1960): 53–60.

Locher, A. "The Structure of Pliny the Elder's Natural History." In *Science in the Early Roman Empire: Pliny the Elder, His Sources and His Influence,* ed. Roger French and Frank Greenaway, 20–29. Totowa, N.J.: Barnes and Noble, 1986.

Lowry, Edward G. "The White House Now." *Harper's Weekly,* 15 May 1909, 7–8.

Mabie, Hamilton Wright. "John Burroughs." *Century Magazine,* August 1897, 560–68.

"Making Science Ridiculous." *Literary Digest,* 2 September 1922, 62–64.

Maltz, Albert. "Man on the Road." *New Masses,* 8 January 1935, 19–21.

Martin, John Bartlow. "The Blast in Centralia No. 5: A Mine Disaster No One Stopped." *Harper's,* March 1948, 1–28.

Mathews, John L. "The Ballinger-Pinchot Controversy." *Hampton's,* November 1909, 659–74.

Mazur, Allan. "Global Environmental Change in the News." *International Sociology* 13, no. 4 (December 1998): 457–72.

McKibben, Bill. "The Call of the Not So Wild." In *Sharp Eyes: John Burroughs and American Nature Writing,* ed. Charlotte Zoe Walker, 12–18. Syracuse, N.Y.: Syracuse University Press, 2000.

McMahon, A. M. "'Small Matters': Benjamin Franklin, Philadelphia, and the Progress of Cities." *Pennsylvania Magazine of History and Biography* 66, no. 2 (April 1992): 157–82.

McMahon, Michael. "Dock Creek and the Origins of Urban Technology." In *Early American Technology: Making and Doing Things from the Colonial Era to 1850,* ed. Judith C. McGaw, 114–47. Chapel Hill: University of North Carolina Press, 1994.

McQuaid, John, and Mark Schleifstein. "In Harm's Way." *New Orleans Times-Picayune,* 23 June 2002, 1ff.

———. "Left Behind." *New Orleans Times-Picayune,* 24 June 2002, 1ff.

Meats, Stephen E. "Henry William Herbert." *The Literary Encyclopedia.* 24 June 2004. http://www.litencyc.com/php/speople.php?rec=true&UID=2099.

Meine, Curt. "Moving Mountains: Aldo Leopold and *A Sand County Almanac.*" In *Aldo Leopold and the Ecological Conscience,* ed. Richard L. Knight and Suzanne Riedel, 14–33. New York: Oxford University Press, 2002.

Miller, Stephen R. "Disappearing Green Ink." *Sierra,* November/December 2003, 50.

Mirando, Joseph. "Embracing Objectivity Early On: Journalism Textbooks of the 1800s." *Journal of Mass Media Ethics* 16, no. 1 (2001): 23–32.

Mooney, Chris. "Blinded by Science." *Columbia Journalism Review,* November/December 2004, 26–35.

Morton, A. G. "Pliny on Plants: His Place in the History of Botany." In *Science in the Early Roman Empire: Pliny the Elder, His Sources and His Influence,* ed. Roger French and Frank Greenaway, 86–97. Totowa, N.J.: Barnes and Noble, 1986.

Mueller, Gene. "Izaak Walton League Helps Hunters and Landowners Cooperate on Access." *Washington Times,* 17 June 1998, B8.

Muir, John. "Snow-Storm on Mount Shasta." *Harper's New Monthly Magazine,* September 1877, 521–30.

"Naked He Plunges into the Maine Woods to Live Alone Two Months." *Boston Post,* 4 August 1913, 1ff.

Nalder, Eric. "Covering Valdez: No Place for Those Bean Counters." *SEJournal* 1, no. 1, Fall 1990, 1, 5–6.

Nash, Roderick. "Aldo Leopold and the Limits to Liberalism." In *Aldo Leopold: The Man and His Legacy,* ed. Thomas Tanner, 53–85. Ankeny, Iowa: Soil Conservation Society of America, 1987.

"National Journal Group Announces Sale of Greenwire to E&E Publishing." *PR Newswire,* 5 October 2000.

"Nature Man." *Hearst's Magazine,* 13 December 1913, 954ff.

"Nature's Finest." *Sierra,* November/December 2000, 48–55.

Neuzil, Mark. "The Great Moon Hoax of 1835." *History Channel Magazine,* September/October 2005, 34–37.

Norris, Ruth. "More Than a Nature Show." *Audubon,* March 1985, 22ff.

"Notes and News," *Auk,* April 1905, 232.

"Oil Slick Fire Damages 2 River Spans." *Cleveland Plain Dealer,* 23 June 1969, 1c.

Olien, Clarice, George A. Donohue, and Philip J. Tichenor. "Conflict, Consensus, and Public Opinion." In *Public Opinion and the Communication of Consent,* ed. Theodore L. Glasser and Charles T. Salmon, 301–22. New York: Guilford, 1995.

Oppenheimer, Michael. "The Heat Is On." http://www.environmentaldefense.org/article.cfm?contentid=505.

Otterbourg, Robert K. "Gifford Pinchot: Conservationist and Publicist." *Public Relations Quarterly,* Summer 1974, 19–23.

Palen, John. "Objectivity as Independence." *Science Communication* 21, no. 2 (December 1999): 156–72.

Park, Robert L. "The Fizzle in Fusion." *Washington Post,* 15 May 1991, B4.

Pawelski, Natalie. "Networks Aren't Tuned into the Environment." *Nieman Reports,* Winter 2002, 69–70.

Payne, Jon. "Creating and Reporting the News." *Nuclear News,* February 1991, 27.

Pearson, Michael. "John McPhee." In *American Nature Writers,* ed. John Elder, 583–98. New York: Scribner's, 1996.

Peavey, Shannon. "Outdoor Focus: Cable Networks Zero in on Niche Events, Athletics." *Television Week,* 12 July 2004, 18.

Pennsylvania Gazette, 23–30 August 1739, 1.

"Pigeon Matches." *Forest and Stream,* 17 February 1879, 145, 171.

Ponder, Stephen. "'Nonpublicity' and the Unmaking of a President: William Howard Taft and the Ballenger-Pinchot Controversy of 1909–1910." *Journalism History* 19, no. 4 (Winter 1994): 111–21.

Pope, Carl. "Television Misses the Picture." *Sierra,* March/April 1996, 12–14.

Price, Jennifer. "Hats Off to Audubon." *Audubon,* November/December 2004, 45–50.

"Pupils Kept in Ignorance of Facts of Life Sciences." *Science News Letter,* 14 January 1939, 23.

"Quake Predicted; Vacations Suspended." Associated Press, 19 March 1990.

Quebral, Nora C. "Wilmer Atkinson and the Early Farm Journal." *Journalism Quarterly* 47, no. 1 (Spring 1970): 65–70.

Quenqua, Douglas. "Raelian Clone Claim Earns Serious Copy." *PR Week,* 6 January 2003, 24.

Reisner, Ann, and Gerry Walter. "Agricultural Journalists' Assessment of Print Coverage of Agricultural News." *Rural Sociology* 59, no. 3 (1994): 525–37.

Rivard, Jacques. "Fighting to Get Environmental Stories on Television." *Nieman Reports,* Winter 2002, 74–75.

Rogers, Charles E. "Agricultural News and Comment." *Journalism Bulletin* 4 (March 1927): 8–10.

———. "Survey of Agricultural Journalism." *Journalism Bulletin* 4 (January 1928): 44–46.

Rogers, Paul. "Complexity in Environment Reporting Is Critical to Public Decision-Making." *Nieman Reports,* Winter 2002, 32–34.

————. "Should They Drain Hetch Hetchy?" *San Jose Mercury News,* 20 July 2006, 1ff.

Ropeik, David. "The Challenge to TV." *Nieman Reports,* Winter 1996, 21–23.

Ryan, Teya. "Network Earth: Advocacy, Journalism and the Environment." In *Media and the Environment,* ed. Craig L. LaMay and Everette E. Dennis, 81–89. Washington, D.C.: Island, 1991.

"Sad, Soiled Waters: The Cuyahoga River and Lake Erie." *National Geographic,* December 1970, 743–44.

Sanders, Scott Russell. "Introduction." In *Aldo Leopold: For the Health of the Land,* ed. J. Baird Callicott and Eric T. Freyfogle, xiii–xix. Washington, D.C.: Island, 1999.

Sargeant, Frank. "Study Shows Mortality Rates High Despite Catch-and-Release Plan." *Tampa Tribune,* 12 March 2006, 14.

Schapsmeier, Edward L., and Frederick H. Schapsmeier. "The Wallaces and Their Farm Paper: A Story of Agrarian Leadership." *Journalism Quarterly* 44 (Summer 1967): 289–96.

Scheese, Don. "Annie Dillard." In *American Nature Writers,* 2 vols. ed. John Elder, 1:213–30. New York: Scribner's, 1996.

Schoenfeld, A. Clay. "The Environmental Movement as Reflected in the *American Magazine." Journalism Quarterly* 60, no. 3 (Autumn 1983): 470–75.

————. "The Press and NEPA: The Case of the Missing Agenda." *Journalism Quarterly* 56, no. 2 (August 1979): 577–87.

Schullery, Paul. "Hope for the Hooks and Bullet Press." *New York Times,* 22 September 1985, sec. 7, p. 1ff.

"Scientist Expects New Madrid Tremors in '90." Associated Press, 29 November 1989.

Showalter, Pamela Sands. "One Newspaper's Coverage of 1990 Earthquake Prediction." *Newspaper Research Journal* 16, no. 2 (Spring 1995): 2–13.

Shulman, Stuart W. "The Progressive Era Farm Press." *Journalism History* 25, no. 1 (Spring 1999): 27–36.

Sill, Melanie. "Needed: Long-Haul Commitment." *Nieman Reports,* Winter 1996, 17–20.

Simon, Clea. "It's a Tough Sell for Stations, But 'Living on Earth' Returns." *Boston Globe,* 13 August 2005, D7.

Smith, Crosbie, and Ian Higginson. "'Improvised Europeans': Science and Reform in the *North American Review,* 1865–1880." In *Science Serialized: Representations of Science in Nineteenth-Century Periodicals,* ed. Geoffrey Cantor and Sally Shuttleworth, 149–79. Cambridge, Mass.: MIT Press, 2004.

Smith, Doug. "About 2,000 Fish-Eating Birds Shot Near Leech Lake." Minneapolis *Star Tribune,* 22 May 2005, 13C.

Smythe, Ted Curtis. "The Reporter, 1880–1900: Working Conditions and Their Influence on the News." *Journalism History* 7, no. 1 (Spring 1980): 1–10.

Spectator, 16 January 1886, 82.

"'State of Beat' Report Paints Grim Picture of Broadcast, Cable TV Coverage." *Environment Writer,* October 2004. http://www.environmentwriter.org/.

Stegner, Wallace. "The Legacy of Aldo Leopold." In *Companion to A Sand County Almanac,* ed. J. Baird Callicott, 233–45. Madison: University of Wisconsin Press, 1987.

Steinhart, Peter. "The Longer View." *Audubon,* March 1987, 10–13.

Stewart, Larry. "OLN Switches to 'Versus.'" *Los Angeles Times,* 25 September 2006, 7.

Stone, Witmer. "Report of the A.O.U. Committee on Protection of North American Birds." *Auk,* January 1900, 51–58.

"Taming H-Bombs." *Wall Street Journal,* 24 March 1989, 1ff.

"They Walk the Line." *Grist.* www.grist.org.

Thomas, Stacie. "The Cuyahoga Revisited." *The Freeman: Ideas on Liberty,* May 2000, 37–38.

Thomson, Peter. "Radio Uses Sound and Script to Transport Listeners to a Place." *Nieman Reports,* Winter 2002, 70–72.

Thoreau, Henry David. "Walking." *Atlantic Monthly,* June 1862, 657–74.

Tichenor, Philip J., and Mark Neuzil. "Advocacy, the Uncomfortable Issue." *Nieman Reports,* Winter 1996, 41–44.

"Tides Foundation Honors Chip Giller, Founder and President of *Grist Magazine,* with the Prestigious Jane Bagley Lehman Award for Excellence in Public Advocacy." *Grist.* www.grist.org.

"Top Ten Missouri Stories." Associated Press, 30 December 1990.

"The Truth About Knowles." *Boston American,* 28 November 1913, 1ff.

Turney, Jon. "Lost in Limbo." *New Scientist,* 22 March 2003, 48.

Waitt, Paul. "Knowles, Clad in Skins, Comes Out of the Forest." *Boston Post,* 5 October 1913, 1ff.

Walker, Jerry. "Ex-N.Y. Times Reporter to Edit Newsletter." *Jack O'Dwyer's Newsletter,* 15 May 1991, 4.

Weatherby, W. J. "Iben Browning: Under the Volcano." *Guardian,* 10 September 1991, 35.

West, Krista. "The Billionaire Conservationist." *Scientific American* 287, no. 2, August 2002, 34–35.

Wikle, Thomas A. "A Comparison of Geographic Membership Patterns in Three National Environmental Organizations." *Journal of Environmental Education* 29, no. 3 (March 1998): 39–48.

Wilson, R. R. "Interpreting Israel's Religion: An Anthropological Perspective on the Problem of False Prophecy." In *The Place Is Too Small for Us: The Israelite Prophets in Recent Scholarship,* ed. Robert P. Gordon, 332–44. Winona Lake, Ind.: Eisenbrauns, 1995.

Winegar, Garvey. "Izaak Walton League Doesn't Conserve Noise This Time." *Washington Post,* 1 August 1999, D12.

Witt, William. "The Environmental Reporter on U.S. Daily Newspapers." *Journalism Quarterly* 51, no. 4 (Winter 1974): 697–704.

Zarek, Corinna. "Katrina Clampdown." *News Media and the Law* 29, no. 4 (Fall 2005): 4–7.

WEB SITES

Aldo Leopold Foundation. http://www.aldoleopold.org.

American Philosophical Society. http://www.amphilsoc.org/about/.

Boone and Crockett Club. http://www.boone-crockett.org.

Charleston Gazette. http://www.wvgazette.com/section/Series/Beyond+ Sago/.

Economic Research Service, U.S. Department of Agriculture. http://

Great Lakes Radio Consortium. http://www.environmentreport.org/.

Grist. www.grist.org.

MediaChannel. http://mediachannel.org.

National Audubon Society. http://www.audubon.org/bird/cbc/history
.html.

Outdoor Writers Association of America. http://www.owaa.org/about
_owaa.php#PositionOnHunting.

Quicksilver. http://kaspit.typepad.com/weblog/2005/09/new_orleans
_and.html.

Sierra Club. http://www.sierraclub.org/history/origins/chapter7.asp.

PANEL DISCUSSION

Schleifstein, Mark. Society of Environmental Journalists plenary session, Lyndon Baines Johnson Library and Museum, University of
Texas–Austin, 30 September 2005.

RECORDED MUSIC

Jones, Grandpa. "Jonah and the Whale." In *16 Sacred Gospel Songs.* Cincinnati, Ohio: King Records, 1963.

The New Lost City Ramblers. "The Old Fish Song." In *The Early Years
1958–1962.* Washington, D.C.: Folkways Recording, 1991.

Newman, Randy. "Burn On." In *Sail Away.* Los Angeles: Rhino Records
#78244, 1972.

INTERVIEWS

William Allen
Steve Anderson
Perry Beeman
Margaret Broeren
Matt Crawford
Jim Detjen
Peter Dykstra
Den Gardner
Mary Manning

Robert McClure
Jim Motavalli
Beth Parke
Kevin Rhoades
Karen Schaefer
Mark Schleifstein
Seth Slabaugh
Peter Thomson
Bud Ward
Ken Ward Jr.

THESES AND DISSERTATIONS

Schwartz, Debra A. "In the Lion's Mouth: Advocacy and Investigative Reporting About the Environment in the Early 21st Century." Ph.D. diss., University of Maryland, 2004.

Wood, Janice Ruth. "The Foundation Years of American Journalism Education, 1908–1930." M.A. thesis, University of South Carolina, 1981.

SPEECHES

Clay, John. "The Plough and the Book." Address to Iowa State College, May 30, 1905, Agricultural Communications Documents Center, University of Illinois.

CONFERENCE PAPERS

Sachsman, David, JoAnn Valenti, and James Simon. "Regional Issues, National Norms: A Four-Region Analysis of U.S. Environment Reporters." Paper presented at the annual meeting of the International Communications Association, May 2005.

INDEX

Mark Neuzil is a professor in the Department of Communication and Journalism at the University of St. Thomas. He is the author of *Views on the Mississippi: The Photographs of Henry Peter Bosse* and a coauthor of *Mass Media and Environmental Conflict: America's Green Crusades* and *A Spiritual Field Guide: Meditations for the Outdoors.* He lives in St. Paul, Minnesota.

Russell E. Train is a chairman emeritus of the World Wildlife Fund, a former administrator of the U.S. Environmental Protection Agency, and the author of *Politics, Pollution, and Pandas: An Environmental Memoir.*